NEIL GAIMAN is a
journalist, short stor
whose articles on sc
things) have appeare
house. He also reviews books for the British Fantasy Society.

KIM NEWMAN is a film critic for *City Limits* and author of a number of coffee-table film books. A freelance journalist and an aspiring fiction author, he also reviews films for the British Fantasy Society, also amongst other things.

Ghastly Beyond Belief

by Neil Gaiman and Kim Newman

Introduction by Harry Harrison

ARROW BOOKS

Arrow Books Limited
17–21 Conway Street, London W1P 6JD

An imprint of the Hutchinson Publishing Group

London Melbourne Sydney Auckland
Johannesburg and agencies throughout
the world

First published in Great Britain 1985

Set in Linotron Sabon by
Input Typesetting Limited, London

Printed and bound in Great Britain
by Anchor Brendon Limited, Tiptree, Essex

ISBN 0 09 936830 7

'All science fiction is comic. Five percent of it is consciously comic and ninety-five percent of it is unconsciously comic. But to laugh at the often very funny ninety-five percent of it is to be put into mortal peril. The 'True Believers' would kill us if they could, and perhaps they can.'

R. A. LAFFERTY, *True Believers*

'You could compile the worst book in the world entirely out of selected passages from the best writers in the world.'

G. K. CHESTERTON

Contents

Foreword and Acknowledgements

It was the authors' original intention to write the definitive book of science fiction and fantasy quotations, a deathless compendium that would be used in academic circles for years to come; something like the Oxford Book of Serious Literary Quotations, only snappier.

When the publishers pointed out that this would have the sales appeal of a book on 'Yak-herding for Bank Managers', the idea was regretfully abandoned.

The book you are holding is entirely useless as a work of reference.

It doesn't even have an index.

The authors owe thanks – for quotes, suggestions, leads, help, advice, coffee, and other things – to:

Forrest J. Ackerman
Douglas Adams
Andromeda Books (Birmingham)
Isaac Asimov
Clive S. Bennett
Robert Bloch
Faith Brooker
The British Fantasy Society
The British Film Institute Library
Joyce Day and the Science Fiction Foundation
David Dickson
Jo Fletcher
Forbidden Planet (London)
Gamma
Colin Greenland
Harry Harrison
Joan Harrison
Richard Holliss
Stefan Jaworzyn
Alan Jones
Rodney Jones
Steve Jones
Knave

Harry Adam Knight
David Langford
Peter Lavery
Martyn Lester
Chris Lloyd
Mary McGrath
Peter Nicholls
John Peel
Ian Pemble
Charles Platt
Steve Roe
Dean Skilton
Tise Vahimagi
A. E. van Vogt
Di Wathen
Mike Wathen

and the authors of the films and books quoted herein, all of whom have brought so much pleasure to so many.

Introduction

by Harry Harrison

Many, many years ago when there wasn't a single college professor in the world who taught a science fiction course – I told you that this was very long ago – Brian Aldiss and I decided that what the world really needed was a little magazine devoted to SF criticism. Since no one in the world cared much about this idea, Brian and I, acting as both editors and publishers, brought this project to fruition. *SF Horizons* was born, and, for good or evil, reasoned criticism entered the science fiction scene for the first time. The relevance of these exciting facts will become clear when I mention that this journal contained a series of short items, very handy to fill in the bits of white space at the end of articles, that were labelled Cabinet of Curiosities. These consisted of fragments of SF stories ripped out of context and dutifully commented upon. I recall one, from a story by Poul Anderson, that read 'He swept the room with the eyes of a trapped animal.' After which Brian commented 'A gnu broom sweeps clean?' I am most pleased to see that the spluttering torch of hilarious disrespect has been seized by the short hairs and thrust up to public view in the volume that you are holding in your hand. How, you might ask, is such mockery and disrespect of any value? Should we really make fun of the things we love? The answer to this must be a resounding YES! Science fiction in general – and the readers in particular – can only benefit by any improvements made in the abysmal writing standards that we have come to accept all too mildly in our beloved field of literary and cinematic endeavour.

Also – no justification is really needed. Just relax and enjoy the mind-boggling hilarity that follows. Turn the pages and lose yourself in the side-splitting galaxy of guffaws culled from all the films you were ashamed to see, the books that you were too disgusted to read.

PART ONE

The Books

Attention Please

ATTACK OF THE KILLER BLURBS

A blurb is a brief description of the contents of a book, designed to tease or entice a casual browser into buying it. A blurb should be short, accurate, tantalizing, and give some evidence that the blurb writer has actually read the book being described.

However, even a cursory glance at a few book jackets shows that such blurbs are in the minority.

Science fiction is, of course, not the only literary genre to suffer. Veteran SF author Frederik Pohl worked as an advertising copywriter in the late 1940s and mentions in his autobiography *The Way the Future Was* that he was responsible for gems such as:

In the wickedest city in the world this copper-haired giant built an empire out of gunplay, gambling and the eager hearts of women.

And the classic:

He knew the whole town's secrets but he had one secret of his own: the huge white bride's bed that he kept for the wife of another man.

These clearly demonstrate that, like all advertising, the blurb attempts to appeal to humanity's basic drives – the most accessible being SEX.

THE BLURB SEXUAL

Every woman in the city was his!

BRIAN ALDISS, *The Male Response*

It proclaims on the front cover. And on the back:

This timely story is destined to become the top *adult* science fiction novel of the year. Mr Aldiss' treatment of the many problems of sex and superstition met by a modern scientist in darkest Africa is startling. How a modern Englishman copes with the pagan passions and primitive perversions of today's torrid continent will keep your interest at fever level.

***The Male Response* is *not* science fiction, and bears little resemblance to the plot description given here.**

His fancies had come true – he was a lone man on a planet entirely inhabited by women.

POUL ANDERSON, *Virgin Planet*

WOMEN'S LIB GONE WILD. Dr. Henrietta Carey, Leader of the *FEMS*, the first woman candidate for president and the perfector of VITA-LERP, the biological skin cream designed to do away with superfluous men, it spelled WAR BETWEEN THE SEXES.

JOHN BOYD, *Sex and the High Command*, (Bantam)

Under the surgeon's knife, Griff Sheridan had become more than any woman dared hope for . . . a superhuman twenty-fifth century lover capable of driving all girls wild!

ROSS CAMRA, *Assault*

LOUIS CHARBONNEAU, *Corpus Earthling*. **In the British edition (Digit) the cover shows a man, and the message:**

He was marked for extermination by the invaders from Mars.

The American cover is almost the same, but the man had been replaced by a full-breasted young lady and the blurb now reads:

She was marked as the first victim of the Martian invaders.

(Remarkably, both blurbs are accurate.)

He defied the twenty-fifth century with a woman who was NOT HIS WIFE – and a WIFE who was NOT A WOMAN!

PHILIP JOSE FARMER, *A Woman A Day* (also known as *Timestop* or *The Day of Timestop*), (Beacon)

Forced to make love to beautiful women! This is adult science fiction at its best.

RANDALL GARRETT AND LARRY M. HARRIS, *Pagan Passions*

The young earthmen explored a fascinating planet, twin to the sun, where one-eyed runts played endless games of sex.

JAMES GRAZIER, *Runts of 61 Cygni C.* (Belmont)

(Actually the planet was twin to the Earth, not the sun; however the blurb is far more exciting than the book it comes from.)

The Major Cult Author of our time challenges the concepts of morality and social organization in *Podkayne of Mars*. Through the eyes of beautiful adventuress and beautiful Podkayne, Robert Heinlein examines the worlds of tomorrow.

ROBERT A. HEINLEIN, *Podkayne of Mars*, (NEL)

(A blurb designed to make the book, a fairly staid juvenile, sound rather naughtier than it in fact is.)

He came from Mars and changed EARTH'S IDEAS OF MORALITY!

ROBERT A. HEINLEIN, *Stranger in a Strange Land*, (4-Square)

On a world older than time, built upon dope and vice, this was . . . SIN IN SPACE! An exposé of the Scarlet Planet!

CYRIL JUDD, *Sin in Space*

While most of these books are very innocent and just repackaged to appeal to 'adult' buyers, there have been a few SF porn books, such as the next two.

She was all woman. Ask the men who made her!

JACK KAHLER, *Latex Lady* (AKA *Rubber Dolly*), (Carousel Books)

Harder than human! A bionic man with a computer crotch satisfies the lust cravings of a super feminine world. More than Mortal Meat!

HORST KLEPPLE, *Hard On*, (Spicy Reader)

Bizarre! Uproarious! Chilling! The most extraordinary things happen when French l'amour meets SF.

DAMON KNIGHT, ED., *13 French SF Stories*, (Corgi)

(One of the few known examples of a franglais SF blurb . . .)

Satyrs from outer space on a lusty earthbound spree.

FRITZ LEIBER, *The Green Millenium*

Potions in the house . . . Evil in the air . . . And a Witch in his bed!

FRITZ LEIBER, *Conjure Wife*

Sex kittens from outer space send two Earthmen into an orbit of eternal ecstacy.

VICTOR LOMAN, *Starship Women,* (Hustler Books)

What happens when the world's most brilliant mind, inside the world's finest body, is thrown for a loop by a mere woman?

FELIX MENDELSOHN JR., *Superbaby*

(The assumptions about men and women implicit in this blurb are staggering.)

Janet's mission is to find a planet where sex reigns – and when she does, you can imagine her bodily gains!

MONICA MOUNDS **(Do you think that could be a pseudonym?)**, *Outer Space Embrace* (AKA *Pleasure Planet* AKA *Janet's Sex Planet* AKA *Intergalactic Orgy* – etc.) (Bee Line Books)

A startling view of life in 1984! Forbidden love! Fear! Betrayal!

GEORGE ORWELL, *1984,* (Signet – 1953 edition)

The scourge had spread all over Earth – killing all but a few women, for whose favours the price was DEATH!

LEONARD PRUYN AND DAY KEENE, *World Without Women*

('Yeah,' he muttered, 'but what a way to go!')

A sexy young witch can get into all sorts of trouble these days.

KEITH ROBERTS, *Anita,* (Ace)

It was love – between a mad scientist and a degenerate speck of hypermatter.

RUDY RUCKER, *The Sex Sphere,* (Ace)

Free Drugs! Easy Sex! No Job Hassles! Some people just don't know when they're being oppressed!

RUDY RUCKER, *Spacetime Donuts,* (Ace)

He had to be stopped, for all women were his playthings and all men his pawns!

OLAF STAPLEDON, *Odd John,* (Beacon)

(The cover shows a naked man chasing a naked woman. One suspects that neither the cover artist nor the blurb writer had read *Odd John*, a pleasant tale of a spiritual and intellectual superman, who founds a Utopian community on a Pacific island.)

She Was A Century Ahead Of Her Sex!

JACK WILLIAMSON, *Dragon's Island,* (Paperback Library)

THE BLURB RHETORICAL

Following the Blurb Sexual there is the Blurb Rhetorical. This sort of blurb hooks the reader by asking a question which *might* be answered somewhere in the book . . .

How can you be sure that the man you live with is not a murderer? CAROLYN BANKS, *The Dark Room*

(Ask him?)

What was the Earthmen's answer to the chilling menace from the skies?

PAUL CAPON, *Phobos the Robot Planet*

(Er . . . forty-two?)

If they were not extra-terrestrial whence did they come?

BRON FANE, *U.F.O. 517,* (Badger)

(Whence indeed!)

What was the rational scientific explanation for the thing that looked like an eye?

JOHN E. MULLER, *Dark Continuum*, (Badger)

(It was a nose in disguise?)

Who were these fantastic women . . . why did they disturb his eternal rest?

JOHN E. MULLER, *1,000 Years On*

(John E. Muller, like Bron Fane, Karl Zeigfreid, Lionel Roberts and many other names, is a disguise for the indefatigable Lionel Fanthorpe).

Could Science reclaim their GOLDEN AGE or was EVIL their inheritance?

ROLF GARNER, *Resurgent Dust*, (Panther)

Would the disembodied minds – doomed to eternal slavery – overthrow the corrupt System?

RAYMOND F. JONES, *The Cybernetic Brains*, (Paperback Library)

(Yes, well actually they would.)

Was he human or alien – sent to save the Earth – or destroy it?

DAMON KNIGHT, *Beyond the Barrier*

Past, present and future. Does it have to be in that order?

GEORGE LANGELAAN, *Out of Time*, (4-Square)

Was he a human meteor or a time bomb from the stars?

URSULA K. LEGUIN, *City of Illusions*, (Ace)

(Actually he was an amnesiac alien come to free Earth from the reign of the evil Shing, but whether that would make him a human meteor or a time bomb I have never discovered.)

For what dreaded purpose did the tentacles of the Invaders snatch man after man from Life?

PHILIP LEVENE AND J. R. MORRISSEY, *City of the Hidden Eyes*

(They wanted to take over the world, of course.)

Could one man survive the destruction of Earth and find sanctuary on another planet whose terrors might be worse than death?

SAM MOSCOWITZ, *The Vortex Blasters* (Anthology)

(I'm sure he could, but unfortunately none of the stories in the anthology ever let on.)

Was this brain of pulsating cells completely indestructible, this formless horror which threatened the world?

VICTOR NORWOOD, *Night of the Black Horror,* (Badger)

(No. It wasn't. Did you guess?)

How would it end, this strange forever, they were prisoners of time?

LIONEL ROBERTS, *Time-Echo,* (Badger)

If the computer had a mind of its own, what did it plan for humanity?

KARL ZEIGFREID, *Protection Infinity,* (Badger)

If Man can mutate – why not the universe itself?

KARL ZEIGFREID, *Escape to Infinity,* (Badger)

THE BLURB PARADOXICAL

Close cousin to the Blurb Rhetorical is the Blurb Paradoxical, in which the blurb writer poses a paradox so cunning that the browsing reader, intrigued, promptly buys the book to resolve it.

A super warrior walks the world, armed with the power to save mankind – or destroy it!

PIERS ANTHONY, *Sos the Rope,* (Pyramid)

(Which will he do? you ask yourself, stunned.)

The formula would give the possessor eternal life . . . yet both sides were willing to die to own it.

RICHARD ASHBY, *Act of God,* (5 Star)

With her lay the destruction – or the fulfillment – of the human race.

JAMES BLISH, *Titan's Daughter,* (Avon)

The Truly Amazing Story of a World Much Like Our Own, Only Startlingly Different.

J. HARVEY BOND, *The Other World*

(Non-committal blurbs of this kind lead one to suspect that the blurb writer might not actually have read the book.)

Shackled by an accident of birth, he struck for freedom by unlocking the mysteries that had scourged the past.

KENNETH HARKER, *The Symmetrians,* (Compact)

World Opposition – to oppose them meant death. Their aim – the destruction of civilization.

GEOFFREY HOUSEHOLD, *The High Place*

The frightening story of a split personality security man, whose developing fear of himself entangles him in a world of mounting violence.

ROBERT MAUGHAM, *The Man With Two Shadows,* (Ace)

(Does he beat himself up? one wonders.)

He came back from Mars, with a secret too terrible to remember.

JUDITH MERRIL, *The Tomorrow People,* (Pyramid)

Planet Ericon's life-or-death battle to rule the universe or disintegrate into cosmic dust.

C. L. MOORE, *Judgement Night*

His mind was disintegrating . . . the face couldn't be real, but it was.

John E. Muller, *The Uninvited*

There has been an accident – the Galaxy itself is doomed!

STANLEY SCHMIDT, *Lifeboat Earth,* (Berkley)

This incredible fantasy world had everything he could want and more than he could handle.

THORNE SMITH, *Rain in the Doorway,* (Del Ray Ballantine)

2045 AD. He was offered eternal life. The price – a living death!

JERRY SOHL, *The Altered Ego,* (Pennant)

Alive, he was just another human being – dead, his mind was a weapon that could destroy the world.

NICHOLAS YERMAKOV, *Jehad,* (Signet)

THE BLURB IMPROBABLE

Then there are those blurbs which *may* mean something, but probably don't.

Star Trek One – A chilling journey through worlds beyond imagination. Circling the solar sphere in search of new worlds and high adventure.

Star Trek Two – A galactic ticket to infinite adventure.

Star Trek Three – A mind-reeling journey! Eerie excursions into galaxies beyond probability!

JAMES BLISH, *Star Trek*, (Bantam)

Weird ... unearthly ... terrifying ... The creature VOR the first alien from outer-space. The terrible stranger from worlds beyond the unknown – V-O-R – the ultimate frightening crisis on Earth.

JAMES BLISH, *VOR*, (Corgi)

A milestone in the annals of science fiction. The 100th issue of the Sci Fi magabook from the land that gave US Metropolis, Fritz Lang, The Woman in the Moon ... and the legendary Marlene Dietrich: Germany, via Clark Dalton, Wendayne Ackerman, et al, has given the Time and Space opera Fans of the English-reading world! PERRY! PUCKY! THORA! ...

CLARK DALTON, *Desert of Death's Domain*

Now the trilogy expands to encompass a story too large to be contained.

FRANK HERBERT, *God Emperor of Dune*,
(G. P. Putnam's Sons)

A million-to-one odds on the Earth's alternate masters.

FRANK HERBERT, *Green Brain*

(What the blurb writer is trying to say – I think – is that there are a lot more insects than people.)

Firm and Earth are on a time track to destruction and Denning and Liston are asked to face the Alien, armed only with their brains!

PHILLIP E. HIGH, *Twin Planet*, (Paperback Library)

('Well, Liston, my brain missed. Throw yours.')

Life without annihilating was depended upon finding another earth-like planet in the Galaxy.

J. R. POWERS, *Black Abyss*

(Not only improbable but incomprehensible.)

An agonizing science fiction adventure.

NORMAN SPINRAD, *Agent of Chaos,* (Belmont)

And finally –

Isn't that the number in the Apocalypse. The Number of the Beast. Russian scientists go to inhuman lengths to plan a race of SUPERMEN.

JOHN TAINE, *G.O.G. 666*

THE BLURB HORRIFIC

This sort of blurb writing seems to be flourishing on both sides of the Atlantic. The name of the game is to send a shiver of fear down your browsing reader's spine before he or she has even opened the book.

(In huge red letters) WHERE TERROR STALKED CHARLES BIRKIN INFECTS ONE WITH CREEPING FEARS.

CHARLES BIRKIN, *Where Terror Stalked,* (Tandem)

Just when you thought it was safe to go back in the shower.

ROBERT BLOCH. *Psycho II*

In the charnel house of science *anything* can happen.

STEPHEN GALLAGHER, *Chimera,* (Sphere)

Fashioned from flesh, baptised in blood . . . THE CREATURE OF VENGEANCE IS COME!

BILL GARNETT, *The Crone,* (Sphere)

They dared invade the Beast's realm and saw things no human should ever see. Some of them even came back – seemingly alive.

VIC GHIDALIA AND ROGER ELWOOD, *Beware the Beasts* (Anthology)

Welcome to Starburst . . . a quiet seaside resort where the people of the future escape to the past, and where only four things are certain . . . (1) Four people are dead. (2) You are next. (3) The murderer isn't human. (4) Night is falling.

CHARLES L. GRANT, *A Quiet Night of Fear,* (Berkley)

Turn on the tap . . . and die of terror.

JOHN HALKIN, *Slime,* (Star)

From the blackest pits of hell, insatiable evil creeps forth to claim men's minds and souls.

JAMES HERBERT, *The Dark,* (Signet)

Frenzied mutant super-rats bloodlusting for human flesh.

JAMES HERBERT, *Lair,* (Signet)

(The author took 244 pages to say what the blurb writer managed to convey in eight words.)

The soul-freezing shock of unholy savage rites and infinite evil.

JAMES HERBERT, *Spear,* (Signet)

They thought the worst was over . . . and it had only just begun . . .

THOMAS O'D. HUNTER, *Softly Walks the Beast*

The people of Wakely are pale and gaunt. They have

abnormally long fingernails and prominent teeth – and some of them have hair on the palms of their hands . . . What is poisoning the lifeblood of Wakely town? What evil force has it in thrall?

SHAUN HUTSON, *Erebus,* (Star)

(Hair on the palms of their hands? No . . . it can't be . . .)

. . . and death was only the beginning.

HARRY ADAM KNIGHT, *Slimer,* (Star)

Every night the children met to play the game. Whether they wanted to or not. ARCADE. They had nothing to lose but their minds.

ROBERT MAXXE, *Arcade,* (Granada)

A mass murder. A disappearance. A cemetery ransacked. It looked like another ordinary day in Los Angeles. Then night came . . .

ROBERT MCCAMMON, *They Thirst*

(Was this book sponsored by the L.A. Tourist Board?)

Icy fangs of the night tearing deep into the flesh of the soul! **it proclaims on the front cover. And on the back of KURT SINGER'S *Horror Omnibus, (Panther):***

. . . Supreme magicians of fear. Stories to make you shudder, shriek and scream. Ghosts ghouls gargoyles gorgons voodoo satanism occult magic uncanny chilling bizarre weird malignant impossible. Look out behind you, IT has arrived.

(A blurb writer is expected to use a thesaurus, but this seems a little excessive.)

A seafood cocktail for the strongest stomachs.

GUY N. SMITH, *Night of the Crabs,* (NEL)

Its fragrance was ripe with evil blood . . .

GUY N. SMITH, *Satan's Snowdrop,* (Hamlyn)

(Nonsense, of course . . .)

Death clung to her like a *Haute Couture* shroud.

GUY N. SMITH, *Blood Circuit,* (NEL)

(But nonsense in French?)

A journey into terror that demands all of your mind and – SOME OF YOUR BLOOD.

THEODORE STURGEON, *Some of Your Blood,* (Ballantine)

THE BLURB MISLEADING

Blurb writers, like all of us, are only human. (At least, I think they are. I *hope* they are.) And sometimes they make mistakes. Or try and sell a book as something it isn't. Or appear not to have read the book in question. Hence The Blurb Misleading.

His nightmare journey through space took him to Solaria where robots ruled and earthmen lived in terror.

ISAAC ASIMOV, *The Naked Sun,* (Panther)

(The blurb writer *might* have thumbed through the first chapter . . .)

Super science and fantastic death launch a rocket to the morgue! Was it murder through the fourth dimension? It's funny and fantastic, grim and gory, when a gentle-spoken nun and a bunch of whacky super-science writers try to educate and enlighten the puzzled cop.

ANTHONY BOUCHER, *Rocket to the Morgue*

(It doesn't actually say it's SF but it does imply strongly that it's more than just the detective story it turns out

to be. In the same way the following volume of autobiography, about a year in a New York commune, seems to be hedging its bets . . .)

A Nebula Award-winning author of *Nova*, *Dhalgren* and *Tales of Neveryon* returns to the source of his vision.

SAMUEL R. DELANY, *Heavenly Breakfast*, (Bantam)

And on the back:

Samuel R. Delany takes a long look back at the mythic scenes of his youthful adventures. The launching pad for the psychedelic voyages that shaped his phenomenal SF. This is the story of a mind being born, the dawn of a new awareness that set loose the fantastic imagination of 'the best science fiction writer in the world' – *Galaxy*.

(He'd already written six novels by the time the book begins . . .)

Stranger In A Strange Land, then *Dune*, and now the major novel of love and terror at the end of time.

SAMUEL R. DELANY, *Dhalgren*, (Bantam)

(Delany wrote *Dhalgren*, all right, but certainly neither of the other 'major novels' mentioned.)

He offered to sell them the secret of eternal life. All he asked in return was their souls.

PHILIP K. DICK, *The Three Stigmata of Palmer Eldritch*

(Actually a novel about Martian colonists, the drugs they take to make life tolerable, and Palmer Eldritch, whose drugs are stronger than reality.)

Two young children saw a strange object land in the middle of a wheatfield, and decided to hide and watch.

Two beings with the appearance of tall blond men emerged from the craft and walked away. What happened when the children decided to hide the space ship is a story not even the aliens could believe.

NANCY AND FRANCIS DORER, *Two Came Calling*

(Also a story not told in the book.)

Stories by the best-selling SF writer in the world.

HARLAN ELLISON, *From the Land of Fear,* (Belmont)

(Asimov, Arthur C. Clarke and Robert A. Heinlein have outsold Harlan Ellison by many millions of books, to name just three.)

In the end, only the remarkable scientist-dragons of a rebellious Mars can resolve the conflict within a man who cannot live within the society he knows is killing him.

ROBERT HEINLEIN, *Between Planets,* (NEL)

(It's elegant. It's well written. It's also on the cover of a book that is entirely devoid of Martian dragons, scientists or otherwise, and inner conflicts are not something that Heinlein is usually known for.)

A rare excursion into time travel.

ROBERT A. HEINLEIN, *Assignment in Eternity,* (Digit)

(A case of guessing what the book *ought* to be about from the title, and guessing wrong.)

Robert Heinlein is the acknowledged master of space-age fiction. He is also coming to be recognized as the spokesman to a generation searching for new concepts of honour and courage.

ROBERT A. HEINLEIN, *Glory Road,* (NEL)

(The blurb doesn't mention who recognized him.)

By popular demand, the master of supernatural horror is back, with one of his best novels.

H. P. LOVECRAFT, *The Case of Charles Dexter Ward* (1970 edition)

(Not only was it his *only* novel, but he'd been dead for over thirty years.)

For sheer inaccuracy the following takes a lot of beating:

It is sometime in the distant future. (**About 2020 AD.**) Society as we know it no longer exists (**it does so**), at least not on the moon where a colony has been established complete with technical advances that have made daily life a near Utopia (**there is a small scientific outpost on Earth's** other **moon – Diana – under menace from a saboteur**). Good health, resources and prosperity belong to all. (**No they don't.**) Then, purely by accident, a scientist develops a tree capable of growing treasure on its branches. (**An old wildlife artist finds a native plant with 'penny-like' leaves.**) Greed and a lust for power seize the inhabitants. (**No, they don't.**) Momentum builds up until an inter-galactic war is on the verge of erupting. (**The saboteur strikes again, and a lot of people on the base are getting worried.**) Only one man, the unfortunate inventor can prevent the holocaust. But, it already seems to be too late. (**The lovable old wildlife artist tricks the naughty saboteur into revealing his identity, the saboteur repents and everybody goes back to Earth the best of friends.**)

PHILIP SHORTER, *Handful of Silver*, (Manor Books)

A remarkable and terrifying novel of how Life Might Be for the Space Travellers of the future.

KURT VONNEGUT JR, *Sirens of Titan,* (Dell, 1st edition)
(A rather funny novel about the manipulation of human history; God; luck and free will. It has little to say about how Life Might Be for the Space Travellers of the future.)

A disturbing recreation of the Dracula legend.

CHELSEA QUINN YARBRO, *Hotel Transylvania*

(Actually, a love story in eighteenth-century France, in which one of the protagonists happens to be a vampire.)

Some of you may have read the blurb to this book, and the book itself, and you may be wondering about any discrepancies between the two.

1. *Buy this book or your head will explode.*
   This statement is patently untrue.
2. *Who said: 'I'll meet you at the Frug-a-go-go when I've finished with the cyclotron, baby'?*
   The authors have not answered this question. They suggested offering a Mars bar to the first reader who came up with the right answer. After the publishers explained the harsh economic realities of publishing today, the authors were forced to abandon this idea, and will now reveal all.
   It was Tony Stark, playboy millionaire industrialist, who, when he donned a suit of armour, was known to Marvel Comics' readers as Iron Man.
3. *Veteran authors Gaiman and Newman have spent aeons in compiling this mighty tome of reference.*
   Well it *seemed* a long time, anyway.
4. *Included are: The World's Most Memorable Titles.*
   This is also patently untrue. We couldn't remember any of them.

The authors

THE BLURB OVERBLOWN

Sometimes the claims made by blurb writers for their books are so grandiose as to result in the Blurb Overblown.

When Man bites Dog it's news. When the greatest writer of the new science fiction brings out a new book it's history. Aldiss is back with the biggest SF book of 1975. You may have to wait until 2001 to read a better Aldiss but don't count on it.

BRIAN ALDISS, *The Eighty Minute Hour,* (Leisure Books)

(Actually, Arthur C. Clarke wrote 2001 . . .)

The most famous science fantasy novel of all time . . . A searing indictment of Western civilization. A staggering, shocking, revealing look at the fundamental urges in our way of life.

ROBERT A. HEINLEIN, *Stranger In A Strange Land,* (NEL)

The freshest, funniest work of fiction about America since the drafting of the US Constitution.

THOM KEYES, *The Battle of Disneyland,* (Star)

This and only this is the genuine novel of our times. Accept no substitutes.

JOHN SLADEK, *The Muller Fokker Effect*

Kilgore Trout, 'One of the most beloved and respected human beings in history.' So said Kurt Vonnegut in *Breakfast of Champions*. Snaggle-toothed, white-haired, long and tangled, a product of the imagination . . . a man whose exploits have been the focal point of one of our greatest contemporary writers, Kurt Vonnegut. For the first time without lurid covers . . .

KILGORE TROUT, *Venus on the Half Shell,* (Star)

The most dazzlingly prophetic novel ever written in America. The all-time great which ranks with *Brave New World* and *1984.*

PHILIP WYLIE/EDWIN BALMER, *When Worlds Collide,* (Paperback Library)

THE BLURB BARBARIAN

In writing blurbs for sword and sorcery novels, blurb writers try to appeal to another basic human interest: violence. The urge to hack one's way through the underground clutching a broadsword . . .

The biggest and best of the barbarian horde is Robert E. Howard's Conan. He gets his fair share of the action in his blurbs.

Conan the Wanderer (Sphere)—The Mighty Barbarian from beyond time carves his way through four fantastic stories.

Conan the Warrior (Sphere)—Conan wades through rivers of blood and overcomes foes both natural and supernatural

and in *Conan the Usurper* (Sphere)—He battles murderous demons and incredible monsters as he cuts his bloody swath through the Hyborian Age.

('Crom!' swore Conan. 'I've cut my bloody swath!')

Kadji, the young warrior, axed a path through a hundred adversaries.

LIN CARTER, *Quest of Kadji,* (Belmont)

The mighty barbarian hacked his way through a thousand adventures.

GARDNER F. FOX, *Kothar of the Magic Sword,* (Belmont)

(I wonder if the same person wrote both blurbs.)

Some Barbarian blurbs are a little more specific than the all-purpose ones above:

To rescue a banished princess, Vantro the Barbarian turns his mighty powers against the sinister Fanes!

GEOFFREY N. WALLMAN, *Death Trek*

Sometimes you even get something rather more interesting:

Thunderbolts flashed from his fingertips and the Universe trembled with the sound of his satanic laughter.

DAVE VAN ARNHAM, *Wizard of Storms,* (Belmont)

(Would that the book were a fraction as interesting.)

THE BLURB BIZARRE

That science fiction stories are often slightly different from the mainstream is something that blurb writers tend to take advantage of; it gives them a break from the monotony of writing for love sagas and epics.

Home is the hunter, home from the hull.

BRIAN ALDISS, *Nonstop,* (Pan)

ISAAC ASIMOV, *Foundation,* (Panther)

In the fifties it read:

A million worlds made up their society – now the threat of thirty thousand years of anarchy loomed large.

And in the sixties, it was fashionably reduced to:

The galaxy was crumbling into thirty thousand years of anarchy.

Science fiction at its most thrilling! Giant metal-hungry Bats in spaceships invade the Earth. Called in to investigate, Neal Vaughan, the hero of this story, finds himself involved in some strange and terrific adventures including a journey to the moon!

SYDNEY J. BOUNDS, *The Moon Raiders*

(Who says science fiction isn't the literature of ideas?)

'READ AND DESTROY' **is 'stamped' on the cover.**

RAY BRADBURY, *Fahrenheit 451,* (Corgi)

Weird, wild, stunning – will make your pulse rev up and your brain stand on end!

JOHN BRUNNER, *Time-Jump,* (Dell)

They were little green men with a difference . . . and what a difference! They were green. They were little. They were bald as billiard balls. And they were EVERYWHERE!

FREDRIC BROWN, *Martians Go Home*

TERROR! CONFLICT! OPPRESSION! and a Galaxy in CHAINS!

H. K. BULMER, *Empire of Chaos,* (Panther)

FEAR! DOUBT! INSANITY! as Earth faces invasion from outer space.

H. J. CAMPBELL, *Another Space – Another Time,* (Panther)

FOR HIS SECRET PLAN . . . these LIVING, bodiless, BRAINS.

H. J. CAMPBELL, *Brain Ultimate,* (Panther)

(Their capitals, not mine.)

Only one man could save the world and he was dead. Again.

PHILIP K. DICK, *Now Wait For Last Year,* (Granada, Manor)

. . . Now Captain Kirk and his friends face their greatest challenge – to repair the fabric of the Universe before Time is lost forever.

DIANE DUANE, *Wounded Sky,* (Pocket)

(Pass the puncture repair kit, Scotty.)

Forget the Kid Stuff.

DAN GOULOYE, *The Last Leap*

Would you believe it? Only an intergalactic guerilla force of pigs could destroy the monsters of the Ghost Plateau!

HARRY HARRISON, *The Man From P.I.G.,* (Avon)

(A blurb none the less weird for being perfectly accurate.)

The Space probe returned to Earth carrying a cargo of writhing death!

HARRY HARRISON, *Plague From Space*

('Anything to declare?' 'Just a cargo of writhing death.')

HARRY HARRISON, *Skyfall,* (Corgi)

On the front cover:

A novel of almost unbearable suspense.

While the back cover reads, in case anyone failed to get the point:

'In the almost unbearable suspense genre.'

MARTIN AMIS

A 'yarn' for science fiction enthusiasts.

GEORGE HAY, *Flight of the 'Hesper'*

To thwart the deadly menace of Impulsatia, they probed the endless voids of hyper-space.

JOHN ROBERT HAYNES, *Scream from Outer Space*

He Was A Destroyer From Another Planet, Bent On The Destruction of the World.

J. HUNTER HOLLY, *Encounter*

(Good to see someone doing their job . . .)

Linc Hostler was sitting in a packed stadium when the Flying Eyes appeared and cast their hypnotic power over half the crowd. Thousands of people suddenly began marching zombie-like into the woods where they vanished into a black pit.

J. HUNTER HOLLY, *The Flying Eyes*

(One solution to violence on the terraces.)

An alien from another world. A visitor from space. An intruder from the cosmos. So how do you imagine him? Five heads, seven arms, a death-ray gun in every hand? Eight feet tall, handsome as hell, dressed in gold with an enigmatic smile? Well you'd be wrong. It looks like a chair. An armchair. A comfortable old purple armchair. But it can still scare the daylights out of you. Who knows what it will do?

ELGAR HOSKY, *The Purple Armchair,* (Mayflower)

(For a start it can clash with the wallpaper . . .)

In this book, John D. Macdonald turns from suspense to a story of ~~fanta~~ . . .
This book is about a m~~ysteri~~ . . .
This is a novel of wild ~~adventu~~ . . .
If Thorne Smith and Mickey Spillane had collaborated on . . .
It's a *story*. By one of America's greatest story-tellers. Read it.

JOHN D. MACDONALD, *The Girl, The Gold Watch and Everything*, (Gold Metal)

This novel was written inside a capsule travelling through space to a dimension we should hope never to know!

FRANK BELKNAP LONG, *The Horror from the Hills!!!!!!*

JOHN LYMINGTON, *Froomb!*

It simply carries this message:

Fluids running out of my brakes.

(?)

Missing: Believed . . . eaten?

EMIL PETAJA, *The Nets of Space*, (5 Star)

ONE NEUROTIC AMOEBA casually placed can alter the entire course of world history. Robert Sheckley says it's like that tiny pebble that sends ripples to the edge of the lake. And since Sheckley figures absolutely anything can happen the possible futures he envisions romp buoyantly all the way from wretched to raucus. If you balk and boggle at some of his predictions think of it this way: THE FUTURE WON'T JUST HAPPEN. IT WILL SNEAK UP ON YOU a little at a time.

ROBERT SHECKLEY, *Store of Infinity*, (Bantam)

They were furry things over seven feet tall and they came down to earth with a diabolical plan!

RUSS WINTERBOTHAM, *The Men From Arcturus*

THE BLURB PROFESSIONAL

He was a conscript astronaut; a galley-slave of space . . .

JOHN E. MULLER, *Perilous Galaxy*, (Badger)

THE BLURB PRACTICAL

Take a piece of bent copper wire and conquer the universe.

ERIC FRANK RUSSELL, *Next of Kin*, (Mayflower)

To create a new Metropolis press the right button . . . and run!

LOUIS TRIMBLE, *The City Machine*

THE BLURB PHILOSOPHICAL

Death is the only answer to war.

LEO P. KELLEY, *Odyssey to Earthdeath*

THE BLURB SARTORIAL

Across the galaxy to universes populated by the tailed, the scaled, and the properly tentacled.

KEITH LAUMER AND ROSEL GEORGE BROWN, *Earthblood*, (Coronet)

Terror in Needlepoint.

JOHN KEIR CROSS, *The Other Passenger*, (Ballantine)

THE BLURB DOOMSDAY

They alone, of all humanity, escaped destruction in the cosmic catastrophe that swept all life from the globe when the untried thorium bomb exploded prematurely.

WILLIAM DEXTER, *World In Eclipse*

When the first Pagbeast escaped from the mad scientist's laboratory, terror was loosed upon the world. Man faced complete annihilation. He had once again created the means of his own destruction.

J. T. MCINTOSH, *The Rule of the Pagbeast*, (Crest)

(First the atomic bomb, now the Pagbeast . . .)

THE BLURB DESCRIPTIVE

The blurb that does away with any need to ever read the book in question.

Was this brain of pulsating cells completely indestructible, this formless horror which threatened the world . . .

From the gloom of sinister swamp it devastates the peaceful farming area around Booger's Marsh, enormous, threatening to engulf the whole of doomed mankind . . . Science is baffled. Atomic holocaust fails to destroy the alien spawn or check its loathsome spread . . . One man – and a courageous girl, in the midst of the shrieking terror, stand between the black horror and total annihilation, finding in a quest for knowledge whereby to destroy the hideous slime monster a supreme test for love and endurance . . . And from the ashes and ruin gropes this same indomitable man and girl struggling desperately to preserve sanity amid utter chaos, sustained by an idea, a mere spark, fostering it, developing reason until, finally, ingenuity prevails, and love, with courage, conquers fear and solves the demoralising problem . . . What it was, its origin, no-one will ever know. For the answer could only be found—in hell . . .!

VICTOR NORWOOD, *Night of the Black Horror*, (Badger)

Alex was a pioneer. Like other pioneers he had problems. He had more problems than most. When things start to go wrong in space they go wrong in a big way. One by one the perils of the void took their toll of his companions. Alex was alone, alone with a vision, a vision of a town, home.

Only thoughts of home kept him alive. He remembered trees, houses, shops, churches, people . . . *people*.

At last he reached earth . . . or perhaps it wasn't earth? Things had changed unbelievably. Perhaps he had changed? How long had he been away? How far had he drifted? There was a sinister possibility that this wasn't home at all. If the things that looked like people weren't people, but aliens, what was he to do?

Alex was a realist. He knew what space could do to a man's mind. He was disinclined to trust the evidence of his own senses. A mind that has had more than it can take can produce some very peculiar perceptions . . .

PEL TORR, *The Last Astronaut*, (Badger)

The final blurb type is rather rare. In an attempt to find a new way to get a book off the shelves and into the buyer's pockets, Panther created:

THE BLURB NONEXISTENT

The publishers regret to announce that there is no blurb to inform prospective readers about the contents of *The Opener of the Way*. Unfortunately the person designated to write the blurb was found dead after reading the book, having apparently suffered some mysterious kind of severe shock . . .

ROBERT BLOCH, *The Opener of the Way*, (Panther)

BEFORE THE BEGINNING

'It is good to renew one's wonder,' said the philosopher. 'Space travel has again made children of us all.'

RAY BRADBURY, Epigraph to *Silver Locusts (Martian Chronicles)*

Authors often take the opportunity of saying something before the book actually starts. However, few have ever played around with the copyright notices . . .

Next of Kin is extended from a story entitled Plus X Copyright © Street and Smith Publications Inc. (actually Eustace Snarge), New York.

ERIC FRANK RUSSELL, *Next of Kin*

(In a story about imaginary symbiotes, called Eustaces, of which Russell said in his introduction:)

Apart from the typing of it I had nothing whatever to do with the book. It was ghost-written for me by my next of kin. Or perhaps I should say it was kin-written for me by my next of ghost.

(ibid.)

Other authors have rewritten the 'All persons etc. are imaginary' line:

Note: All characters in this novel are fictitious except possibly the Martians.

EDGAR PANGBORN, *A Mirror for Observers*

All persons, places, and events in this book are real . . . No names have been changed to protect the innocent, since God Almighty protects the innocent as a matter of Heavenly routine.

KURT VONNEGUT JR, *Sirens of Titan*

Others write forewords and author's notes. Pretentious:

Author's note: It is suggested that the reader not attempt to read this book at one sitting. The intellectual content of these stories, taken without break, may cause brain damage. This note is intended *most* sincerely, and not as hyperbole.

ARTHUR BYRON COVER, *The Platypus of Doom and Other Nihilists*

Honest:

Particularly disliking forewords, I seldom read them; yet it seems that I scarcely ever write a story that I do not inflict a foreword on my long-suffering readers. Occasionally I also have to inject a little weather and scenery in my deathless classics, two further examples of literary racketeering that I especially deplore in the writings of others. Yet there is something to be said in extenuation of weather and scenery, which, together with adjectives, do much to lighten the burdens of authors and run up their word count.

EDGAR RICE BURROUGHS, from foreword of *Skeleton Men of Jupiter*

And embarrassing:

Come with us, O readers, to a world where gleaming cities raise silver spires against the stars, sorcerers cast spells from subterranean lairs, baleful spirits stalk crumbing ruins . . . and the fate of kingdoms is balanced on the broadswords brandished by heroes of preternatural might and valour. In this world men are mighty, women are beautiful, problems are simple, and life is adventurous, and nobody has ever heard of inflation, the petroleum shortage, or atmospheric pollution!

L. SPRAGUE DECAMP, Introduction to *Conan The Barbarian*

Characters, Human and Otherwise

HEROES

'Today's hero is tomorrow's thug.'

HARLAN ELLISON, *SF Voices 3*

Everybody needs heroes. And the heroes of science fiction have always had a pretty good idea of their role in life.

Tough, noble, indestructible and able to wipe the floor with a dozen dirty aliens before breakfast.

Men like Tony Brant:

Tony Brant, lean and tough as a whipcoard (**sic**), with that sharp ageless cast of feature that personified the men of the 25th century. Neither physically, mentally nor biologically, Brant hadn't aged a day since he was twenty.

TREBOR THORPE, *Lightning World*

Men like Lt John MacGregor:

'I'll introduce myself. Name's Lt John MacGregor, as a matter of fact, in the I.P.F.'

'Interplanetary Force,' goggled Fred.

'Precisely,' said MacGregor with an exaggerated bow. 'My man, you are now in the presence of the John

MacGregor who has shot down seventeen of the Martian invasion fleet.'

LIONEL FANTHORPE, *Flame Mass*

They are modest:

Doc nodded. He had already noticed that, but he did not say so. He made it a policy never to disillusion one of his men who thought he had been first to notice something or get an idea, although Doc himself might have discovered it far earlier. It was this modesty of Doc's which helped endear him to everybody he was associated with.

LESTER DENT, *Doc Savage: The Man of Bronze*

'I have never known her to be wrong. She knew *you* were good, Blade!'

Richard Blade was, after all, an Englishman. Now he was embarrassed.

JEFFREY LORD, *Blade, The Jade Warrior*

'Hell's – jingling – bells!' he wrenched out, finally, and waved a hand at the points of light crowding so thickly his tactical tank. 'A thing that the whole damned Grand Fleet couldn't do, and he does it alone, and then he *apologizes* for it as thought he ought to be stood up in a corner or sent to bed without any supper!'

'Uh-huh, that's the way he is,' Kinnison breathed, in awe. 'What a brain! . . . What a man!'

E. E. 'DOC' SMITH, *Second Stage Lensman*

A murmur ran through the listeners. Heads turned to look at Cliff Davenport. For once in his life he felt slightly embarrassed. Proud too. The safety of the human race lay in his hands. He was being asked to deliver them from this peril of the deep. It was one helluva responsibility.

GUY N. SMITH, *Night of the Crabs*

They have incredible powers, such as telepathy:

'I am a mind reader par excellence. I intend to use my ability to work a great deal of good in the world, such as in detecting criminals and in showing up corrupt public officials.'

WILLIAM K. SONNEMANN, *The Master Minds of Venus*

The ability to move at speeds often considered impossible without a TARDIS:

Seeing escape impossible, the stranger halted, sank to one knee and levelled a ray-gun at the approaching figure of the earthman. Carter saw his finger whiten as he squeezed the trigger.

'Carter!' Kantos Kan shouted, 'Throw yourself to the floor.'

With the speed of light, Carter dropped prone. A long blade whizzed over his head and buried itself to the hilt in the heart of the stranger.

EDGAR RICE BURROUGHS, *John Carter of Mars*

And they spend their time having quite a number of harrowing, death-defying adventures and thrills:

'I've been all over the three worlds and three moons, and in my time I have enjoyed quite a number of harrowing, death-defying adventures and thrills, but in all my career I profess I haven't had one which matches that of the death's head meteor.'

NEIL R. JONES, *The Moon Pirates*

They may not be great conversationalists:

'Here we go again,' agreed the co-pilot; it didn't seem a particularly original remark, but he couldn't think of anything else to say. A conversational gambit like 'here we go again' isn't the kind of scintillating witticism that calls for a reply which would have delighted Dr Johnson or Voltaire!

PEL TORRO, *The Last Astronaut*

They may not be very bright:

'Let me tell you here and now, the Chief is far from being "bonkers" as you so respectfully suggest! He's got a theory . . .'

Paul laughed. 'You mean the old rumours about the Yellow Peril and all that? We used to read paperbacks about it, when I was a kid. A bit far fetched, isn't it?'

Barry grunted. 'Maybe. Maybe not. Something about making a world filled with their own sort of people. Asians.'

LUAN RANZETTA, *Yellow Inferno*

But they are quick to point out their personal failings (if any) to love-struck young heroines:

(Elric, tortured albino prince:) 'I should admit that I scream in my sleep sometimes and am often tortured by incommunicable self-loathing. Go while you can, lady, and forget Elric for he can only bring grief to your soul.'

MICHAEL MOORCOCK, *While the Gods Laugh*

And they bow to no man:

The Khad twisted on his throne and there was mingled rage and amazement in his tone. 'You *dare* to stand before me.'

Blade now was playing it by intuition. 'I stand,' he said calmly. 'Sir Blade bows to no man.'

JEFFREY LORD, *Blade, The Jade Warrior*

They are quick on the draw:

'I find your voice rather pleasant.'

'It's a good job somebody does,' said Salford. 'There have been occasions when my voice has been the last sound that some people hear.' He sounded grim.

'How is that? Please explain?' asked the robot.

'Perhaps the meaning will make itself evident when I say that the last words they heard were, "Reach for your blaster!"'

LEO BRETT, *Power Sphere*

In a difficult situation you can rely on a hero to remain unruffled:

'How much air have we got left in our emergency supplies?' asked Conrad Danes.

'Three, four hours, perhaps.'

'As narrow as that!' exclaimed Alex.

''Fraid so,' replied Jerry. 'Pretty grim, isn't it?'

PEL TORRO, *The Last Astronaut*

To square his jaw:

'I talk to you first, because I gather that you are the commander of your party . . . I know that you must be a man of some courage, and I hope that you will consider it sweet to die for your country, when the time comes.'

Barry squared his jaw. It sounded bad. Very bad.

LUAN RANZETTA, *Yellow Inferno*

And to smile:

'I'm not getting at you. I'm glad to know a man who can take things with a smile. Take it on the chin with a grin. Stiff upper lip, and all that jazz.' Hal Delaney smiled too. A cynical smile, there were too many blisters on his face for it to be anything else. It was one of those wry, painful smiles that only a hero can produce, in moments of extremity.

LIONEL FANTHORPE, *Flame Mass*

Even after they've been bumped off (valiantly, of course) heroes keep an eye on the raw recruits:

'Rasczak's Roughnecks have got a reputation to uphold. The Lieutenant told me before he bought it to tell *you* that he will always have his eye on you every minute . . . and that he expects your names to *shine*!'

ROBERT HEINLEIN, *Starship Troopers*

In a hero's life there is only room for two women. His true love, and his mother:

He had gained fame, and lost the trust of the one person in the world, apart from his mother, on whom he could really depend.

TERENCE HAILE, *Space Train*

Women who have very clearly defined roles:

'Sending a woman to talk about rocket-engines! The man must be off his head! See you later, Mum!'

(*ibid.*)

A hero *can* be a scientist, but if he is, he makes sure that everyone knows he's just one of the boys at heart:

'I'm just about done here. I'll be ready tomorrow, I think, to visit their library and tape up some planetographical and planetological – notice how insouciantly I toss off those two-credit words? – data on this here planet Hodell.'

E. E. 'DOC' SMITH, *The Galaxy Primes*

A hero is a diplomat:

'My name is Brant,' said Tony. 'I'm the leader of this expedition. We come from the planet earth. It's so far away I don't suppose your half-wit chemists have ever heard of it!'

'That's the stuff!' applauded Joe. 'Put the fatheads in their place! Did you ever see such a crummy lot of 'em?'

TREBOR THORPE, *Lightning World*

And, at the end of the day a hero always stops to reflect on what he's gained:

A universe for his freedom. And a woman like Mai Valoris to call his own. It was a good exchange, Reed Norvack thought. It was worth the killing of an evil god.

JAMES HARVEY, *Titans of the Universe*

WOMEN

Science fiction is one of the few places where a pretty girl can be a damned nuisance.

JOHN TAINE, *Of Worlds Beyond*

Many of the women in science fiction find themselves tacked on as an afterthought. Something for the men to return to. Something to keep the hero mindful of his job in moments of stress. Something to be kidnapped at the start of the book and rescued at the end.

Let's meet a few:

The first was a woman of about forty-five and she'd been attractive until someone had hewn her almost in half.

LIONEL AND PATRICIA FANTHORPE, *The Black Lion*

She was so pretty, just the kind of girl he liked best – dark hair curling softly around her face, big brown eyes . . . a mouth just meant for kissing.

ROBERT FRENCH, *Now the Gods*

He gazed down at her face from his six feet two inches of strongly muscled frame. She was pretty in a dainty, delicate kind of way, with a pale face from which Arthur assumed that she had perhaps recently had a severe illness, which might account for her presence on the bracing, but gusty, east coast, so early in the year.

TOM WADE, *The World of Theda*

Some have sexy, truck-like bodies:

This body was built for intercontinental hauling and had the apparatus that was made for endurance. It had everything a man could want in a woman. It was the wanton, uncivilised body that all men had longed to possess since the days of the cave man. It exuded purely animal sexuality.

SUE PAYER, *Second Body*

But they are usually good eggs:

'Don't be dumb, Norman. That woman's a knockout – a riot – a regular tri-planet call-out!'

'Oh, she's all x, as far as that goes. She's a good little egg, too – not half as dumb as she acts – and she's one of the squarest little aces that ever waved a plume.'

E. E. 'DOC' SMITH, *Spacehounds of IPC*

A few are icebergs – at least until the hero thaws them out:

'Still, if that's actually your picture of Brownie, just what kind of a woman *could* you love? If any?'

'Belle.'

'*Belle*? Belle *Bellamy*? For godsake! That iceberg? That egomaniac? She's a pure, unalloyed bitch!'

'Right, on all counts. She's also crooked and treacherous. She's a liar by instinct and training. I could add a lot more. But she's got brains, ability, and guts. She's got the spine and the bottom and the drive. So just imagine her, thawed out. Back to back with you when you're surrounded – she wouldn't cave and she wouldn't give. Or wing and wing – holding the beam come hell or space-warps. Roll that one around on your tongue, Jim, and give your taste-buds a treat.'

E. E. 'DOC' SMITH, *The Galaxy Primes*

Some aren't even human:

The huge electronic brain was a matter for constant concern. She was new and raw and sometimes temperamental. That was a trait which was almost expected in anything feminine, even if only declared so arbitrarily, as was the case with the big brain.

A. A. GLYNN, *Plan for Conquest*

When women *do* go into space, they have clearly defined roles:

'This little jaunt of ours is strictly business, and don't any of you forget it! I mean about Mandy. She's coming as our secretary. She's fully trained for space travel. She's tough as they come.'

LUAN RANZETTA, *Yellow Inferno*

(For a secretary, anyway.)

But as soon as they've found their heroes they give all that sort of thing up for good:

'[The space ship] has been given to the five of us,' he concluded.

'Four of you,' smiled Ena. 'A woman has more important work to do on Earth, than wander around in space . . . especially a married woman.'

VICTOR WADEY, *The United Planets*

Women have a number of instinctive skills that men don't, and science fiction writers are quick to recognize this:

'I let them dry. But I wash now. I think I do more better than you.'

He laughed. 'It's instinctive, I guess – something carried in the genes that make women want to wash clothes!'

RENA VALE, *Taurus Four*

Helen Powell kept her head and began working away bravely at the gag. She was glad that she had washed her cardigan in soft, gentle soap flakes, in accordance with the instructions on its ticket. She would not have fancied chewing her way through wool that might have been flavoured with powerful detergent!

KARL ZEIGFREID, *Projection Infinity*

And it's not just washing:

She frowned. 'I've felt so guilty and useless, running about cleaning house, while you two were fighting for my life.'

J. HUNTER HOLLY, *The Flying Eyes*

He read the note she had left him: '*Darling Alex, Something had to be done. I have destroyed the thing in the engine room. Unfortunately there was rather a lot of radiation and I didn't fancy going that way, so I went through the lock instead. I expect it will be quite fun in hyper-space.*'

PEL TORRO, *The Last Astronaut*

On the outside they may seem tough:

She would be betraying her friends who expected so much from her. Too much, she often thought. Did they forget she was a mere woman?

LUAN RANZETTA, *Yellow Inferno*

But even when fighting the forces of gravity their minds are never far away from the way they look:

Orlande Price struggled with forces that were pulling her facial contours out of shape. Her struggles seemed to epitomise woman's life-long struggles to keep up with fashion and not to keep up with the passage of the years.

PEL TORRO, *The Last Astronaut*

Obviously, no matter what happens in future society, women will stay the same:

The cybernetic control of New Society had not prevented its housewives from calling on each other at odd times of the day while their mutual menfolk were working. Like housewives everywhere, they had snippets of mutually interesting information to exchange. Like housewives everywhere, they rushed into each other's kitchens in times of crisis when the men were absent.

A. A. GLYNN, *Plan for Conquest*

Women aren't men. They do things that men wouldn't do. Like run away:

This running away was not in their line of duty. How could they ever contact their home base if they remained hidden in the hills for ever, dependent upon the whims and the know-how of a female scientist with the welfare of Tibet and China at heart?

LUAN RANZETTA, *Yellow Inferno*

Or use feminine wiles:

Consequently she hadn't been in Horton's Crossing more than a few hours before in addition to gleaning considerably more information than her contemporaries by virtue of vastly differing approach and unscrupulous methods only a woman could employ she established her first conquest in the stocky, hairy-chested person of Corporal Danny Mareno . . .

VICTOR NORWOOD, *Night of the Black Horror*

In the instant that our glances had met I had seen that she, whom I took to be a woman, would, if she had had the power, make men slaves, but in that same instant she had seen, in my eyes, that it was men who were the stronger, who held the power, and that it would be she, if any, who would be the slave.

JOHN NORMAN, *Raiders of Gor*

They aren't all brainless:

'You do know my name,' the stranger's thought came clearly now. 'I am the "Toots", the "Rep-Top", the "Queen of Sheba", the "Cleopatra", the Elder Person of Lyrane II. Do you remember me, Kinnison of Tellus?'

'I certainly do!' he shot back. What a brain – what a *terrific* brain – that sexless woman had!

E. E. 'DOC' SMITH, *Second Stage Lensman*

And although sometimes they object to the way that men are always fighting:

'Weapons, weapons – always *weapons*! The eternal *male*! If it were not for your huge vessel and the peculiar airplane hovering over us I would claw your eyes out and strangle you with my bare hands.'

(*ibid.*)

When the chips are down, they appreciate it:

'If I do not please you,' she screamed, 'beat me or kill me!' He kissed her swiftly, and turned to defend a wall.

JOHN NORMAN, *Raiders of Gor*

Then have a good cry afterwards:

She held Hilda to her and let her have a good cry, and this was a wonderful relief after all the pent up feelings of those last few days of prison and cruel treatment by the octopoids.

TOM WADE, *The World of Theda*

Some women are unduly forward:

'And I suppose you got the thought – it must have jumped up and smacked you' – Lola's hot blush was visible even through her heavy tan – 'how many times I've felt like running my fingers up and down your ribs and grabbing a handful of those muscles of yours, just to see if they're as hard as they look?'

E. E. 'DOC' SMITH, *The Galaxy Primes*

Men don't always give them what they want:

He released me quickly, for I was left standing, kissless.

ANNE MCCAFFREY, *Restoree*

But at least in Port Kar they know how to treat them:

The men of Port Kar, I said, know well how to treat women. The men of Port Kar, I said to myself, know well how to keep women.

As slaves and slaves alone!

Worthless are they for aught else!

JOHN NORMAN, *Raiders of Gor*

Scientists, Mostly Sane

'Technology! How can any man who means to keep his sanity go far in such an art?'

FRED SABERHAGEN, *Empire of the East*

The scientist is a stock figure in SF. Whether physically deformed:

His Lordship, J conceded, looked full of beans today . . . The yellow eyes were clear and even the polio-stricken legs had a new energy. Today Lord L was wearing a discreetly chalk-striped grey lounge suit that somewhat mitigated his hump. His tie was a horror, of course, but then it always was.

JEFFREY LORD, *Blade: The Jade Warrior*

Physically perfect (and a dab hand at fisticuffs, no doubt):

She flipped the coin dexterously. 'Heads it is, Lola, so I get Jim – James James James the Ninth himself. You have the honor of pairing with Clee – or should I say His Learnedness Right the Honourable Director Doctor Cleander Simmsworth Garlock, Doctor of Philosophy, Doctor of Science, Prime Operator, President and First Fellow of the Galaxian Society, First Fellow of the Gunther Society, Fellow of the Institute of Paraphysics, of the Institute of Nuclear Physics, of the College of Mathematics, of the Congress of Psiontists, and of all the other top-bracket brain-gangs you ever heard of. Also, for your information, his men have given him a couple of informal degrees – P.D.Q. and S.O.B.'

E. E. 'DOC' SMITH, *The Galaxy Primes*

Elderly and academic:

'And now tell us of yourself,' said 25X-987, 'and about your world.'

Professor Jameson, noted in college as a lecturer of no mean ability and perfectly capable of relating intelligently to them the story of the Earth's history, evolution and march of events following the birth of civilization up until the time when he had died, began his story.

NEIL R. JONES, *The Planet of the Double Sun*

Practical:

He was a practical electrician . . . He doubted the existence of the Deity but accepted Carnot's cycle, and he had read Shakespeare and found him weak in chemistry.

H. G. WELLS, *Lord of the Dynamos*

Sweaty:

Locksley had won every single letter by the sweat of his brow and that was literal, for profuse perspiration was a by-product of his keen thought process.

LIONEL FANTHORPE, *Flame Mass*

Half-crazy:

'He was easy to care about. Half-crazy sometimes, maybe. But I guess you can't be a seven-foot tall genius and not be.'

LARRY NIVEN AND STEVEN BARNES, *The Descent of Anansi*

Gayle dropped the wrench with a sigh of satisfaction and stepped back to view the latest product of his delusion-tormented mind.

MILTON KALETSKY, *The Beam*

Many are vague and elderly:

'The professor was muttering contentedly in the brush, pocketing plant specimens and dissecting small vermin with his nail clippers.'

JOHN SILBERSACK, *No Frills Science Fiction*

Some charming with it:

When the inventor, Patsy Kelly, was asked how ships could move at seven times the speed of light when the limiting velocity of matter, according to Einstein, was the speed of light, he responded in his droll Goidelic way, with a shrug, 'Well – sure and I guess Einstein was wrong.'

HARRY HARRISON, *Space Rats of the CCC*

Scientists know the value of the spoken word, and are forever mystifying the poor mortals around their laboratories. Not just with scientific double talk, either:

'Oooohhh!' the psychiatrist's voice was loaded with meaning, and interrogation.

LIONEL FANTHORPE, *Flame Mass*

'Understanding one madman throws light on others. There are no sacred cows in the laboratory.'

'I will not follow the capitalist herring,' Lepilov growled.

FRANK HERBERT, *The White Plague*

Sometimes they can be alarmingly straightforward. Here a lady genius explains a batch of super-chlorophyll she's just knocked together to save everyone on a spaceship from expiring from lack of air:

'I've never seen anything like them before,' said Jerry.

'No, they're a new species,' said Ursula. 'I've just made them.'

'Fantastic!' said Jerry.

PEL TORRO, *The Last Astronaut*

This particular lady genius also has an uncanny knowledge of the working of the human mind. Like many other SF characters (Hari Seldon and co) she is able to predict how people will react in a given situation:

'In a moment I predict that you will do one of two things. You will either get up and hit me, or you will burst into jolly, jovial, tension-releasing laughter, and we may soon be the best of friends . . .'

(*ibid.*)

Scientists love explaining:

Kel produced a bottle of powerful antibiotic. 'This kills nearly every known bug in the universe, let's hope it's going to work.'

TREBOR THORPE, *Lightning World*

(**The Professor explains . . .**) 'For a person travelling at or near the speed of light, which, as you know, is just slightly over a hundred and eighty-six thousand miles per second, the difference in time flow would be so great that during what would appear to him as the passage of one year, something like two hundred and fifty million years would pass on earth.'

'You can't be serious,' Eve said.

'If this is true how come the public doesn't know about it?' Jonathan demanded.

JOHN MANTLEY, *The 27th Day*

Unfortunately, unless a scientist is also the hero, he is going to be unreliable. When threatened with an operation that would leave his head in one room and his body in another (with pipes connecting the two) most heroes would merely square their jaws and grin manly grins. Scientists are made of baser stuff:

'But who will submit to such an experiment?' queried the professor weakly, plainly aghast at this man's inhuman attitude, with its cruel disregard for human life and suffering.

'You will!' snapped the human-robot with terrible finality in his tone, and a merciless sneer of contempt upon his pale features.

'No – no – no, not that!' pleaded Crayton, shivering so dreadfully that he tottered weakly to his knees and sought support by grasping a near-by table. 'I'll do — anything but that!'

NEIL R. JONES, *The Moon Pirates*

The common people don't trust them:

'I've never really agreed with that harmless, crazy scientist picture,' Peruge said. 'I don't think they're all innocent and harmless. To me no atomic physicist is completely responsible and trustworthy.'

'Ohh, come now, Mr Peruge . . . the doc makes movies about bugs.'

FRANK HERBERT, *Hellstrom's Hive*

Unless they read Lionel Fanthorpe:

'Some kind of force field – these boffins are experimenting with them, I believe.' Jinks was an intelligent man. He read and understood the novels of Fanthorpe, Muller and Fane.

KARL ZEIGFREID, *Projection Infinity*

Bits of some professors will keep dropping off:

. . . the professor's eyebrows came crashing down.

SAMUEL DELANY, *Ballad of Beta 2*

When confronted by a menace, scientists tend to be overconfident:

'In that case,' the scientist said, 'mankind and normal life here on earth is doomed — But such pessimism is totally unwarranted. I've had considerable experience in similar fields of research, sheriff. Delving into mysteries and unknown nuclear forces is my province, and I shall, I promise you, devote my undivided attention to solving the strange enigma of this incredible spawn . . .'

VICTOR NORWOOD, *Night of the Black Horror*

Some are so set in their ways that they are just not open to new ideas:

The professor was on the verge of exploding. 'No man can have lived since the days of Moses. Four thousand years! It's absurd. I happen to be an anthropologist, and I know!'

P. SCHUYLER MILLER, *Old Man Mulligan*

I have no doubt that it was such professors that prompted Arthur C. Clarke to write:

Scientists of over fifty are good for nothing except board meetings and should at all costs be kept out of the laboratory.

ARTHUR C. CLARKE, *Profiles of the Future*

But at the end of the day, if the scientist is pure in heart, and engaged to another scientist, and doesn't have a hunchback or a Central European accent, he can say things like:

'Diana's a smart girl, and a damn fine chemist, and she learned a lot from her father. So did I, and if Diana's theory about vibrations is correct, and I can't find a single flaw in it taking it at face value, between us we can contrive the destruction of that creature this very afternoon . . .'

VICTOR NORWOOD, *Night of the Black Horror*

and be right.

THE BAD GUYS

Unlike in films, where the bad guys get most of the good dialogue and all of the fun, bad guys in SF books tend to get a very rough deal – especially in the looks department.

Sakya went a sickly green, whether from anger or from a guilty conscience, Barry could not tell.

LUAN RANZETTA, *Yellow Inferno*

On a green crystal throne, on a huge raised dais, surrounded by silk and satin, surrounded by all the fabrics that go to make up voluptuous luxury, sat a green humanoid figure. Flesh hung in rolls on its evil face. Little piggy eyes gleamed and glared at them . . . The little eyes in the fleshy face turned into two ice-cold diamonds; bitter, savage, hard . . . burning with a fire of hatred and an evil sense of power.

TREBOR THORPE, *Lightning World*

His little bloodshot eyes regarded them – curious, cunning, hopeful, rather like the eyes of an intelligent pig calculating its chances of eating the baby.

AVRAM DAVIDSON, *Mutiny in Space*

The Irishman's bullet-hard head crashed straight into the soft jowls of the pudding-like jelly that called itself Blenkinsop.

LIONEL FANTHORPE, *The Golden Chalice*

And his ears – there was something very odd about the lobes of his ears. They lay close to his head, and they were very, very long – unnatural lobes, appended to unusual ears. Wherever you went it seemed that great-uncle Roderick's ears were following you.

(*ibid.*)

Under that nose his teeth . . . they were the two things you noticed about his face first – there was a third thing, but I'll come to that in a minute – but his nose and his brown teeth, all colours, horrible colours like a mouthful of evil growing out of his gums when he parts his lips in a snarl.

(*ibid.*)

His was the most repellent face Bert had ever seen. Close-set yellowish eyes stared from it ferociously, and a livid scar extended from below the right eye to his chin, deforming both lips as it crossed the hard mouth – a face never to be forgotten.

HARL VINCENT, *The Barrier*

All they want is to be Masters of the Entire Galaxy:

DuQuesne cut off his forces and sat back at the controls, relaxed, his black eyes staring into infinity. Earth was his, to do with as he wished; and he would soon have it so armed that he could hold it against the universe. Master of Earth! His highest ambition had been attained – or had it? The world, after all, was small – merely a mote in space. Why not be master of the entire galaxy?

E. E. 'DOC' SMITH, *Skylark of Valeron*

Bad guys are pitiless:

Utterly callous, DuQuesne neither felt nor expressed the slightest sign of pity for the race of beings so suddenly snuffed out of existence. 'Their removal at this time will undoubtedly save me a lot of trouble later on,' he added.

(*ibid.*)

'You fool!' Bleeko gloated from behind his massive desk. His face flamed with sadistic joy and anticipation. 'You trusting, greedy fool! I have you exactly where I want you now. How easy! How simple! This entire building is screened and shielded – by *my* screens and shields. Your friends and accomplices, whoever or wherever they are, can neither see you nor know what is to happen to you. If your ship attempts your rescue it will be blasted out of the ether. I will, personally, gouge out your eyes, tear off your nails, strip your hide from your quivering carcass . . .'

E. E. 'DOC' SMITH, *Second Stage Lensman*

And sadistic:

It was obviously Larsen's intention to flog the engineer as ship captains back in the age of sail, half a thousand years ago, used to do. But Larsen didn't look like a man preparing even zestfully to enforce discipline. He looked like a man lustfully anticipating murder.

MURRAY LEINSTER, *Invaders of Space*

They say things like:

The pirate stared suspiciously, then, eyes firmly on Lucky's blaster, yelled, 'Blinking Space, there's a ripper with a gat here.'

ISAAC ASIMOV, *Pirates of the Asteroids*

'He has the mind of a fiend!'

'That comes of bringing the dead back to life,' said Quendan cryptically.

NEIL R. JONES, *The Moon Pirates*

'You are too soft with the accursed Mona people, Congnicubbicca,' Brandicca sneered. They exchanged hateful looks.

DAVID R. MORGAN, *The Strange Case of William Whipper-Snapper*

Pograt staggered for a moment and then turned.

'You die for that, Earthling!' But before he could fire several of the slaves jumped on him.

(*ibid.*)

'Don't threaten me with that thing,' said the dreadful bacteriologist, 'I can fire mine as quickly as you can fire that!'

JOHN E. MULLER, *Micro Infinity*

They menace their women:

'Carlos!'

'Ahhh, my love, someday I shall teach you to say that exquisite name with true passion.'

FRANK HERBERT, *Hellstrom's Hive*

And fink on their friends:

'Calot!' he hissed. 'Ever did I think you carried the heart of a sorak in your putrid breast. Often have you bested me in the secret councils of Issus, but now in the field of war where men are truly gauged your scabby heart hath revealed its sores to all the world. Calot, I spurn you with my foot,' and with the words he turned to kick Xodar.

EDGAR RICE BURROUGHS, *The Gods of Mars*

Noor Kama said casually, 'To convince you I speak the truth, let me tell you that Felton Pratt was killed because he is the murderer of Nels Larsen. Or at least, this is what the rumour says. He got to be too big for his clingpants and—had to be removed.'

JAMES HARVEY, *Titans of the Universe*

However, most bad guys have one good quality: whenever the hero is in their power, they stop to gloat and then considerately explain how their evil plans can be thwarted:

'Why do you Englishmen always think we are so stupid? I have merely to pull down this red lever, and the whole fleet of over a thousand satellites would be blown to smithereens, as you say.'

LUAN RANZETTA, *Yellow Inferno*

ALIENS

'The great roe is a mythological beast with the head of a lion and the body of a lion, though not the same lion.'

WOODY ALLEN, *Without Feathers*

Mythological creatures were the first aliens—but what about *real* aliens? *Alien* aliens from other planets. Beings that, on first contact, provoke remarks like:

'Maybe these creatures will be aesthetic marvels, nice and friendly and polite – and underneath with the sneaking brutal ferocity of the Japanese. Or maybe they'll be crude and gruff as a Swedish farmer – and just as decent underneath.'

MURRAY LEINSTER, *First Contact*

What will they *look* like?

To staid, Earthly inhabitants of forty million years past, Zora would have appeared as a weird monstrosity. Yet her features, her curved, undulating lines and graceful, waving tentacles were harmonizing and symphonious to the eye.

NEIL R. JONES, *Space War*

Hanging in the air, suspended without visible means of support, was a gigantic brain, approximately two feet in diameter. A naked brain, with the convolutions exposed. It was a ghastly thing.

The horror of it was heightened by the two tiny, pig-like, lidless, close-set eyes and a curving beak which hung directly below the frontal portion of the brain, resting in what was apparently an atrophied face.

CLIFFORD D. SIMAK, *The World of the Red Sun*

Men, upon Lyrane II, were dwarfs about thirty inches tall. They had the temper and the disposition of a mad Radeligian cateagle, the intellectual capacity of a Zabriskan fontema.

E. E. 'DOC' SMITH, *Second Stage Lensman*

She paused in the operation of starting, however, for there drifted down in front of her the most grotesque figure she had ever seen outside the theatre.

WILLIAM K. SONNEMANN, *The Master Minds of Venus*

The eyes, at this close range, seemed quite cold and pitiless; and Arthur seriously doubted, as he gazed at these strange being, possessing, as they did their type of features, the two protuberant, almost jet black eyes, set at the extreme outward edge of the curved head, together with, as he was now able to see, a tiny slit about four inches below them, which was presumably the mouth, whether the creatures were able to express emotion of any kind. Compassion, at least, would be most difficult.

TOM WADE, *The World of Theda*

Will they have names or numbers?

Among the adventure-scarred veterans still pregnable to the lure of the mysterious cosmos, and who had come through the war with the Mumes with undamaged heads were 6W-438, 20R-654, 41C-98, 29G-75, 6N-24, 47X-09 and 2Y-4. Then there were three of the converts from the ranks of the Tripeds, Glrg, Ravlt and Jbf, known among the Zoromes as 454ZQ2, 92ZQ153, and 5ZQ35.

NEIL R. JONES, *Space War*

'Shart, Melath, Odioth,' B'lerion closed a finger onto his palm with each name. 'Nabeth, as you suspected, Ponteth and Bidorth. That seven, and if my memory serves me, N'mool, Bidorth's rider, comes from Telgar Upper Plains . . .'

ANNE MCCAFFREY, *Moreta – Dragonlady of Pern*

'L'vin, W'ter, and H'grave attended both Gathers. I've recommended M'gent.'

(*ibid.*)

Might they be eels?

'Mistress Sin. Her talents are equally unique. Her specialities are seduction and erotica, which have powers in certain human situations where even force of arms might fail. However, lest anyone should be tempted to jump into bed with her, they should be warned that she also has an electro-muscular system donated by her fishy ancestry.'

COLIN KAPP, *Cageworld No 1: Search for the Sun!*

Or crustaceans?

Such crabs! They were as large as 'buses . . . He realised that they were what he had mistaken for mist.

TERENCE HAILE, *Space Train*

Are they immortal?

'Some of the Proavitoi say they do not die, Nokoma. Is this true?'

'How is not be true? If they die, they not be here to say they do not die. Oh, I joke, I joke. No, we do not die. It is a foolish alien custom which we see no reason to imitate. On Proavitus, only the low creatures die.'

R. A. LAFFERTY, *Nine Hundred Grandmothers*

Are they sane?

'He's either the most hopeless raving lunatic I've ever heard,' commented John, 'or else he's some incredible entity from beyond the hyperdrive lanes.'

LIONEL FANTHORPE, *Flame Mass*

Or socially acceptable?

[**Re evil Green aliens:**] They might form an object lesson in how-not-to-run-a-society, but as travelling companions they were very definitely non-U.

TREBOR THORPE, *Lightning World*

Are they beatable?

'The alien enemy . . . that we will be facing in a few hours is tough. We might as well accept that fact. But – being an Alien, he is not as tough as we are.'

GORDON DICKSON, *Naked to the Stars*

Will they understand such concepts as compassion, help and niceness?

'It would seem self-evident that all intelligent races, whatever their outward form or mental status, should work together harmoniously for their mutual advancement.'

'Bah!' snapped the amoebus savagely. 'That is the talk of a weakling – the whining, begging reasoning of a race of low intelligence, one which knows and acknowledges itself inferior. Know you, feeble brain, that we of Chlora' – to substitute an intelligible word for the unpronounceable and untranslatable thought-image of his native world—'neither require nor desire cooperation. We are in no need either of assistance or of instruction from any lesser and lower form of life. We instruct. Other races, such as yours, either obey or are obliterated.'

E. E. 'DOC' SMITH, *Skylark of Valeron*

'In our world,' replied Arthur, 'it is the normal thing for one who is able to give help to go to the rescue of one of our race who might be in some trouble or difficulty. Is that not done here?'

'I cannot understand such a stupid idea; that is not reason, it is merely a form of low instinct,' continued the monstrous ruler. 'You people must be very low in the scale of evolution to have such impulses.'

TOM WADE, *The World of Theda*

Could they be regular guys underneath?

'Good grief! They're intelligent!' gasped Tony to Ray. 'Turn around and look. There's the guy who got you out! So he's got a flat head and green skin. So what? He saved your life.'

TREBOR THORPE, *Lightning World*

Or not?

A solitary 'Venusian' on an alien Earth behaves as humans consciously or subconsciously *expect* a blob from outer space to behave . . . in his guts he *knew* I wanted to eat his brain.

RUDY RUCKER, *Jumpin' Jack Flash*

What kind of weaponry will they have? What kind of protection?

'They are eyes. And they're like human eyes. Therefore, they should be as vulnerable as human eyes.'

'Right,' Wes said. 'Nothing's more vulnerable than an eye. It has no armour – nothing but a blink to protect it.'

J. HUNTER HOLLY, *The Flying Eyes*

His only thought was a bemused observation that aliens were supposed to have ray-guns, and not sword-sticks.

JAMES WHITE, *The Secret Visitors*

Will they say things like:

'Man is a joke, a clown, a parasite. He is nothing; he will be less.

'*Come and go mad.*'

FREDERIC BROWN, *Come and Go Mad*

'Where have you been, my earth lover? Have you been away? The long passionate night is calling. The sublime flowers of the forest smile on us. Together, we must lie down to sleep.' Oon's language was simple, natural and direct.

JAMES GRAZIER, *Runts of 61 Cygni C*

'Already he speaks our not-so-easy language.'

ANNE MCCAFFREY, *Decision at Doona*

'We juggle priceless eggs in variable gravity. I am afraid. I will taste fear until I die.'

JERRY POURNELLE AND LARRY NIVEN, *The Mote in God's Eye*

'Keep away from each other,' daleked the splodge.

FIONA RICHMOND, *Galactic Girl*

Wilson looked at Ly-shan and said, 'The Wykzl here can tell you what I'm saying is true. The Dynarx use this drug as an integral part of their deepest religious rites.'

'They are drug-crazed heathens,' Ky-shan confirmed.

E. E. 'DOC' SMITH, *Lord Tedric: The Space Pirates*

But above all – *will they play cricket?*

The new cricket enthusiast now proceeded to purchase a stock of bats, balls, bails, stumps, gloves and nets, and a great quantity of cricketing manuals to take back to Terra.

'And when I have formed a first class team on Terra,' he announced, 'Terra will challenge the best team that Earth can muster.'

VICTOR WADEY, *The United Planets*

MAN – THE MEANEST CRITTER IN THE WHOLE UNIVERSE!

Chiefly propagated by *Astounding Science Fiction*, the philosophy that man is the master-race, and that critters that squirm, crawl, undulate, wiggle or flop should be blasted, flamed, toasted, or blatted—and that the alien races could not best mankind, because we are the only race with a sense of humour, the ability to do long division, or to dream, was a popular one with adolescent readers.

E. E. 'Doc' Smith's rallying cry seems a trifle disturbing in the light of mid-twentieth century events:

'I'll bet my shirt that the chlorins are wiping out the civilization of that planet – probably people more or less like us. What d'you say, folks – do we declare ourselves in on this, or not?'

'I'll tell the cockeyed world . . . I believe that we should . . . By all means . . .' came from Dorothy, Margaret, and Crane.

'I knew you'd back me up. Humanity *uber alles* – *homo sapiens* against all the vermin of the universe! Let's go, *Two* – do your stuff!'

E. E. 'DOC' SMITH, *Skylark of Valeron*

Here Keith Laumer and Rosel George Brown explain the difference between Gooks and Geeks:

'You've got a lot to learn, lad. Most of the boys are humanoids; I've even got a couple that call themselves Terries; I guess they've got some Terry blood, but it's pretty badly mutated stock. They don't like having us damn near pure breeds around. It makes 'em look like what they are. Gooks.' He took a swallow from his glass, blew air over his teeth.

'I don't like to work around Gooks, but what the hell; it's better'n living with Geeks.'

'What's the difference between a Gook and a Geek?'

'I stretch a point: if a being's humanoid, like a Minid or a Chronid, O.K., give him the benefit of the doubt. Maybe he's descended from mutated stock. You got to make allowances for Gooks. But a life-form that's strictly non-human – that's a Geek.'

'Why do you hate Geeks?'

'I don't really hate 'em – but it's them or us.'

KEITH LAUMER AND ROSEL GEORGE BROWN, *Earthblood*

Put more simply:

An Earthman is an Earthman the universe over. No other planet seems to produce men of quite the same type or of quite the same calibre.

LEO BRETT, *Power Sphere*

And what about the jolly bad show of trying to pass yourself off as a genuine Earth stock, then?

Being of genuine Earth-stock, Salford found that pseudo-terrestrial accents really irritated him. It was like running into a man wearing a cheap impersonation of a school tie to which he was not entitled.

(*ibid.*)

Here a Heinlein hero does a spot of toasting:

So I merely blinked hard – opened my eyes and stared straight at a local citizen just coming out of an opening in the building ahead of me. He looked at me, I looked at him, and he started to raise something – a weapon, I suppose – as Jelly called out, 'Odd numbers! *Advance*!'

I didn't have time to fool with him; I was a good five hundred yards short of where I should have been by then. I still had the hand flamer in my left hand; I toasted him and jumped over the building he had been coming out of, as I started to count.

ROBERT A. HEINLEIN, *Starship Troopers*

To put it another way:

'For his own peace of mind, the space sociologist should sometimes kick the dirty savage on his bare butt.'

RENA VALE, *Taurus Four*

It was Kingsley Amis, in his seminal critique of SF who observed that:

In space-opera, Mars takes the place of Arizona with a few physical alterations, the hero totes a blazer instead of a six-gun, bad men are replaced by bad aliens looking just like bad men with a perfunctory sixth digit, and

Indians turn up in the revised form of what are technically known as bug-eyed monsters.

KINGSLEY AMIS, *New Maps of Hell*

Try the experiment on the following passages:

'Be smart, kid,' Henry Dread said between gritted teeth. 'Drop it, before I have to burn you . . .' He was tall and solid, with a scarred face and thick fingers. He stood, two guns aimed at Roan, tense and ready, and the sweat trickled down his face.

'Try it,' Roan said.

Henry Dread's mouth twisted in a sort of smile. 'Yeah, you're fast, kid. Nobody ever took a gun away from Czack like that before. I don't think he likes you for it –'

'Why don't you kill the muck-grub . . .!' The horned one stood in a half-crouch, eyes on Roan.

KEITH LAUMER AND ROSEL GEORGE BROWN, *Earthblood*

Before he would be accepted as a 'regular' he knew that he would have to prove his quality. Buckos and bullies would be sure to try him out. This way was much better. The tale would spread; and any gunman who had drilled two hi-jackers, dead-centre through the face-plates, was not one to be challenged lightly.

E. E. 'DOC' SMITH, *Grey Lensman*

Real Spacemen don't waste time Seeing if The Quiche is Friendly:

There was a satisfying crack as his mighty right exploded like a tornado on the point of Blenkinsopp's jaw – if such a fat-shrouded protuberance could be said to have a 'point'. Whatever the anatomical mystery beneath that layer of fat, the result was equally satisfactory, and spectacular. Blenkinsopp's eyes glazed and then closed about a fifth of a second before that bloated body crashed to the floor and lay very, very still.

LIONEL FANTHORPE, *The Golden Chalice*

To those who had no reason to fear the Guards, he was honest, tough, steely-eyed, lantern-jawed, righteous, self-righteous and a Good Guy. To those who had reason, he was honest, tough, steely-eyed, lantern-jawed, righteous and a moron.

THOM KEYES, *The Battle of Disneyland*

Davis saw Slip Hanlan's lips curl in a snarl of fury. No dame laughed at him!

P. SCHUYLER MILLER, *Old Man Mulligan*

'Anything is better than sitting around here waiting for it to flop over those hills,' Colonel Jamison snapped.

VICTOR NORWOOD, *Night of the Black Horror*

'I think I have a realistic view of human nature. Isaac Asimov has an asinine motto, "Violence is the last refuge of the incompetent." I agree with it completely – if it's read properly. That is, only the incompetent wait until it's the last resort.'

JERRY POURNELLE, in *Dream Makers 2* by CHARLES PLATT

Bruce the pilot acknowledged this with a bit of a grunt. 'Uh huh . . .' he managed to let out between his teeth.

NEAL RAFCAM, *The Troglodytes*

'Step up, step up and kill a woman! Get rid of a load of repressions! Squeeze the trigger and feel the old anger ooze out of you! Better than a massage! Better than getting drunk! Step up, step up and kill a woman!'

ROBERT SHECKLEY, *Love Incorporated*

ROBOTS

'I made you, don't you understand? I'm human, I made you —'

WALTER M. MILLER JR, *I Made You*

Science fiction robots come in all shapes and sizes. They can be cute or menacing, intelligent or stupid, cheerful or depressed. Initially, robots were more monstrous than otherwise, but Isaac Asimov and John W. Campbell changed their image somewhat when they created the Three Laws of Robotics.

Asimov's Three Laws of Robotics:

1. A robot may not injure a human being, or, through inaction allow a human being to come to harm.
2. A robot must obey the orders given it by human beings except where such orders would conflict with the First Law.
3. A robot must protect its own existence as long as such protection does not conflict with the First or Second Law.

Although later writers noticed a flaw in the rules:

'Asimov's first law is unrealistic . . . If a millionaire builds a robot his first thought will be to protect his investment. So the robot's first law will be to protect his investment. So the robot's first law will be to protect itself – not other people. And since a principal interest in building robots is likely to be military, those robots are certainly going to harm human beings as much as they can.'

JOHN SLADEK, in *Dream Makers 2* by CHARLES PLATT

As a self-willed robot puts it:

The mass of humans were born slave-drivers. Just look at the Asimov priorities: Protect humans, Obey humans, Protect yourself. Humans first and robots last? *Forget it! No way!*

RUDY RUCKER, *Software*

Some early robots were cyborgs; this one is an early forerunner of the Six Million Dollar Man:

'Did you ever hear of the case of Nez Hulan?' queried Crayton.

'You mean the man who lay dead in space for three years, and was brought back to life again after having been given a new heart made of rubber and his fractured skull replaced by an aluminium brain case?' queried Clarkford.

'Yes,' replied Sorelle. 'Who hasn't heard of it – the most famous surgical operation in history. His arms and legs were found so torn and mangled that their amputation was necessary. It seems that he was supplied with mechanical legs and arms as well as with metal radiophone ears built into his aluminium skull.'

NEIL R. JONES, *The Moon Pirates*

What is a robot? Here Lionel Fanthorpe explains:

Terrifying things, steel things; metal things; things with cylindrical bodies and multitudinous jointed limbs. Things without flesh and blood. Things that were made of metal and plastic and transistors and valves and relays, and wires. Metal things. Metal things that could think. *Thinking metal things*. Terrifying in their strangeness, in their peculiar metal efficiency. Things the like of which had never been seen on earth before. Things that were sliding back panels . . . *Robots*! Robots were marching . . . Robots were marching; and were about to spread havoc and destruction across the earth, and as yet the sleeping earth knew nothing of their coming. As mysterious as anything in the great universe.

LEO BRETT, *The Coming of the Robots*

(Any questions?)

Bad robots do two things:

1. They kill people:

'What did you find?' asked the pilot, still watching the wreck.

Instead of an answer, metal tentacles gripped the pilot by his neck and slowly twisted his head off, then pulled him from his seat.

NEIL R. JONES, *Space War*

2. They build more robots:

'Servos working on servos,' he rumbled. 'Producing their own kind. If we don't stop this, we'll be outnumbered by them!'

A. A. GLYNN, *Plan for Conquest*

Humans can amuse them:

The robot pilot turned from his controls and said calmly, 'Our present velocity represents the peak N-space performance of this craft.'

'Then exceed it,' said Melor.

'I am not programmed!'

'Do it anyway.'

'The master jests,' said the robot, with a mocking smile.

E. E. 'DOC' SMITH, *Lord Tedric, The Space Pirates*

Robots come in many designs:

Something came in through the door and I recoiled, thinking the war was on. It was only a robot, but it made such a hideous amount of hissing and clanking that I wondered what was wrong with it . . . The Count ordered the ghastly thing to wheel over the bar; as it turned away I saw what could only have been a *chimney* projecting behind one shoulder. There was the distinct odor of coal smoke in the air. 'Does that robot burn *coal*—?' I gurgled.

HARRY HARRISON, *The Stainless Steel Rat*

They have their problems:

'And then of course I've got this terrible pain in all the diodes down my left-hand side.'

DOUGLAS ADAMS, *Hitch Hiker's Guide to the Galaxy*

'The first ten million years were the worst,' said Marvin, 'and the second ten million years, they were the worst too. The third ten million I didn't enjoy at all. After that I went into a bit of a decline.'

DOUGLAS ADAMS, *The Restaurant at the End of the Universe*

Some concepts elude them:

'You do not perceive any beauty?'

'Perhaps none remains after so long a time,' said Frost.

'It is not supposed to be the sort of thing which gets used up,' said Mordel.

ROGER ZELAZNY, *For A Breath I Tarry*

The late Philip K. Dick's robots and machines are often as human – or more so – than the flesh-and-blood people in his stories. Where else could a conversation of this sort occur, between a man . . . and a taxi?

To the cab he said suddenly, 'If your wife were sick –'

'I have no wife, sir,' the cab said. 'Automatic Mechanisms never marry; everyone knows that.'

'All right,' Eric agreed. 'If you were me, and your wife were sick, desperately so, with no hope of recovery, would you leave her? Or would you stay with her, even if you had travelled ten years into the future and knew for an absolute certainty that the damage to her brain could never be reversed? And staying with her would mean –'

'I can see what you mean, sir,' the cab broke in. 'It would mean no other life for you beyond caring for her.'

'That's right,' Eric said.

'I'd stay with her,' the cab decided.

'Why?'

'Because,' the cab said, 'life is composed of reality configurations so constituted. To abandon her would be to say, I can't endure reality as such. I have to have uniquely special easier conditions.'

PHILIP K. DICK, *Now Wait For Last Year*

Someday a human being may shoot a robot which has come out of a General Electrics factory, and to his surprise see it weep and bleed. And the dying robot may shoot back and, to its surprise, see a wisp of grey smoke arise from the electric pump that it supposed was the human's beating heart. It would be rather a great moment of truth for both of them.

PHILIP K. DICK, *The Android and the Human*

Language!

FUTURESPEAK

One way of giving the reader the impression that he or she is reading about something set in the future, is to update the jargon and the dialogue. Although the adventure could be occurring just as easily in the present day, simply replacing *pen* with *stylo*; *glass* with *glassite*; *glue* with *adhesi-ray*; *gun* with *blaster,* etc. shows you that this is, in fact, the twenty-fifth century.

There was no other ship but Alton Raymond's saucer to break the stretch of macadamite.

JAMES HARVEY, *Titans of the Universe*

Their plotel room – every hotel that catered to the planetary trade was a plotel.

(*ibid.*)

A series of exercises follows, most of which Rogan could have done with one optic closed, they were so easy for him.

PAUL JAMES, *Rogan*

While characters comment on the quaint, old-fashioned way people did things way back in the twentieth century . . .

'Go on, old man of mystery, shoot the works. Make with the facts. And all that jazz . . . as they used to say in the old days.'

LIONEL FANTHORPE, *Flame Mass*

Alex R13Pk, ARC Captain, and his mate Diana, T-T11C, a dietetic-navi-scientist, also were readying themselves for the journey in their Palisades bubblevilla.

JAMES GRAZIER, *Runts of 61 Cygni C*

She kicked off her tight nilex flight slacks and lay back on the spume-foamed airbed excitingly nude from waist up, clad only in the new xnile, glow-blue g-panties that made her panty area pulse.

(*ibid.*)

'You're funny, Steve – like a crutch,' she rebuked him, but smiled back sunnily, an elusive dimple playing in one lovely brown cheek.

'Looking right through anybody is too ghastly for words, but I think they're perfectly all x, anyway, in spite of their being so hideous and so cold-blooded, so there!'

E. E. 'DOC' SMITH, *Spacehounds of IPC*

NATIVE ACCENTS

'That affair that's going on up yon is unnatural!' declared Albert, waving a finger towards the window. 'It's wrong, I tell you. Summat queer'll come of it all.'

A. A. GLYNN, *Plan for Conquest*

This is the kind of remark that locals make, normally in village inns, as they eye the castle on the hill with suspicious eyes, and try to remember if they need to lay

in a store of firebrands for the late night rampage at the end.

Somerset-cum-all-purpose-bumkin seems to be the favoured accent to imply dark and dreadful doings are afoot.

'That b'ain't no joke, bless my heart and sould, zur, that b'ain't no joke!' retorted the old station master. 'There's some things a man do joke about, and there's some things a man don't joke about – and Long Barrow 'All ain't got nothin' to do with a sense of humour! Nothin' to do with a sense of humour at all. You couldn't find two things farther apart. Poles apart, they are, poles apart! Ha, there's been dark doin's up there! Dark and dreadful doin's. Anyway we can't stand a-jawin' here in the cold, come you into my office. There won't be no more trains through here for a time, zur. Come you into my office and have a cup o' tea. When we've had a yarn I dare say you'll change your mind about goin' up the 'All, arter I've told you some o' the things what happen up there!'

LIONEL FANTHORPE, *The Golden Chalice*

The same British Rustic (illustrating the remarkable ability of even the most banal science fiction to prophesy the future):

'Boy George, he's down the line a few mile, and he sorta come over here now and agin just to have a look and give a helpin' hand, like. I ain't so young as I used to be, as I said afore. Now, you can have that old Coronation mug, here y'are!'

(*ibid.*)

And an interplanetary Rustic:

'Mates, he says his business be not ours.'

There was a laugh from behind him and a voice

sounded. 'Right he be, for his business be book-mucking and 'puter-rubbing, and that be naught for true men.'

ISAAC ASIMOV, *Foundation's Edge*

(**Aaar!**)

Other accents are more sinister:

There were a lot of stories about him and when anybody asked him directly how he got out of Commie-land, he'd give a mysterious smile and say, 'A lodt of beeple vould get in trouble if I told.' Gradually folks stopped asking.

J. HARVEY BOND, *The Other World*

(**Who could blame them?**)

The upper-class Brit:

Merrivale was describing what he called 'Hellstrom's cover', which turned out to be the making of documentary films about insects. 'Deucedly curious, don't you think?' Merrivale asked.

FRANK HERBERT, *Hellstrom's Hive*

'I tried to reach old Fin earlier. Can't raise a peep. Bad show over there, I'm afraid. But Barrier Command now has your serum formula and the jolly old biochemical picture, all that.'

FRANK HERBERT, *The White Plague*

Normally he wouldn't have dreamed to call anybody . . . old fruit . . . but Boxer would have been disappointed if he didn't say at least *one* thing a day, which to him was . . . typically English (**sic**).

ROBERT RAY, *No Stars for Us*

'There's a gentleman on the line who simply will not be put off. He says he must speak to you at once on a matter of national urgency.'

'Does he, by jove!' Grisedale's jaw tightened. 'A crank, no doubt.'

GUY N. SMITH, *Night of the Crabs*

The Hillbilly Yokel:

'It'll take me ten years and as many barrels of rot-gut liquor to clear that stink outen my nostrils,' he declared. '. . . From now on all I want is to sit down by yon creek with a fishin' pole and sniff the fresh smell of juniper and sagebrush till I can convince myself there's more'n just stinks left in my bailiwick . . . One thing's for sure, Colonel – it'll cost a packet to fill yon hole with concrete.'

VICTOR NORWOOD, *Night of the Black Horror*

The American negro – here portrayed as both cowardly and incomprehensible:

'We didn't stop it,' a negro yelled. 'Ain't nuthin' gonna stop that hell-spawn! We is all gonna die . . .!' A rock-hard fist smashed him flat, but panic spread like wildfire.

VICTOR NORWOOD, *Night of the Black Horror*

'To tell tha truf, Chief, Ah was scared,' he admitted. 'When Ah fin' tha bandits shootin' at we, Ah say to me feet, "Feet, tha Lord put yo' on me legs fo' to run, an' now feets do yo' duty" Yaas sir, Chief.'

A. Hyatt Verrill, *Through the Andes*

The English Cockney – also a figure of fun, with his quaint way of speaking:

'Cor lumme, Delia Doris, this ain't 'arf a rum go!' replied the Green Martian. 'They does talk summat like the tame 'oomans, but not so plummy, like. An' these duds o' theirn – there ain't noffin' like 'em on all Barsoom. The Masters could 'ardly care less wot their slaves wears – if anyfing – an' they'd never go ter all the trouble o' setting up a factory ter turn out rags like these . . .'

A. BERTRAM CHANDLER, *The Alternate Martians*

(A Green Martian Cockney? I'm afraid so.)

'Don't get working on any of that supercodology when I'm around, mate, or you'll get a bunch of fives in the fag-hole.' ANTHONY BURGESS, *1985*

Human colonies that have been lost in space for many years evolve their own way of speaking. This is a typical example:

Carefully he fingered the plasti-leather cover and bent to examine the faded lettering.

'It is called the Book,' Billim said proudly.

'What is it for?'

'It gave us all the words we use for talk. If we not had the Book we be like the little bocks and only say *baaa*.'

Dorian was deeply touched. He could think of no better way to appraise the value of the human communication system. RENA VALE, *Taurus Four*

The Scots – often to be found in engine rooms:

Clavering slowly straightened, a puzzled expression on his seamed, dirty face, muttering, 'What the hell's wrong wi' the bastard noo?' And then he saw Wilkinson, and what he had done. He snarled, 'Ah'll thank ye tae keep yer scabby honds off *my* switchboard, Skipper!'

A. BERTRAM CHANDLER, *The Alternate Martians*

The cunning linguistic skills of this would-be saboteur are something of a *tour de force*:

Despite his Central European origins, Zakminsky was a brilliant linguist. He could not only speak impeccable English, he could put on a Scottish accent so effectively that it sounded plausible and natural to the English sailors on board the gunboat.

'Hoots! I thoct I was lost the noo!' exclaimed Zakminsky with a tight-lipped smile.

KARL ZEIGFREID, *Projection Infinity*

MIGHTY OATHS

Blast was a weak, prissy, Eagle-Scoutish word for Constant to use – and it took him a moment to realise why he had used it. Blast was what space cadets on television said when a meteorite carried away the control surface, or the navigator turned out to be a space pilot from the planet Zircon.

KURT VONNEGUT JR, *Sirens of Titan*

Although Kurt Vonnegut felt that space cadets only ever said 'Blast', many SF authors have done their best to expand the vocabulary of spacefarers who hit their fingers with iridium sonic hammers.

E. E. 'Doc' Smith broke new ground in his Lensman series, coming up with:

Holy-Klono's-Iridium-Intestines!
Holy Klono's whiskers!
'Thank Klono and Noshabkeming! You're QX, then?'
Hell's Brazen Hinges!
By Klono's emerald-filled gizzard!
'KLONO'S tungsten TEETH and CURVING CARBALLOY CLAWS!!!'

Which Harry Harrison in *Space Rats of the CCC* parodied as:

> By Mrrdl's holy name!
> Holy Kolon!

Sword and Sorcery tends to be a more fruitful area for full-bodied oaths. There is Robert E. Howard's Conancuss 'Crom!' of course, and then there's:

> By Astis' ivory Teats!
> By Zevata's golden whiskers!
> By Nobalyaga's cleft!

L. SPRAGUE DECAMP, *The Clocks of Iraz*

> By Vaisu's brazen arse!
> By Franda's Golden Locks!
> By Astis' coynte!
> By Heryx's iron yard!
> By Thio's horns!

L. SPRAGUE DECAMP, *The Fallible Fiend*

> By Arioch!

MICHAEL MOORCOCK, *Elric* stories

> 'Oh, bird sweat!'

PAUL O. WILLIAMS, *The Fall of the Shell*

Cordwainer Smith's Norstrilians could be quite coarse on occasion:

'How do you know so mucking much?' said Bill, speaking up. 'And why waste our time with all this crutting glubb?'

'Watch your language, man,' said John Fisher. 'There are some mucking ladies present.'

CORDWAINER SMITH, *Norstrilia*

E. E. 'Doc' Smith was also responsible for:

'Great Cat!'
Spacehounds of IPC

and:

'Sweet spirits of niter!'
Skylark of Valeron

and even:

His rage mounted higher and higher, visibly. 'Did I *ever* ask you for a drink, you (unprintable here, even in a modern and realistic novel, for the space of two long breaths) . . .?'

Grey Lensman

The technique of leaving out the actual words said was fairly common:

'Stop,' snarled Stewie. 'Stop, you waddling blankety blank blanks! Take it you hell-gulping blobs of stink. *Stop*!'

L. RON HUBBARD, *The Invaders*

and still continues to this day. For example, in Douglas Adams' book *Life, the Universe and Everything*, the line 'He had won an award for the most gratuitous use of the word fuck in a serious screenplay' **became, in the American edition,** '. . . the word "Belgium" in a serious screenplay'. **And the ubiquitous sound effect** 'wop!' **became** 'whop!' **presumably to avoid offending any Italian-Americans that might read it.**

It is often assumed that spacemen will swear about space things:

'Oh, Great Stars and Small Planets, I don't!'

ISAAC ASIMOV, *Foundation's Edge*

Great Space! Great Galaxy!

ISAAC ASIMOV, *Pirates of the Asteroids*

'Where in sunspots did you find him, Holla?'

J. HARVEY BOND, *The Other World*

'Jeepers-creepers!'
'By the great spiral nebula of Andromeda!'
'By all the twinkling stars of heaven!'
'Would you adam-and-eve it?'

TREBOR THORPE, *Lightning World*

Future oaths could be acronymic – 'Tanj!', a Larry Niven coined acronym: There Ain't No Justice!, in the *Known Space* series – or refer to purely local problems:

'Bleb!'

SAMUEL DELANY, *Empire Star*

(As in 'What the bleb?')

'Mist Demons!'

LARRY NIVEN, *A Gift From Earth*

Larry Niven is particularly active when it comes to coining future obscenities. In *The Integral Trees* he came up with 'Treefodder' – anything that might feed the tree: excrement, or garbage, or a corpse:

'Your tribe is dead! Your tree is torn apart! *We* could have been your tribe, you treefeeding mutineer you!'

INSULTS

The hurling of insults is a traditional spacefaring practice. Why call somebody an idiot or a jerk, when you can call them a jelly-livered son of an Arcturan dung beetle? (Apart from anything else, these guys are paid by the word . . .)

'So you *do* know me, you bedroom-eyed Aldebaranian hell-cat,' he remarked, evenly. 'I thought you would.'

'Yes, you sweet, uncontaminated sissy, you overgrown superboy-scout, I do!' she hissed, malevolently, and made a quick motion towards her corsage.

E. E. 'DOC' SMITH, *Grey Lensman*

'Clam it, you squint-eyed slime-lizard!'

E. E. 'DOC' SMITH, *Second Stage Lensman*

'If this is insubordination and if you want to make something out of it, you pussy-gutted, pusillanimous, brainless tub of lard, cut in your jets!'

(*ibid.*)

Aliens have their own insults:

'You make me ill!' Volmik said harshly and uttered the most insulting statement known to Alphirkians: 'You make my guts tired.'

SILAS WATER, *The Man With Absolute Motion*

as do other space-travelling folk:

'I've said you're a chancroid, Hook, and a burst ulcer, and a candidate for advanced pustular syphiloderma, and I'll go on telling you you're a Pasturella pestis . . .'

TULLY ZETFORD, from the *Hook* series

'Don't *touch* her, you slat-headed ape!' Czack's voice crackled from his Bolo. 'I don't want nobody's filthy hands on her, until I see her.'

Henry Dread laughed. 'It's not a woman, you rack-skull. And it's *my* freaking tank and *I'll* see it first.'

KEITH LAUMER AND ROSEL GEORGE BROWN, *Earthblood*

some of them quite familiar:

Bigman said, 'Which one of you knotbrains called me Shortie?'

ISAAC ASIMOV, *Pirates of the Asteroids*

The army is still the best source of ear-blistering insults:

He looked at us. 'You apes – No, not "apes"; you don't rate that much. You pitiful mob of sickly monkeys . . . you sunken-chested, slack-bellied, drooling refugees from apron strings. In my whole life I never saw such a disgraceful huddle of momma's spoiled little darlings in – you there! Suck up the gut! Eyes front! I'm talking to *you*!'

ROBERT A. HEINLEIN, *Starship Troopers*

'Back in line there, you bone-skulled sons of one-legged joy-girls!'

KEITH LAUMER AND ROSEL GEORGE BROWN, *Earthblood*

But the *Ghastly Beyond Belief* prize goes to John W. Campbell Award-winner Paul O. Williams:

'I say you are the remnants of old vomit, occupied only by maggots. You mistake your ordure for ideas. Your breath is a pile of fish entrails. The vile ugliness of your entire being might make one mistake you for rich fertiliser, but you would kill my garden.'

PAUL O. WILLIAMS, *The Fall of the Shell*

FUNNY YOU SHOULD SAY THAT

There have been very few full-length modern fantasy or science fiction novels which contain *no* dialogue. (Richard Lupoff's *The Sword of the Demon* is the only one that springs to mind.)

The following fragments have little in common with each other; they come from stories as frequently anthologized as Asimov's *Nightfall*, authors as prestigious as Frank Herbert and Aldous Huxley, Jack Vance and Robert A. Heinlein, as well as some others less well-known.

He doubled his knee and drove it hard into his assailant. 'Let me up or I'll kill you.'

Theremon cried out sharply and muttered through a blinding haze of pain, 'You double-crossing rat!'

ISAAC ASIMOV, *Nightfall*

'Hello, hello, hello!' It came in a high tenor, and the plump cheeks of the newcomer expanded in a pleased smile. 'What's this morgue-like atmosphere about here? No one's losing his nerve, I hope.'

(*ibid.*)

'Funny you should speak English and not know who Hitler was,' I said.

J. HARVEY BOND, *The Other World*

'I'm afraid it's no use, John Carter,' he said. 'Even though your plan is most ingeniously conceived, it will avail naught against that horrible monstrosity.'

EDGAR RICE BURROUGHS, *John Carter of Mars*

'Take your filthy paws off me, you Slavonic dike!'

A. BERTRAM CHANDLER, *Empress of Outer Space*

Doc turned to pretty Princess Monja. He hesitated, then said: 'Monja, you've been a brick.' 'What's that?' she asked. Evidently her supply of English slang was limited.

LESTER DENT, *Doc Savage: Man of Bronze*

'Kermit,' she gasped. 'it won't be necessary, because I know where they are right now.'
'You're getting omniscient?'

NANCY AND FRANCIS DORER, *Two Came Calling*

'Strike me pink!' ejaculated Delaney. 'Nut case, is he?'

LIONEL FANTHORPE, *Flame Mass*

'This damned asteroid belt is full of . . . asteroids.'

ROBERT FRENCH, *Now, The Gods*

'As soon as the crocks are washed up Mom, I intend to carry out a trial run with my rocket engine.'

TERENCE HAILE, *Space Train*

'We're rapidly approaching something which looks like a small planet!' she cried. 'I suggest everyone ties himself down to minimise the shock of entering another atmosphere.'

(*ibid.*)

Enthusiastic cabin boy: 'Excuse me, Sir – what's it like in that abyssal ooze?'

FRANK HAMPSON, *Dan Dare Comics*

A single inhalation by thousands, then came the everywhere voice in soft, reverent tones: 'Look at that bastard *go*!'

ROBERT A. HEINLEIN, *The Happy Days Ahead*

'The eroded sculpture of canyons and cliffs and galaxies has imprinted upon me the certain knowledge that I am a mote.'

FRANK HERBERT, *God Emperor of Dune*

'I'm authorized to tell you that we are South Africans, you Irish bog-trotter! You are ordered to lower your sails!'

FRANK HERBERT, *The White Plague*

'Golly!' the little nurse exploded, when the door was safely closed behind them.

'I entirely agree with you,' Will said.

ALDOUS HUXLEY, *Island*

'Spool it!' said Cherry wearily. 'Wait till I get my hands on that rat-faced runt Castor. That must be the lousiest stinking trick he ever pulled. I'll shake that old skeleton until his eyeballs rattle in their sockets.'

COLIN KAPP, *Cageworld No 1: Search for the Sun!*

'What can you do with a man who tells you not to worry and if the worse comes to the worst he'll call in his fucking Starfleet and save the world?'

THOM KEYES, *The Battle of Disneyland*

'There are shadows in yon hollow doughnuts,' Sinclair stated. 'And they move.'

JERRY POURNELLE AND LARRY NIVEN, *The Mote in God's Eye*

The underpeople spontaneously chorused, 'Put your trust in the joyful lawful, put your trust in the loyal-awful bright blank power of the under-bird!'

CORDWAINER SMITH, *Norstrilia*

'The fuckin' bridge's collapsin'. And God Almighty, look at them bleedin' crabs!' Terror-stricken tones that aptly summed up what was happening.

GUY N. SMITH, *Crabs on the Rampage*

'What is it these beatniks have been saying for about a thousand years, they do it for kicks? I can't understand that generation at all.'

PEL TORRO, *The Last Astronaut*

Sthelay said: 'Mirk approaches; dark hideous mirk when the gharks and hoos come forth and all the world is dead!'

JACK VANCE, *Marune: Alastor 993*

'I don't think you've completely got over that grimly frightening and horrifying experience you had last week,' commented Ralston sympathetically.

KARL ZEIGFREID, *Projection Infinity*

SMART-ALEC COMMENTS

Banter and smart-alec comments are usually inserted into a book to heighten moments of tension, show what stern stuff the hero is made of, or simply to prove that people cannot resist making awful jokes:

'Scrounge some breakfast. We've got to eat, even if this is Armageddon.'

'And Armageddon sick of it,' Karen offered.

ROBERT A. HEINLEIN, *Farnham's Freehold*

Hugh put his hand on her belly, felt her womb harden as increasing pain showed in her face. 'Bear down, baby,' he told her. 'And pant; it helps.'

She started to pant, it turned into a scream.

Endless seconds later she relaxed, forced a smile and said, 'They went that a-way! Sorry about the sound effects, Daddy.'

(*ibid.*)

Snaggle-head stepped in front of him; his grimy finger prodded Roan's chest. Roan looked into the oversized face, spotted here and there with coarse hairs sprouting from inflamed warty blemishes.

'What you think you're looking at, punk?'

'It looks like the hind end of a crundle-beast,' Roan said clearly, 'only hairier.'

KEITH LAUMER AND ROSEL GEORGE BROWN, *Earthblood*

He laughed uncertainly and licked at a moist patch on her neck. 'Well . . . I'll have to volunteer for suicide duty more often.'

LARRY NIVEN AND STEVEN BARNES, *Descent of Anansi*

'Do you have a red birthmark shaped like a star on your . . . on your . . .'

'On my what, Jack?' I guess I was thinking of my shoulders or my back or maybe my foot.

'On the lower left side of your fanny?'

I gasped. 'Jack! What a question to ask a woman!'

He looked grave. 'It's important that I know, Wendy.'

'Why? Are you doing research on fannies for your Ph.D?'

SUE PLAYER, *Second Body*

'I say, Barry. What about a medico of some sort? It's a bit wild where we're going isn't it? There just *might* be some diseases an aspirin can't cure.'

LUAN RANZETTA, *Yellow Inferno*

'What I keep saying is, why send us to *Tibet*? Surely it would be the last place to have atomic secrets! The people there can hardly rub two pieces of yak together.'

(*ibid.*)

'I am the boy who has all the in-for-mation about oxygen and CO2 . . . of which Diana is bereft, unfortunately . . . and any other gases you want to mention! Nobody can think of a sober, elegant sounding title for me, so I just call myself the gas man!'

'Would an Alka-Seltzer help?' Richard said slyly.

PHILIP SHORTER, *A Handful of Silver*

'Basically, your trouble is that you want to whistle after crabs. Female crabs, of course. I did not mean to imply there was anything seriously wrong with you.'

JAMES WHITE, *Countercharm*

'Lothar! Ask him what the hell tigers are doing in an African jungle? Doesn't he know that tigers can only be found in Asia?' The tiger roared as Lothar spoke. 'What did he say?' 'He say: "You know it, and I know it – but do tigers know it?"'

J. X. WILLIAMS, *Her*

Preoccupations

FOOD AND DRINK

It's interesting to note that the authors of science fiction have never bothered about the serious business of cooking in space. This attitude is understandable in stories dealing with long, lean, bronzed heroes sworn to wipe out the space pirates swarming in the rings of Saturn – *that* breed never sleeps, much less eats. But what about the short, fat, pasty tourists of AD 2060 who plonk down their $2060 for a first-class seven-day round trip to the moon, including a three-day stop-over at the Lunar Hilton Hotel?

ALFRED BESTER, *Turning Points*

It's true. Little real attention *has* been paid to food in space. What do they eat? Where do they eat? Who eats who? (Actually this last question has been gone into at great length, and, as a general rule, *they* eat *us*.)

But Robert Sheckley gives us another useful general rule:

'I don't eat anything that giggles.'

ROBERT SHECKLEY, *One Man's Poison*

However, some books present a slightly more food-oriented view of life:

'And now, what's this about life on other planets?'

Roger gave him a look of mock astonishment. 'Do

you mean to say you think I would utter one word . . . without a slice of Helen's fine pie under my belt? Drive on. You'll hear it when we get there.'

PHILIP SHORTER, *A Handful of Silver*

Accidental italics gave some little cheese sandwiches unwanted significance:

'Every syllable, Willard . . . but *I don't remember any gun . . . do you?' Don pushed the plate across the table. 'Did you try those little cheese sandwiches yet . . . great!'*

ROBERT FRENCH, *Now, the Gods*

Some extol the merits of health foods:

'Will you step into my panel room, madame . . . lovely madame?'

April positively purred at him. 'Ohhhh, you sweet man! Do you know how many times I hear that, since I got to good eating?'

NANCY AND FRANCIS DORER, *Two Came Calling*

Richard Seaton eats goulash in space:

'The idea is, Doll, not to take any unnecessary chances. Ah, this goulash hits the spot!'

E. E. 'DOC' SMITH, *Skylark of Valeron*

While other heroes enjoy stranger menus:

'What do we eat?'

'The eternal question of the hungry labouring man! I've got a roasted bongo, a fried filamaloo bird, and a boiled warple for the meat dishes. For vegetables, mashed hikoderms and pimola greens. Neocorn bread.'

E. E. 'DOC' SMITH, *Spacehounds of IPC*

Thomas M. Disch managed to sum up an entire lifestyle in the inventory of one kitchen:

Catsup, mustard, pickle relish, mayonnaise, two kinds of salad dressing, bacon grease and a lemon. Oh yes, two trays of ice cubes. In the cupboard it wasn't much better: jars and boxes of spice, flour, sugar, salt – and a box of raisins!

An empty box of raisins.

THOMAS M. DISCH, *Descending*

The Blessed Leibowitz's shopping list became a holy relic:

'*Of course*,' Cheroki said sharply, 'you could NOT POSSIBLY be trying to say that – you have received – from the Blessed Leibowitz, dead now, lo, the last six hundred years – a handwritten invitation to profess your solemn vows? And you, uh, deplored his handwriting? – Forgive me, but that's the impression I was getting.'

'Well, it's *something* like that, Father.'

Cheroki sputtered. Becoming alarmed, Brother Francis produced a scrap of paper from his sleeve and handed it to the priest. It was brittle with age and stained. The ink was faded.

'*Pound pastrami*,' Father Cheroki pronounced, slurring over some of the unfamiliar words, '*can kraut, six bagels – bring home for Emma*.'

WALTER M. MILLER JR, *A Canticle for Leibowitz*

James Herbert adds to the list of Things to Say after World War Three:

'Don't scoff them all, Bunter, you'll make yourself sick,' Culver advised, unable to stop himself from smiling.

'Crunchie bars, Fruit and Nut, Walnut Whips – Christ, I'm dead and this is heaven.'

JAMES HERBERT, *Domain*

(Thus adding tooth decay to his other problems . . .)

Drink is another matter. A list of exotic alien-and-future alcohols could fill a book, from Old Space Ranger hooch and Martian *jabra* water on up (or down).

But how about this:

'Whatever rhythmic clock is calling you, those gin and tonic pills will give you a good appetite.'

JAMES GRAZIER, *Runts of 61 Cygni C*

(Ice and lemon, anyone?)

Tea is mentioned rarely:

'You get a cup o' that inside you, and you feel a different man altogether! Altogether different you feel! You can feel it goin' round your veins like fire! That'll get you back on the deck, that'll put the feelin' back in your fingers and toes. That'll get the salt out o' your beard, boy. Old salt won't mix along o' that, that's too strong for him! Well, railwayman's tea ain't so strong as what that is, but it's very near! There's three kinds o' tea worth drinking, trawlerman's tea, sergeant major's tea, and railwayman's tea, and we're havin' railwayman's tea tonight.'

LIONEL FANTHORPE, *The Golden Chalice*

Coffee is much more popular. It can be taken by tube:

Amos, with a tube of coffee in his hand, gestured to Diana.

'You know, Diana, foodtubes are neat and easy to

handle, but I would like to know why people gave up utensils and quit eating natural foods.'

'As a matter of fact, I happen to know the whole history of it,' Diana replied.

JAMES GRAZIER, *Runts of 61 Cygni C*

Or while falling into a small lump on a chair:

She continued to weep quietly, falling into a little lump on a chair, until I thought to have her go with Ittlo and get quantities of the stimulating beverage.

ANNE MCCAFFREY, *Restoree*

And it markedly increases one's interest in the workings of a spaceship's engines:

Every man who drank coffee wanted to ask about the engines.

MURRAY LEINSTER, *Invaders of Space*

In conjunction with steak, a corrosively strong cup of coffee can even get your lens flaming again:

The Lensman made his way to the gallery. He could walk without staggering already – fine! There he fired himself a big, thick, rare steak – his never-failing remedy for all the ills to which flesh is heir – and brewed a pot of Thralian coffee; making it viciously, almost corrosively strong. And as he ate and drank his head cleared magically. Strength flowed back into him in waves. His Lens flamed into its normal splendor. He stretched prodigiously; inhaled gratefully a few deep breaths. He was QX.

E. E. 'DOC' SMITH, *Second Stage Lensman*

So remember —

'Go on. Have a zestful cup of Fleet-issue Caffo-Stim.'

NEVILLE KEA, *The World of Artemis*

LOVE AND MARRIAGE

A purpose of human life, no matter who is controlling it, is to love whoever is around to be loved.

KURT VONNEGUT, JR, *Sirens of Titan*

So said Kurt Vonnegut, Jr, although he didn't bother to define the word *love*. Other science fiction writers have repaired that deficiency:

Professor Jameson regarded her a bit pathetically, then whimsically, before forming his reply. 'Stripped of its glamor, its falsities, its hypnotic fascination, love is the irresistible instinct to fulfill a biologic urge, half a species seeking the other half, bringing about the eventual propagation of the species and fulfilling nature's law. Love rarely yields its fluorescent promises, for – like the bright petals of a carnivorous flower – it entices its victims to serve the wholesale ambitions of a far-seeing destiny.'

NEIL R. JONES, *Space War*

Most authors don't bother to define it. They *show* it. After all, we all know love is the moment that the heroine takes off her glasses:

He was astonished at her use of his first name. She was almost pretty when she said it. She had removed her glasses while they were drinking the coffee, and he noticed her eyes were a deep blue. Strange he had never noticed them before.

SUE PAYER, *Second Body*

The goodnight kiss he had given her, the natural manner in which she had received it and kissed him of her own free will, and yet all without a suggestion of looseness or frivolity, convinced him finally that he was indeed not mistaken, she was the girl for him.

TOM WADE, *The World of Theda*

However, the path of true love never did run smooth:

'If I break up with her now, she'll think I'm doing it because she's a werewolf. It's awkward, it feels nasty and middle-class. I should have broken up with her the first time I met her mother, or the second time she served the eggplant . . . Damn, I wish I hadn't found out. I don't think I've ever found out anything about people that I was the better for knowing.'

PETER S. BEAGLE, *Lila the Werewolf*

Rolf got up and stretched his mighty legs. 'I must go forth and slay an evil god,' he said.

Tears came to Freya's eyes. 'Somehow I knew, there in the Common House, that wedded ecstacy was not for me.'

IVAR JORGENSON, *Whom the Gods Would Slay*

'You half-wit, you ninny, you lug!' she stormed, bitterly if almost inaudibly, at that reflection. 'You lame-brained moron, you red-headed, idiotic imbecile, you microcephalic dumb-bell, you *clunker*! Of all the men in this whole cockeyed galaxy, you *would* have to make a dive at Kimball Kinnison, the one man who thinks you're just part of the furniture. At a Grey Lensman . . .' Her expression changed and she whispered softly, 'A . . . Grey . . . Lensman. He *can't* love anybody as long as he's carrying that load. They can't let themselves be human . . . quite . . . perhaps loving *him* will be enough . . .'

E. E. 'DOC' SMITH, *Grey Lensman*

It always spells trouble for their love life if the couple marry too early on in the plot, since it is only at the end of the book that such moments of bliss such as this can occur:

'I think,' Stephen said slowly, 'that you and I may be getting married one of these days.'

'Wow! *That* was the all-time dullest proposal I have *ever* heard!' she laughed.

ROBERT FRENCH, *Now, The Gods*

And for once in her restless, ambitious, studious existence, Diana Waring was supremely content just to relax, secure in the comforting presence of sincere love and admiration, whilst in her serenity Jim Trassidy, man of the future, found, for the moment at least, complete satisfaction . . .

VICTOR NORWOOD, *Night of the Black Horror*

'On Venus we have a ceremony of marriage much like yours . . . we have waited for some time in order that you and Madge might serve as best man and matron of honour, if you will.'

'Will we?' exclaimed Madge and Jim in unison. 'I'll say we will.'

WILLIAM K. SONNEMANN, *The Master Minds of Venus*

An author who has often demonstrated her mastery (mistressy?) of the mysteries of love is Anne McCaffrey – described by Kingsley Amis as 'The Barbara Cartland of Science Fiction':

'I tell you one thing you do Mrrva doesn't – you do fancy sewing. There's not a female in either village that doesn't like something pretty to wear!'

'Of course!' Pat sat up, delighted. 'Just the thing!' But when she tried to rise, heading towards her small chest of treasures brought from Earth, Ken pulled her roughly back into his arms and silenced her protests with deliberately passionate kisses.

ANNE MCCAFFREY, *Decision at Doona*

'Is this body you cared for so long offensive to you?' he asked softly. 'You know it so well.'

'I know it well, yes, but not the man within it,' I whispered.

He smiled then, a wonderful tender possessive smile. 'When the man I am is within you, you will know all of me well and I, all of you. And you will no longer be afraid of me.'

My arms, of themselves, slid up around his neck and our bodies touched. I couldn't control my trembling.

'Dear my lady Sara,' he said softly, his voice rough with passion. 'I'm claiming my own. *Now*!'

ANNE MCCAFFREY, *Restoree*

SCIENTIFIC DOUBLE-TALK

'Science?' said the doctor. 'Why, science is nothing but classification. Science is just tagging a name to everything.'

CHARLES G. FINNEY, *The Circus of Dr Lao*

For every science fiction writer who has an understanding of science, or who is concerned enough to stop and work out the scientific rationale of his story, there are a dozen who cheerfully ignore scientific laws and write down anything that 'sounds right', and contains roughly the right words in the right order:

An alterometer converted the magnetix flux into diometric energies.

JAMES HARVEY, *Titans of the Universe*

Their rocket functions by means of a beam of photons projected fore and aft of the machine. The one serving to reduce pressure in an atmosphere from the nacelle of the craft, the latter to create a molecular pressure against elements in the tail of the craft by which method they were thrust forward much in the fashion of a jet.

NEAL RAFCAM, *The Troglodytes*

New drugs, new processes, new radiation medicine, had prevented arteries from clogging and hardening. Had prevented muscles from clogging the fat. Had prevented old age from destroying a man.

TREBOR THORPE, *Lightning World*

John Sladek joked about trains to the stars . . .

Some doddering scientists sneer at the idea of travel between stars. The nearest star, they say, is 25 trillion miles away. They forget that monorail trains are capable of astonishing speeds (over 200 m.p.h.!). Doubtless, despite the skeptics, we'll have a regular train service to Alpha Centauri and other stars, by the end of the century.

JOHN SLADEK, *Space Shoes of the Gods*

. . . he had obviously not read *Space Train*, by Terence Haile, in which our hero's super-fast train, on its London to Birmingham test-run (with the Prime Minister and many other notables aboard) attains such a speed that it takes off into space! However, we should stop to reflect that *Space Train* was written in the early 1960s, when the possibility that the first man on the moon would get there on the 8:15 from Euston was stronger than it is today.

Here our hero squirts all the bad air into space, after turning on the reserve oxygen supply:

The cloud of foul air hung in space, and Mike wondered, idly, if some future generation of space-adventurers would find that tiny air pocket in the gigantic vacuum of the universe. It might even be the means of saving someone's life!

TERENCE HAILE, *Space Train*

The train is pulled back to Earth when the magnetic train line is once more activated and another train put into action. You see, the first train had picked up a number of giant 'space crabs' on the way, thus making it *different* to the second train, and as everybody knows . . .

Like poles repel; unlike poles attract. The trains were unalike because of the 'Crab-ballast' carried by Mike's rocket. Otherwise, there would possibly have been no smash.

(*ibid.*)

Speed is often explained in 'Scientific' terms:

The ships were so big, so vast, so fast. Faster than sounds. The noise reached you after the ship made it. That was why there was never any warning.

NICHOLAS FISK, *Starstormers*

'My! We are going fast,' Emma said . . . 'Ten parsecs per nanosecond of microdotted time,' Mercurio replied in a very relaxed voice.

DAVID R. MORGAN, *The Strange Case of William Whipper-Snapper*

Still visible were the familiar shapes of the continents. They were travelling away from it at seven hundred times the speed of light. Soon it would be completely lost to view, and a feeling of space isolation would overtake them.

FIONA RICHMOND, *Galactic Girl*

Lots of things are invisible, like air, gas, glass under water, but they exist right enough. Electricity is invisible, but it's there right enough. You can't see it, but you see what it does. And though we cannot see the fourth dimension, that's how the hyperdrive principle works.

TREBOR THORPE, *Lightning World*

Spaceships aren't the only things that travel through space:

' . . . Where do meteorites come from?' 'Space,' said Vawn, in a bored voice. 'Look, I'm hungry—' 'That's it! Space! So that tells you one important thing about meteorites!' said Ispex. 'What important thing? Is anyone else hungry?' Vawn said. But Tsu said, 'Go on!' 'It tells you,' said Ispex, impressively, 'that meteorites are spaceworthy!'

NICHOLAS FISK, *Starstormers*

Few writers can resist the opportunity to speculate about black holes, neutron stars and such:

'We have taken a massive double sun, collapsed it into itself, and forced it through the process of becoming a neutron star, whereby it is packed into neutrons, and then, because of its gravitational mass breaking itself down further, it has changed into something which your Newtonian and relativistic physics have no way of predicting. It has become a miniature monobloc of zero volume and infinite density, able to transpose itself through time and space, a singularity, both existing and not existing.'

'Just like a woman,' thought Raunch.

RAY KAINEN, *Satyr Trek*

Man is an indefinable creature. The Ancient Greeks pondered over the amber glow that emanates from two materials in friction. Today we have the science of electronics.

NEAL RAFCAM, *The Troglodytes*

'—you're right about the boffins. They say the Earth is shrinking at the poles. That makes it feasible that it will bulge in the middle, doesn't it? I can't visualize how that affects us, but I do understand that it slows up the Earth's revolutions. That *could* be important.'

LUAN RANZETTA, *Yellow Inferno*

'You really go in for that teleportation stuff, don't you, Chief?'

'It's a field I'm interested in,' answered Tony. 'That, and psycho-lithography.'

TREBOR THORPE, *Lightning World*

'We landed on a sun,' he said slowly. 'A sun? . . . But why?' 'Probably for safety. What kind of being could come through this heat without a lot of preparation?' 'The dome must be a perfect insulator.' 'Either that, or they use the heat for refrigeration.'

SILAS WATER, *The Man with Absolute Motion*

Maybe, as Dr Asimov has pointed out:

'Science has advanced to the point where the only meaningful questions left are the ridiculous ones. The sensible ones have been thought of, asked, and answered long ago.'

ISAAC ASIMOV, *Jokester*

Questions such as: what makes stars twinkle? Charles Fort said it was the jelly . . .

I shall have to accept, myself, that gelatinous substance has often fallen from the sky – or that far up, or far away, the whole sky is gelatinous? That the twinkling of stars is penetration of light through something that quivers?

CHARLES FORT, *The Book of The Damned*

And what about the gunts?

'Setting this ship down – call it sixty thousand tons for a thousand miles at one gravity – will increase the field's potential by approximately one-tenth of one gunt. Have you studied paraphysics?'

'No.'

Garlock smiled – with a touch of condescension. 'Then I can't even make a stab at explaining instantaneous translation to you.'

E. E. 'DOC' SMITH, *The Galaxy Primes*

Scientific heroes not only double-talk, but they often draw some kind of diagram as they go, on napkins, tablecloths, cuffs or whatever comes to hand:

He shut off the machine. 'It worked,' he said sadly. 'But really, it's hard to make them. Nobody seems to understand the type of wave but myself and I've no mathematics to express it to them. Nobody here ever studied quad-dimensional calculus.'

'I guess he has us there, eh?' said Carlyle.

But it didn't have Kit. He at once began to run through the system and nod his bright hair over it. He took a pencil from his breast pocket and started to make cryptograms on a coil box.

'You've one too many resistances. It will work faster with your eighteenth stage inverted and its amplitude increased. Further, according to this disintegration speed, if you mounted the thing on a force beam so –' and he drew rapidly on a piece of plywood scrap . . .

L. RON HUBBARD, *Kingslayer*

Scientific discoveries are often made in order to save the world. This example contains excitement, drama, and even a little pathos:

'Don't let's gamble for small stakes, Jim. As I've worked it out, the frequency necessary to create vibration at the level we estimated will place such a strain on the generators that they may burn out . . . Why risk that merely to destroy a handful of spores when out there is the terrifying entity that is symbolic of everything loathsome and vile? You said yourself, Jim—we may only have the one chance. Let's get out there and give that foul monstrosity everything we've got—one final, devastating surge of shrieking vibratory sound that will, I feel sure, send it back to where it belongs – straight to hell . . .!'

'Yes, by God!' Colonel Jameson declared passionately. 'And we'll do just that. Diana, child—you know I lost my daughter, Angela, when she was only twelve . . . I'd like you to know that, if she'd lived, the best I could have wished her was to be like you . . .'

VICTOR NORWOOD, *Night of the Black Horror*

LUST IN SPACE

'The methods and mores of sexual copulation are the central feature of all higher developments of life.'

ROBERT A. HEINLEIN, *The Number of the Beast*

'In order to keep the world filled you've got to keep it fooled.'

THORNE SMITH, *Dream's End*

It took a long while for science fiction to recognize the existence of human reproduction. While adverts in the back of the pulps were trying to decrease the reader's ignorance of sex . . .

The Forbidden Secrets of Sex are Daringly revealed!

. . . Homosexuality – Sex abnormalities. Do you know about the astounding world of 'half sexes'? They crave the companionship of their own sex – their practices are unbelievable to the normal mind – yet you should understand them! *Attract the* OPPOSITE SEX! There is no longer any need to pay the *awful price* for one moment of bliss. Read the scientific pathological facts told so bravely by Dr Rubin. The chapters on venereal disease alone are worth the price of the book . . .

From an advert in *Amazing Stories*, 1934.

. . . most SF seemed to be written for adolescent boys, who were, it was assumed, quite content to have their heroes reproduce by binary fission, or any other methods they pleased, just as long as it didn't get in the way of the story.

But in the 1960s the climate of popular opinion changed; SF writers realized that adolescent boys were just as interested in sex as everyone else.

'I shouldn't have said that, Clee, of course.' A light mental laugh came. 'It was just the shock; there wasn't anything in any of my First Contact tapes covering what to do about beautiful and enticing girls who try to seduce our men. She doesn't know, though, of course, that she's supposed to be a bug-eyed monster and not human at all. Won't Xenology be in for a rough ride when we check in? Wow!'

E. E. 'DOC' SMITH, *The Galaxy Primes*

With feelings still of revulsion she told of the cruelty of the octopoids in their treatment of her, and of the callous way in which her clothes had been ripped from her while the repellent tentacles did their probing of her person during that first mental conflict with Dor Kotiv.

TOM WADE, *The World of Theda*

James Tiptree Jr suggested it might be the other way around. Maybe *we* would fancy *them*:

Anything different-coloured, different nose, ass, anything, man *has* to fuck it or die trying.

JAMES TIPTREE JR, *And I Awoke and Found Me Here on the Cold Hill's Side*

Aliens have other problems, apart from randy humans. Some are the wrong shape ever to reproduce:

Being shaped like a squashed accordion did not make for a very full sex-life, and the reason was simple – there was no way to manoeuvre into position. As visions flashed through my head of a couple of beach balls trying to make love, I began to see their problem. Sex had simply fallen by the way, because nobody could figure out how to make it happen.

NANCY AND FRANCIS DORER, *Two Came Calling*

But most of the sex in SF is between two human beings:

With sudden warmth she realized that if Duke Farnham had half the strong masculine charm his father had, a panty girdle wouldn't be much protection.

ROBERT A. HEINLEIN, *Farnham's Freehold*

I was about to ask Aramé once more, whether the use of Snukki for the dirty jobs was really the least of all available evils, when she surprised me by unpeeling her Sari-type dress and calling to me in American, 'C'mon, honey. Watcha waitin' for? Rough me up a l'il. Today, I'm feelin' kinda kinky!'

NEVILLE KEA, *The World of Artemis*

'You filthy lecherous pig!' Her eyes were blazing. As he reared back she rolled beneath him and jumped to her feet. For the first time she noticed the lower half of his body. Fear stabbed at her heart. She almost retched. To think it had been so close!

'You foul demented snake!' she screeched, backing off and putting a packing-case between herself and Glover.

GUY N. SMITH, *The Slime Beast*

SF authors have examined the sexuality of men:

The question 'Has anyone ever told you that you are a very good-looking young man?' lost all of its savour when it was asked only by another very good-looking young man – or, as often or even more often, by a not very good-looking middle-aged man.

AVRAM DAVIDSON, *Mirror Mirror*

US Presidents:

The profound anality of the presidential contender may be expected to dominate the United States in the coming years . . . In assembly-kit tests Reagan's face was uniformly perceived as a penile erection.

J. G. BALLARD, *Why I Want to Fuck Ronald Reagan*

Blue movies:

The blue movie was good too. It gave Buzz a hardon. He had a cock thirteen inches long. It was as tough and flexible as plastic can be and it glowed in the dark.

ALAN MARKS, *The Antenna Syndrome*

And a common problem:

Gavin thought about his hardness which was boring against her thighs.

GUY N. SMITH, *The Slime Beast*

(Well, yes, sex can be boring.)

There is, unfortunately, a certain amount of unwitting *double-entendre* in SF:

Monk stared after her, grinning from ear to ear, carefully tasting the young Mayan princess's kiss on his lips. 'Gosh! What Doc is passin' up!' he ejaculated.

LESTER DENT, *Doc Savage: Man of Bronze*

He wasn't going to leave Pat Benson on her own, crabs or no crabs.

GUY N. SMITH, *Night of the Crabs*

Occasionally writers produce dialogue worthy of a soft-porn magazine letter column:

Her heart was pounding and her breath was coming faster and faster. 'Give it to me properly, Gavin, like every woman wants her man!'

GUY N. SMITH, *The Slime Beast*

'I have to have you right now,' she pleaded. 'My body is on fire.'

'This isn't the right place,' he protested.

'Is *this* the right place?' she asked coyly.

SHARON TAYLOR, *Pleasure Planet*

And:

The bed creaked alarmingly threatening the beams of the living-room ceiling. Five minutes and Clive Rowland's pent-up emotions exploded in hot gushes and his breath came heavily.

GUY N. SMITH, *The Sucking Pit*

. . . of which the alien equivalent might be:

Every time she was penetrated, the queen's huge body rippled and arched and she gave out a hissing, screaming grunt. Steam rose from her straining body, gouts of milky fluid dripped from her immense length, bubbling from her orifices . . .

RICHARD AVERY, *The Deathworms of Kratos*

Sex gives an author a chance to wax philosophical:

One of the heresies of Uqbar had declared that mirrors and copulation were abominable, because they increase the number of men.

JORGES LOUIS BORGES, *Tlon, Uqbar, Orbis Tertius*

My father had once offered the opinion that maturity was reached when sex was more important than chocalate ice-cream, and from what we could gather . . . ours was a mature nation.

NANCY AND FRANCIS DORER, *Two Came Calling*

It took Kurt Vonnegut, Jr, (whose mythical SF writer, Kilgore Trout, wrote SF that appeared in porn mags) to point out the real connection between SF and pornography:

He didn't understand that what Trout had in common with pornography wasn't sex but fantasies of an impossibly hospitable world.

KURT VONNEGUT, JR, *God Bless You Mr Rosewater*

But Lionel Fanthorpe gets the last word:

'That kid knew two things. How to work the computer and sex!'

'Men and computers; and now she's blown herself into space!'

'There's a lesson there somewhere,' said Hilton thoughtfully.

PEL TORRO, *The Last Astronaut*

SPUNG! THE NUMBER OF THE BREAST

Although Robert A. Heinlein mentioned breasts in *Stranger In A Strange Land:*

It was not the figure-eight in which her pert fanny moved when she walked, nor the lush view from the other direction – he was not the infantile type, interested solely in the mammary glands! No, it was herself he loved.

. . . it was not until his mammoth *The Number of the Beast* – that he really took notice of this part of the female anatomy. Most of the following breasts belong to Mrs Dejah Thoris Carter (née Burroughs) – Deety to her friends:

Deety backed off and her nipples showed faintly – not rigid but she was feeling better. My darling keeps her feelings out of her face, mostly – but those pretty pink spigots are barometers of her morale.

ROBERT A. HEINLEIN, *The Number of the Beast*

'I think you're cute, too,' Zebbie answered, grabbed me by both shoulders, dragged me over the table, and kissed me hard. Our teeth grated and my nipples went *spung*! Sometimes I wish I weren't so noble.

(*ibid.*)

Deety did not answer. Her face assumed her no-expression. Her nipples were down. I kept quiet.

(*ibid.*)

Took one last look in the mirror, saw that my scrap of a halter, like a good evening gown, made me nakeder than skin would. My nipples popped out; I grinned and stuck out my tongue at them. They stayed up; I was happy.

(*ibid.*)

In SF before this, the proper attitude to breasts was that displayed by E. E. 'Doc' Smith:

He broke off and stared at her, his contemptuous gaze travelling slowly, dissectingly, from her toes to the topmost wave of her hairdo. 'Forty-two, twenty, forty?' he asked.

'You flatter me.' Her voice was controlled fury. 'Thirty-nine, twenty-two, thirty-nine. Five-seven. One thirty-five. If any of it's any of your business, which it isn't. You should be discussing brains and ability, not vital statistics.'

E. E. 'DOC' SMITH, *The Galaxy Primes*

A few aliens did (or didn't) have them. In L. Sprague deCamp's *Rogue Queen*, only the 'functional' queens of the hive-like aliens possess 'fully developed glands':

'They are mammals; the functional females had fully developed glands – though not so fine as yours, Queen.'

Trust Rodh . . . always to work in some little boot-licking compliment to her superiors.

L. SPRAGUE DECAMP, *Rogue Queen*

But after the (humble, breastless worker) heroine escapes from the hive and EATS STEAK she grows her own, prompting the following comment:

'Great Eunmar! I didn't know you with those bulges!'

(*ibid.*)

Horror writers have their own uses for breasts:

The girl's left breast came away in one piece trailing bloody roots and exposing a pumping gushing heart in a gaping hole.

GUY N. SMITH, *The Slime Beast*

And other writers have explored even more terrifying aspects:

Her breasts looked out at him like some cast-eyed giant.

WILLIAM BARTON, *Hunting on Kunderer*

Terror took her by the tits. Was this another of Tom's evil little aliens?

FIONA RICHMOND, *Galactic Girl*

And the more humorous:

And as the heads turned, Vawn began to giggle. For on top of each female head were the bonnets: and the bonnets resembled nothing so much as – what was the word – *brassieres*, that was it, those things women wore in the twentieth century.

NICHOLAS FISK, *Starstormers*

Her bosom quivered as she chuckled.

Lepilov forgot himself and stared at her breasts, fascinated. *A magnificent giantess*!

FRANK HERBERT, *The White Plague*

Meanwhile, I'm still trying to work out what this young head-transplant victim actually *looked* like, following her diet:

Her dieting had paid off, and she was flat where women ought to be flat and curvy where women should be curvy. Doubly so, in fact, in both directions.

SUE PAYER, *Second Body*

ATOMIC WAR

'The best defence against the atom bomb is not to be there when it goes off.'

British Army Journal, 1949

'Ever since the day that I first heard that an atomic bomb had been exploded over Japan I have had the disturbing conviction that we are all living in a science-fiction story.'

DONALD A. WOLLHEIM, **quoted in** *Encyclopedia of SF*

Although the atomic bomb brought a new rationale for the post-holocaust novel, there is little SF that has approached the subject directly.

Some thought it would *not* be a Good Thing:

In the event of attomigeddon, all men will be cremated equal. FORREST J. ACKERMAN

Atomic energy is powerful medicine. It can make the dead walk – or it can make the walking dead.

J. W. CAMPBELL JR

'You seem a very superior type of man to be a tramp . . . what brings a man of standing into this disreputable state?' . . .

'My name is Erasmus John Mediu . . . an atomic scientist for many years. I was engaged on so many projects of devilish weapon-forging that I was nauseated beyond description. I managed to swallow this sickness for a long time, but the cumulative effect was so great that finally I had to make a break. Not wishing to be stricken with the mark of Cain a million times over, I gave up atomising and turned to the simple, honest pleasures of the open road.'

TERENCE HAILE, *Space Train*

While others were not too sure:

There are so many, many things in this so-termed civilization of ours which would be mightily improved by a once over lightly of the Hiroshima treatment.

ROBERT A. HEINLEIN, *Pie from the Sky*

If not, in fact, advocating it:

He frowned. 'Barbara, I'm not as sad over what has happened as you are. It might be good for us. I don't mean us six; I mean our country.

She looked startled. 'How?'

'Well – it's hard to take the long view when you are crouching in a shelter and wondering how long you can hold out. But – Barbara, I've worried for years about our country. It seems to me that we have been breeding slaves – and I believe in freedom. This war may have turned the tide. This may be the first war in history which kills the stupid rather than the bright and able – where it makes any distinction.'

'How do you figure that, Hugh?'

'Well, wars have always been hardest on the best young men. This time the boys in the service are as safe or safer than civilians. And of civilians those who used their heads and made preparations stand a far better chance. Not every case, but on the average, and that will improve the breed. When it's over, things will be tough, and that will improve the breed still more. For years the surest way of surviving has been to be utterly worthless and breed a lot of worthless kids. All that will change.'

She nodded thoughtfully. 'That's standard genetics. But it seems cruel.'

'It *is* cruel. But no government has yet been able to repeal natural laws, though they keep trying.'

She shivered in spite of the heat. 'I suppose you're right. No, I *know* you're right.'

ROBERT A. HEINLEIN, *Farnham's Freehold*

Some authors seem unable to make up their minds:

This was it. The 'impossible' war had been possible after all. The 'absolutely unthinkable' had been so easily thinkable after all. For now, oddly enough, this was the only thinkable thing – the only course of action to take; insane and hopeless though it all seemed.

JULIUS P. NEWTON, *The Forgotten Race*

But if it happens they know which side they're on:

'And what if the Communist powers win?' asked Amos.

Alex answered calmly. 'In that case, we stay here until we can contact anti-Red powers and attempt to organize a counter-Red guerrilla special force. I am sure you realize, luckily, we have the only extra-long-range interstellar spaceship in existence . . .'

JAMES GRAZIER, *The Runts of 61 Cygni C*

Not that he had believed in 'Better red than dead' – or believed in it now. The aggression had been one-sided as hell – and he did not regret a megaton of the 'massive retaliation'.

ROBERT A. HEINLEIN, *Farnham's Freehold*

More things to say after WW3:

'It was a pretty nice world, even if I did crumb up my marriage.' (*ibid.*)

'Have you seen any of my friends? They look like me.'

. . . 'No, I haven't seen your companions, ever . . . We will walk until we are tired. Then we will eat ripe blue berries and make blissful love. After that, if you like, we will walk some more.'

'I like you, Nona! I like to walk!' Alex replied, his hand trembling with the touch of the C female.

JAMES GRAZIER, *Runts of 61 Cygni C*

Nuclear war raises some interesting theological questions:

Could God and the hydrogen bomb both exist, and if so, was it the kind of God that he had always been taught to believe in?

LIONEL FANTHORPE, *The Golden Chalice*

Brother Francis visualized a Fallout as half-salamander, because, according to tradition, the thing was born in the Flame Deluge, and as half-incubus who despoiled virgins in their sleep, for, were not the monsters of the world still called 'children of the Fallout'? That the demon was capable of inflicting all the woes which descended upon Job was recorded fact, if not an article of creed.

WALTER M. MILLER JR, *A Canticle for Leibowitz*

Interstellar nuclear war is another matter:

'There can be circumstances when it's just as foolish to hit an enemy city with an H-bomb as it would be to spank a baby with an ax. War is not violence and killing, pure and simple; war is *controlled* violence, for a purpose. The purpose of war is to support your government's decisions by force. The purpose is never to kill the enemy just to be killing him . . . but to make him do what you want him to do. Not killing . . . but controlled and purposeful violence. But it's not your business or mine to decide the purpose or the control. It's never a soldier's business to decide when or where or how – or *why* – he fights; that belongs to the statesmen and the generals. The statesmen decide why and how much; the generals take it from there and tell us where and when and how. *We* supply the violence.

ROBERT A. HEINLEIN, *Starship Troopers*

‘In an interstellar war planets cannot be captured, Doctor. They can only be detonated.’

JAMES WHITE, *Star Surgeon*

The question of whether or not we *will* kill ourselves off in a nuclear war remains undecided, at the time of writing, but I think John Steinbeck’s answer is as good as any:

It’d be kind of silly if we killed ourselves off after all this time. If we do, we’re stupider than the cave people and I don’t think we are. I think we’re just exactly as stupid and that’s pretty bright in the long run.

JOHN STEINBECK, *The Short-Short Story of Mankind*

GOD AND RELIGION

‘She believed that God liked people in sailboats much better than He liked people in motorboats.’

KURT VONNEGUT, JR, *Cat’s Cradle*

This was Kurt Vonnegut’s brief description of a rich and unpleasant woman. Like many other SF and fantasy authors he has created his own religions: Bokonism (in *Cat’s Cradle*, a religion based on lies, but good lies), and in the *Sirens of Titan,* The Church of God the Utterly Indifferent:

‘O Lord Most High, Creator of the Cosmos, Spinner of Galaxies, Soul of Electromagnetic Waves, Inhaler and Exhaler of Inconceivable Volumes of Vacuum, Spitter of Fire and Rock, Trifler with Millennia – what could we do for Thee that Thou couldst not do for Thyself one octillion times better? Nothing. Oh, Mankind, rejoice in the apathy of our Creator, for it makes us free and truthful and dignified at last.’

KURT VONNEGUT JR, *Sirens of Titan*

Philip K. Dick created a logical religion for his characters in *The Maze of Death*, with a pantheon contactable by radio-broadcast prayer:

His prayer had been simple. 'This damn inventory-control job bores me,' he had prayed. 'Routine work – this ship is too large and in addition it's overstaffed. I'm a useless standby module. Could you help me find something more creative and stimulating?' He had addressed the prayer, as a matter of course, to the Intercessor. Had it failed he would have presently re-addressed the prayer, this time to the Mentufacturer.

PHILIP K. DICK, *The Maze of Death*

Cirocco Jones' funeral prayer adopts a slightly unorthodox stance:

'Whoever or whatever you may be, you might want to take these departed human souls to your breast. I don't know anything about them except one was very young. The others were, for a time, zombies in the service of Luthor, an evil thing, no longer human. No matter what they may have done in life, they must have started out innocent, as do we all, so don't be too hard on them. It was your fault for making them human, which was a dirty trick. If you are out there somewhere, you ought to be ashamed of yourself.'

JOHN VARLEY, *Demon*

A prayer against Fallout:

'From the place of ground zero,
O Lord, deliver us.
From the rain of the cobalt,
O Lord, deliver us.
From the rain of the strontium,
O Lord, deliver us.
From the fall of the cesium,

O Lord, deliver us.
From the curse of the Fallout,
O Lord, deliver us.
From the begetting of monsters,
O Lord, deliver us.
From the curse of the Misborn,
O Lord, deliver us.
A morte perpetua,
Domine, libera nos.'

WALTER M. MILLER, *A Canticle for Leibowitz*

This Roger Zelazny prayer covers all eventualities:

'Insofar as I may be heard by anything, which may or may not care what I say, I ask, if it matters, that you be forgiven for anything you may have done or failed to do which required forgiveness. Conversely, if not forgiveness but something else may be required to insure any possible benefit for which you may be eligible after the destruction of your body, I ask that this, whatever it may be, be granted or withheld, as the case may be, in such a manner as to insure your receiving said benefit. I ask this in my capacity as your elected intermediary between yourself and that which might not be yourself, but which may have an interest in the matter of your receiving as much as it is possible for you to receive of this thing, and which may in some way be influenced by this ceremony. Amen.'

ROGER ZELAZNY, *Creatures of Light and Darkness*

H. G. Wells' Beast-Men had their own religion, the worship of the sinister Dr Moreau, with their own gospel:

Not to go on all-Fours; *that* is the Law. Are we not Men?
Not to suck up Drink; *that* is the Law. Are we not Men?

Not to eat Flesh nor Fish; *that* is the Law. Are we not Men?
Not to claw Bark of Trees; *that* is the Law. Are we not Men?
Not to chase other Men; *that* is the Law. Are we not Men?

H. G. WELLS, *The Island of Dr Moreau*

Robert A. Heinlein pointed out:

'I've never understood how God could expect his creatures to pick the one true religion by faith – it strikes me as a sloppy way to run a universe.'

ROBERT A. HEINLEIN, *Stranger In A Strange Land*

One obvious solution:

'In a crisis it is best not to be pernickety – never mind the religious difficulties, apply all the best rites and remedies and don't worry about how they will combine.'

MANUEL MUJICA LAINEZ, *The Wandering Unicorn*

At this point Ghastly Beyond Belief tackles a Serious Question. Is There A God? And if so, who is He (or She)?

'I think there are innumerable Gods. What we on Earth call God is a little tribal God who has made an awful mess. Certain forces operating through human consciousness control events.'

WILLIAM S. BURROUGHS, *Writers at Work 1967*

A look of awe – almost a look of terror – came upon the captain's face. 'He? Oh, him.' The tone of wonder enriched his voice and made it echo in the small cabin of the spaceboat. 'Sh'san. He is the thinker of all thinking, the "to be" of being, the doer of things. He is powerful beyond your strongest imagination. He makes me come living out of your living minds. In fact,' said the captain with a final snarl, 'he is a dead mouse-brain laminated with plastic and I have no idea at all of who *I* am. Good night to you all!'

CORDWAINER SMITH, *Think Blue, Count Two*

Tarzan had his own ideas:

If he ever met God, Tarzan would be prepared. One could never tell whether a grass rope, a war spear, or a poisoned arrow would be most efficacious against an unfamiliar foe. Tarzan of the Apes was quite content – if God wished to fight, the ape-man had no doubt as to the outcome of the struggle.

EDGAR RICE BURROUGHS, *Jungle Tales of Tarzan*

While Richard Cowper's mad submarine captain realized that *he* was God while doing the crossword:

The moment of ultimate revelation had come to him while he was scouring the pages of his Thesaurus in search of a synonym to help him complete *The Times* crossword. No sooner had his eye alighted upon the catalogue of divine attributes and perfections and he had heard himself intoning 'infinite power, wisdom, goodness, justice, truth, love, mercy, omnipotence, omniscience, etc, etc.' than he knew that what he had stumbled upon was nothing less than a flawless mirror from which his own sublime reflection beamed resplendent. The total absence of any possible reference to humility quite confirmed him in his belief.

RICHARD COWPER, *De Profundis*

Other authors have suggested him to be a hobbyist, a superman, an accountant, a star, a computer . . .

Carefully, AC organized the program.

The consciousness of AC encompassed all of what had once been a Universe and brooded over what was now chaos. Step by step, it must be done.

And AC said, 'LET THERE BE LIGHT!'

And there was light –

ISAAC ASIMOV, *The Last Question*

My favourite view of God comes from Maudsley the Planet Builder:

'A tall, bearded old man with piercing eyes had come to me and ordered a planet. (That was how your planet began, Carmody.) Well, I did the job quickly, in six days I believe, and thought that would be the end of it. It was another of those budget planets and I had cut a few corners here and there . . .'

ROBERT SHECKLEY, *Dimension of Miracles*

Although:

'In organized religion the actual presence of a god is an embarrassment.'

ROBERT BLOCH, *How Like a God*

So does He exist?

'God? I don't know . . . but the Devil? Sure I believe in the Devil. He does commercials.'

WILLIAM PETER BLATTY, *The Exorcist*

But so does God:

'Our first hymn,' he said briskly, 'is sponsored by Manna Bakeries, makers of Angel Bread, the loaf of love with our Supreme Bishop's smiling face on every wrapper and containing a valuable coupon redeemable at your nearest neighbourhood Church of the New Revelation.'

ROBERT A. HEINLEIN, *Stranger In A Strange Land*

According to *Newsweek* magazine, God is somewhere between Superman and Yoda the Jedi Muppet:

People can croak 'Entertainment! Entertainment!' until they're blue in the face. The fact remains that films like CLOSE ENCOUNTERS OF THE THIRD KIND, SUPERMAN and STAR WARS have become jerry-built substitutes for the great myths and rituals of belief, hope and redemption . . .

From a 1979 edition of *Newsweek*

Or as George Bernard Shaw put it:

Beware the man whose god is in the skies.

GEORGE BERNARD SHAW, *Man and Superman*

Where the Bible is concerned, science fiction seems to be divided between those who want to claim the Old Testament as a seminal work of SF:

Adam and Eve also crop up as themselves in a number of allegorical fantasies, notably the book of Genesis, George Bernard Shaw's *Back to Methusalah* (1921) and John Erskine's *Adam and Eve* (1927).

BRAIN STABLEFORD, *Encyclopedia of Science Fiction*

And those who want to rewrite the New Testament:

'Some fell upon the metal deck,' murmured Tom, 'and the andies stomped on it with their steel boots and squashed it flat. And some fell on the pedaways and got itself chomped up in the machinery. But some of it fell right into the sewage tanks and that lot sprouted a hundredfold into God's own holy protein.'

RICHARD COWPER, *De Profundis*

The well-heeled prophet is never without honour in his own country.

(*ibid.*)

'You're the son of God!'
J. C. looked grim-faced.
'Smile when you call me that, stranger.'

PHILIP JOSE FARMER, *J. C. on the Dude Ranch*

'So you would like to resemble Jesus Christ, um?'
'Um, yes.'
'May I ask why?'
'Sure.'
A pause and then an irritated, 'Well, why?'
'So I could consort freely and openly with prostitutes without getting busted.'

LEO P. KELLEY, *The Earth Tripper*

'You know how that camel does it? He just closes one of his own eyes and flops back his ears and plunges right through. A camel is mighty narrow when he closes one eye and flops back his ears. Besides, they use a big-eyed needle in the act.'

R. A. LAFFERTY, *Narrow Valley*

WEAPONS

Weapons fall into three classes. Ravening beams of destruction:

From it there fanned out into space a concentrated beam of destruction – the terrible ray of annihilation, against which no known substance could endure for a moment;

the ray which had definitely outlawed war. But even that frightful weapon was useless – it spent its force harmlessly upon an impalpable, invisible barrier, a hundred yards from its source, and the bold lifeboat disappeared in one blinding explosion of incandescence as the captor showed its real power in retaliation.

E. E. 'DOC' SMITH, *Spacehounds of IPC*

Hand blasters:

Smiling, Roan said, 'Want the gun back?'

Henry Dread's smile was grim. 'Keep it,' he said. 'From now on, you walk behind me. Keep the gun at your hip, and your right hand loose.'

He turned and followed the huddle of pirates, and Roan trailed him, walking with his head up, liking the feel of the heavy gun in his belt.

KEITH LAUMER AND ROSEL GEORGE BROWN, *Earthblood*

Mullan himself used his little pocket atomic firearm . . . when the little mushroom cloud cleared away no-one was hurt at all.

'Even acid, high-explosive, atomic hand-guns, didn't touch these people?'

TREBOR THORPE, *Lightning World*

The customs man recovered his balance and, with the speed of a striking sex-crazed strooka, drew his weapon. The Tonota eighty could vapourize a man's head at six hundred meters.

TULLY ZETFORD, from the *Hook* series

And the improvised:

A weapon! He must repel this loathesome (sic) creature. Then an idea filtered through his fear-crazed brain. He saw the box of matches and the three-day-old news paper. Fire! The scourge of all beasts of the wild . . .

GUY N. SMITH, *The Slime Beast*

Special Effects

HUH?

Occasionally one reads something that leaves one feeling a little disoriented. What *did* the author mean by that?

Sometimes one is merely baffled:

A world in which the human race has been split into several species, while wars are waged over the weather with the aid of gigantic insects, does have parallels to our planet today. I do not predict that this is the future that awaits us. But I do not deny that this is the direction in which we are moving.

STANTON A. COBLENZ, *Pulp Voices*

He had to keep moving, it was like groping your way through a thick fog. The beams of your headlights throwing the fog back at you. It was like that, yet it wasn't.

LIONEL FANTHORPE, *The Asteroid Man*

There was something about his appearance that was almost scrofulous, he might almost have been the spurious founder of the celebrated Disumbrationist school!

KARL ZEIGFREID, *Projection Infinity*

At other times the intention is clear but an extra meaning creeps in:

She paused, her icy-blue gaze sweeping each of her officers in turn.

A. B. CHANDLER, *Empress of Outer Space*

Few townspeople ever came near the collapsed timbers, except maybe to pick up charred kindling from among the long-dead ashes, or courting couples.

VICTOR NORWOOD, *Night of the Black Horror*

(One wonders if the courting couples burned anywhere nearly as well.)

There was no time for thought or pity. The Mongs sacrificed dung people as they stepped on beetles.

JEFFREY LORD, *Blade: The Jade Warrior*

METAPHOR AND SIMILE

'Her world exploded': If this sentence appears in mundane fiction it is probably going to be a more-or-less muzzy emotional metaphor, referring to some internal state, whereas in a science fiction text it reserves the right to mean that a planet belonging to some woman blew up. Or 'He turned on his left side' in a text of mundane fiction probably refers to an insomniac; in science fiction it could mean that someone reached down and flipped a switch.

SAMUEL DELANY, quoted in *Who Writes Science Fiction*, by CHARLES PLATT

This section leaves such metaphors alone – otherwise it would leave readers pondering over the significance of commonly-used phrases as 'The sun came in through

the window', 'Her eyes followed him down the road', 'He turned into a driveway', and 'Brownlow gave the girl a hand'.

Thus in the following passage:

Peggy thought longingly of the fat sexual slug that lay curled in a beautiful bird's-nest in the crook of his thigh.

FIONA RICHMOND, *Galactic Girl*

. . . The slug is actually not a slug at all.

And with that, a mixed bag of similes and metaphors that you can use to increase your word-power and astound your friends:

As their lips pressed together and opened he sent his tongue probing into her mouth to find her and felt it squirming out past her teeth like a restless sea-slug.

WILLIAM BARTON, *Hunting on Kunderer*

Her voice was like an iceberg.

J. HARVEY BOND, *The Other World*

'The important thing,' he said, 'is to lay the Brains by the heels.'

SYDNEY J. BOUNDS, *The Robot Brains*

It was as though his soul, like some infernal yo-yo on the end of demonaic string, had been lowered to within inches of the very caverns of Hell itself, and now was reascending by that same strange method.

LIONEL FANTHORPE, *The Golden Chalice*

Am I flotsam and jetsam on the tidal beaches of life?

LIONEL FANTHORPE, *The Triple Man*

She accused him of deliberately cultivating her friendship in order to meet her father and so further his own personal ambition. She stated that she felt like a piece of sullied cloth removed from a boiled pudding.

TERENCE HAILE, *Space Train*

She was beautiful in a grubby sort of way, somewhere between a prissy Lucrezia Borgia and Snow White in orgasm.

THOM KEYES, *The Battle of Disneyland*

I heard voices, and yowls, and echoes, but above all there gently rose that impious, insidious scurrying; gently rising, rising, as a stiff bloated corpse gently rises above an oily river that flows under endless onyx bridges to a black, putrid sea.

H. P. LOVECRAFT, *The Rats in the Walls*

I needed a shot of the *aqua vita* like a three-testicled sailor needed shore leave.

ALAN MARKS, *The Antenna Syndrome*

Her voice grated like a bone saw in Moreta's ear.

ANNE MCCAFFREY, *Moreta, Dragonlady of Pern*

Beams and timbers of misery and wanting clashed within me.

JOHN NORMAN, *Raiders of Gor*

A woman's intuition is sharper than a laser beam.

SUE PAYER, *Second Body*

For three seconds there was deep silence.

It was so deep it had the shape and smell of smog.

Or the curiously distorted, rhomboid lines of a child's scream, kicking in a nightmare.

ROBERT RAY, *No Stars for Us*

'Suffice it to say that your arrival was like a turd falling into a Ming vase.'

JOHN VARLEY, *Demon*

A few literary nasties:

He was dressed in rags and his mouth looked like a hole doing the mambo. But what made Babs scream like a banshee, and made my heart do a couple of back-flips, was a seven foot long pitchfork sticking out of his chest.

Liquid ice shot through my veins. A combine harvester grappled with my guts as I felt myself keeling over.

J. HOGAN, *Pitchforked into Darkness*

A mêlée beneath a crimson fountain of spraying blood, entrails torn from a gaping belly wound and slurped into revolting mouths like strings of spaghetti.

GUY N. SMITH, *Crabs on the Rampage*

The crab moved, a sinister sideways lurch that brought it a foot or so nearer, squatted again. Unblinking eyes that burned hatred like gamma rays.

(*ibid.*)

He fought to free himself from whatever it was that had a hold on his left leg that could only be compared with a pair of garden shears with serrated blades . . .

GUY N. SMITH, *Night of the Crabs*

And some insects and animals:

His gray hair was bristling like the antennae of a Jovian glow-worm in a thunderstorm; his optics were sticking out like they grew on stalks.

NELSON BOND, *Legacy*

Time puffed along like a poisoned caterpillar.

ISIDORE HAIBLUM, *The Wilk Are Among Us*

(**BBC Announcer**) '. . . and in the air, ladies and gentlemen, we can see this amazing train which is not a train, rushing along at fantastic speed, like a caterpillar which has lost nine-tenths of its body and has an overgrown head.'

TERENCE HAILE, *Space Train*

His expression suggested that he was giving birth to a porcupine.

ROBERT A. HEINLEIN, *'The Number of the Beast –'*

Someone was smiling. It was only a small smile but in the midst of a sea of grave faces it stood out like a dead fly in a bowl of cream.

WALTER M. MILLER, *A Canticle for Leibowitz*

'The melbar instantaneous transmitter,' answered Knight, 'is not functioning. So we're like a blind man lost in a desert without a camel . . .'

JOHN E. MULLER, *Micro Infinity*

'She's the one!' Kinnison rasped. 'She looks like an angel, but take it from me, she isn't. She's one of the slimiest snails that ever crawled – she's so low she could put on a tall silk hat and walk under a duck.'

E. E. 'DOC' SMITH, *Grey Lensman*

DEATHLESS PROSE

Deathless prose comes in many forms.

For example, bestseller *Foundation's Edge* contains many passages that . . . or should I say:

Bestseller *Foundation's Edge*
Contains –
A number!
of –
Passages that –
Seem only
Designed!
To use up a great deal of –
***Paper*!**

Branno the Bronze she was sometimes called, and she certainly acted with metallic rigour –
Unless she herself was already in the grip –
No! That way led to paranoia!
And yet –

ISAAC ASIMOV, *Foundation's Edge*

. . . the unmistakable adoration in her voice escaped Doc's notice.

LESTER DENT, *Doc Savage: Man of Bronze*

Doc came back, appearing with the silent unexpectedness of an apparition. (*ibid.*)

His visage was littered with broken possibilities, wrecked faiths and loves, but behind his features his skull shone with pale malice.

STEPHEN DONALDSON, *The Power That Preserves*

Donaldson's later books have actually become even more impenetrable:

They were featureless and telic, like lambent gangrene. They looked horribly like children.

STEPHEN DONALDSON, *The Wounded Land*

(For the discovery of which I am indebted to Dave Langford and *Knave*.)

These space folks were a cool lot.

ROBERT FRENCH, *Now, the Gods*

Buildings spewed out clots of dead.

JAMES GRAZIER, *Runts of 61 Cygni C*

Know, O Prince, that between the years when the oceans drank Atlantis and the gleaming cities, and the years of the rise of the Sons of Aryas, there was an age undreamed of, when shining kingdoms lay spread across the world like blue mantles beneath the stars.

ROBERT E. HOWARD, *The Phoenix and the Sword*

I hate to admit it, but that opera had some real groovy tunes.

NEVILLE KEA, *The World of Artemis*

He went into the misty light with his geranium.

WILLIAM KOTZWINKLE, *ET: The Extraterrestrial*

But there was a cold and acid-thinking part of his brain that spoke icily. No man, drunk with joy over riches, will turn to unrelated enormities until his first intoxication has worn off. The crew of the *Theban* hadn't yet realized that now they must set about murdering each other.

MURRAY LEINSTER, *Invaders of Space*

Praise be to Té, it was a banner year for giant slugs!

JULIAN MAY, *The Adversary*

She gave the porridge a final decisive poke and turned fully toward Moreta. 'How long does it take this sickness to come on people?'

ANNE MCCAFFREY, *Moreta – Dragonlady of Pern*

The fire-height is warm in the full sun, the dragon replied evasively swinging her head toward her rider. The many facets of her eyes were tinged with the blue of longing.

(*ibid.*)

Harry Harrison swears that the greatest line lost to science fiction was cut by Frederik Pohl, from a Sam Moskowitz article on the negro in science fiction; Moskowitz had concluded the piece, 'To call a spade a spade'.

He was also responsible for the following:

Concepts the mind cannot stomach . . .

SAM MOSKOWITZ, *The Immortal Storm*

Victor Norwood – who wrote with what Isaac Asimov might have described as a 'thick layer of fatty adjectival froth'– not only created a remarkable monster:

. . . Helpless for the first time since erring evolution spawned its ghastly composition, the creature, now thoroughly alarmed, floundered impotently, flinging gobs of filth in all directions . . .

VICTOR NORWOOD, *Night of the Black Horror*

but also one of the most remarkable sentences in SF:

Had it persevered – if awful chance had decreed that it escape from the quicksand as nightfall closed in over that foetid marsh, neither Colonel Jameson or Jim Tressidy or anybody in Horton's Crossing or camped in the adjacent hills would have survived to greet Lieutenant Wade Castro when, shortly after dawn the next day, he reported, red-eyed through lack of sleep, to the officer who had received instructions to accompany him in the spacious helicopter waiting on the hard-core, clambered aboard, took the ungainly seeming machine to tree-top level, and, half an hour later, brought it down skilfully in the deserted town's main street within yards of Sheriff Regan's office – just as Colonel Jamison had instructed.

(*ibid.*)

Nothing much happened in those weeks; yet each day and night was pregnant with happening.

SUE PAYER, *Second Body*

Her green dress stuck like glue to her body, making her look lumpy.
'What's wrong, Ann?'
'I'm scared,' she spat out.

ROBERT PETYO, *The Institute*

Love leaked from the green eyes of the recently-returned astronaut. She'd not been expecting his descent so soon . . .

FIONA RICHMOND, *Galactic Girl*

And now not a soul in the world would be any the wiser as to what secret of the speechless minnows he held and had *not* divulged. And all because of the insalubriousness of a rock cavity.

NEAL RAFCAM, *The Troglodytes*

I've heard of the mint with the hole, but . . .

Jupiter. The planet with the orange glow in the centre. Sounded great. A queer feeling of sheer excitement made the blood rush through his veins . . . it was an urge only another cosmonaut could fully understand.

LUAN RANZETTA, *Yellow Inferno*

Every so often he felt the striking claws missing him by inches.

GUY N. SMITH, *Night of the Crabs*

As soon as 'evening had let her curtain down, and pinned it with a star' (as the poet sings), the saboteur slipped away on the pretext of going to the toilet.

KARL ZEIGFREID, *Projection Infinity*

THE SCARY BITS

'Your standard television news show is more horrific these days than any of the gothics.'

GAHAN WILSON, *SF Voices 3*

Suzy McKee Charnas, when asked what inspired her to write a vampire novel:
'Well . . . vampires are such snappy dressers.'

People like to be scared. Especially when it's a *safe* fear. The novels of Stephen King, James Herbert and the egregious Guy N. Smith, and the stories of H. P. Lovecraft, are in essence reassuring.

After all, no matter what happens, *you* aren't going to be eaten by giant rats, bats or cats, find yourself transformed into one of the undead, or, granted a glimpse of the hellish *otherness* of the Elder Gods, wind up in a madhouse, scribbling your story in a notebook. *You* won't have to face Things Man Was Not Meant to Know . . .

Will you?

You could have either werewolves or Pyrex nine-cup percolators in the world, but not both, surely.

PETER S. BEAGLE, *Lila the Werewolf*

'Understand death? . . . sure: that's when the monsters get you.'

STEPHEN KING, *Salem's Lot*

The scary bits generally start slowly, with a few cunningly-dropped hints that All Is Not As It Should Be:

South of Prospect Park the brownstones rise wild, and there are mortgages that no mustard has ever cut . . . The very cats were sickly and stunted and about the tumbled maws and lids of the ancient ash-cans many dead Puerto Ricans tottered or lay rotting . . .

JAMES BLISH, *Getting Along*

The place had not been inhabited since the reign of James the First, when a tragedy of intensely hideous, though largely unexplained, nature had struck down the master, five of his children and several servants; and driven forth under a cloud of suspicion and terror the third son, my lineal progenitor and the only survivor of the abhorred line.

H. P. LOVECRAFT, *The Rats in the Walls*

Gradually things get creepier and creepier:

What the devil could it be? he asked himself over and over again. Only the length of the torch beam separated him from his objective now. He drew closer, and closer still. Then he recognized the peculiar gleaming object for what it was – a door handle!

LIONEL FANTHORPE, *The Asteroid Man*

A cunning use of sound effects builds up tension:

Something was coming up the cellar steps, he could hear it, clump. Clump. Clump. Clump. Clump.

LIONEL FANTHORPE, *The Golden Chalice*

But you can't keep building up the tension for ever. Sooner or later, somebody has to get hurt:

'This was not a deliberate act of vandalism as you may think. You see –' Here he paused almost for dramatic effect, then went on slowly: 'the coffin lid was smashed open from the *inside*!'

JOHN CRAWFORD, *Dark Legion*

'Lover,' she whispers, and closes her eyes.
  It falls upon her.
  Love is like dying.

STEPHEN KING, *Cycle of the Werewolf*

Minutes later it was again on the prowl, its carnal appetite merely whetted, its craving as voracious as before – And wherever it roamed the hideous marauder left only death – and putrid slime, and the evil odour of its slithering passage . . .

VICTOR NORWOOD, *Night of the Black Horror*

'That "thing" —!' she blurted, 'It's got Chase —! It's REAL —! ALIVE —! Out there . . .! THE SWAMP CREATURE —! I've SEEN it —! All black and shiny — and HORRIBLE—! Like a – like – it's – we —'

(*ibid.*)

'What a beautiful night,' Pat remarked as they passed alongside the barbed-wire fence which enclosed War Department property. 'If only we didn't have to worry about giant crabs!'

GUY N. SMITH, *Night of the Crabs*

Liz turned away and retched. Below her the two men vomited showering the monstrosity with spew. The stench was far stronger now, hanging in the windless atmosphere.

GUY N. SMITH, *The Slime Beast*

He lifted him high above his head and then hurled him out as far as he could. There followed the inevitable thud, squelch, slurp, and a final gurgling before complete silence returned.

GUY N. SMITH, *The Sucking Pit*

As one approaches the end, be ready for the sudden italics, the disappearance of the author in mid-sente –

– the cut tentacle, ten feet in length, which had been caught between dimensions when the door had been shut against that monstrous body to which it belonged, the tentacle no living savant could identify as belonging to any known creature, living or dead, on the face or in the subterrene depths of the earth!

AUGUST DERLETH AND H. P. LOVECRAFT, *The Gable Window*

'There is something fumbling at the door-handle. O God, help me now! Jesus! – The door is opening – slowly. Somethi . . .'

WILLIAM HOPE HODGSON, *The House on the Borderland*

And then there was a huge surge of grey vibrating flesh. The smell became a nightmare tide. It was a huge outpouring of a viscid, pustulant jelly, a huge and awful form that seemed to skyrocket from the very bowels of the ground. And yet, with a sudden horrible comprehension which no man can have known, I perceived *that it was but one ring, one segment, of a monster worm that had existed eyeless for years in the chambered darkness beneath that abominated church*!

STEPHEN KING, *Jerusalem's Lot*

Misprints

It is rara that eagle-eyed prufreeders allow mistakes to crepp in.

But mistakes *do* happen, from time to time. And when they occur they do not occur singly and inoffensively, but in clusters, strategically placed where they can do the most damage.

A surprising number of books have misprints in the very first sentence. Like these three:

One thing everybody said about Hartford McBride – in addition to the fact that his name sounded like a publishing house, or an insurance company – was that he manged to survive his father's considerable wealth.

ROBERT FRENCH, *Now, The Gods*

It was not a day for macabre, portenous death.

A. A. GLYNN, *Plan for Conquest*

The corridor walls were made of light green plastic with a matt finish, except at the gently curving corners where they were brought to a high gloss to serve as mirrors so that when their was an alarm and people ran like the very devil to their respective posts, they could see who they were running into.

ROBERT RAY, *No Stars For Us*

Giving rise to Ghastly's Law – No book with a typographical error in the first sentence is going to be enjoyed by anyone except a masochist.

When 'James Harvey' plagiarized Gardner Fox's *Escape across the Cosmos* for Manor Books under the title *Titans of the Universe* he changed very little, but added a new dimension to many of the more prosaic moments . . .

He mader the implositrons work, all right.
. . . He turned the Vrallen to drifting motes of dead energy. He obleatrated them. Ah, but the coat! Every life but three was lost.

JAMES HARVEY, *Titans of the Universe*

In the same motion he was lifting off his feet, turning his body. He drove into the men at knee height. His heavy body and massive muscles crunced across their legs as if he ahd been an iron bar . . . There was a sodden splat an nosen cartilage flattened.

(*ibid.*)

With alien life? Alien life that fasted on . . . human life!

(*ibid.*)

(In the original it *feasted* on it . . .)

There were uncounted billions of men out there on those star worlds living in a fool's paradise, completely unaware of this doom that threatened them. His brother back on the Kansas farm that girl named Hella who had given him the statuette of Excel the woman in the Mews who had told him Lelton Pratt was dead all would be prey to Yeeluth when he crossed the barriers between worlds.

(*ibid.*)

What was done to these smugglers was unspeakable:

England of the seventeenth century practiced a crude method of embalming to serve a grim, practical purpose. Smugglers were hung to gibblets along the coast, their bodies coated from time to time with tar and pitch to preserve them as long standing examples.

NEIL R. JONES, *Space War*

'Oh, stove it,' said the orderly in a disgusted voice. 'What rattles me . . . he doesn't care about that poor bastard next door, but if he catches you with a button undone . . . Gawd help you. You know what? I reckon this bastard hates us.'

ROBERT RAY, *No Stars For Us*

'They resent you harrassing the, Colonel, for minor defractions. The spirit in the Outpost . . .'

(*ibid.*)

Lionel Fanthorpe has had his own troubles with misprints:

'Say! You're sarong for a little guy.'

LIONEL FANTHORPE, *Flame Mass*

'You're no more a solicitor than I am, are you?'
The fat man shook his head. Most of the fight seemed to have gone out of him.
'No, I'm not,' he snarled savagely, 'I'm an occult plilosopher. But you wouldn't understand that.'

LIONEL FANTHORPE, *The Golden Chalice*

Jerry Hilton . . . lived in a world of his own. He was an almost perfect example of the introvert. His was almost a clinical example of introversion. His mind was entirely concerned with its own interval functioning.

PEL TORRO, *The Last Astronaut*

When the heroes come to defeat the awful outer-space menace of the Flame Mass they often do so by using the tried-and-true, how-to-screw-up-a-super-brain method of asking it a silly question. ('Which came first, Brain, the chicken or the egg?' 'The chicken . . . no, the egg . . . this does not compute . . . gggsszzppluzlt!')

Fanthorpe went one better. The question that caused Flame Mass to 'Dissolve in a kaliedescope of stars' was:

'What happens when an irrisitable force meets am immoyable object.'

LIONEL FANTHORPE, *Flame Mass*

'Debbie?'

'How are you feeling?'

'Like I just got shot in the back. What happened?'

'You got shot in the back.' 'Like I just got shot in the back. What

'How are you feeling?'

'Like I just got shot in the back. What happened?'

'You got shot in the back.'

He got up, very slowly this time. 'I know that,' he snapped playfully.

ROBERT PETYO, *The Institute*

Writers and Rules

WHO'S WHO

In advertising jargon they call it *positioning*: making something unknown familiar to the consumer by comparing it with something known: ('I use Skyway Soap because . . . It is as pure as the sky itself.' Robert A. Heinlein, *Have Space-suit Will Travel*).

On book jackets it serves to introduce an unknown author: ('Margie Herfendormer is J. R. R. Tolkien on Acid!') **and unknown but hoped-to-be blockbusting books. (Thus the blurb for Julian May's *Many Coloured Land* informed one that it was in the stirring tradition of *Lord of the Rings* and *The Foundation Trilogy*.)**

So who *is* who?

'Brian Aldiss . . . is Joyce, Huxley, Waugh, on a pot party. With Arthur C. Clarke trying to give a lecture to Isaac Asimov while Noel Coward sings and plays the piano.'

Blurb from *The 80 Minute Hour*

Ron Goulart. 'The Mack Sennet of science Fiction.'
Analog
Blurb from *Shaggy Planet*

'Harlan Ellison – A non-stop controversialist who comes on like an angry Woody Allen.' *New Yorker*

Blurb from *I Have No Mouth and I Must Scream*

'Harry Harrison, the Monty Python of the spaceways.' *Daily Telegraph*

'If Le Carré had made it with Le Guin, their mutant offspring would have written this dandy novel.' *Harlan Ellison*

Blurb from ROBERT A. HEINLEIN'S *Friday*

'Heinlein – The Kipling of Science Fiction.' *Time and Tide*

Blurb from *The Green Hills of Earth*

'J. R. R. Tolkien and C. S. Lewis are not in Mr Herbert's inventive league.' *New York Times*

Blurb from FRANK HERBERT, *Dosadi Experiment*

Harry Harrison, of Adolph Hitler's Hugo-Award-winning SF classic *Lord of the Swastikas:*

'If Wagner wrote SF this is how he would do it.'

NORMAN SPINRAD, *Iron Dream*

'In the tradition of H. P. Lovecraft. The Cosmic Vision of Philip K. Dick. The Savage Humour of Harlan Ellison.'

Blurb from BRIAN LUMLEY, *The Clock of Dreams*

'Anne McCaffrey is the Barbara Cartland of science fiction.' *Kingsley Amis*

'Norman Spinrad is the Norman Mailer of Science Fiction.'

NORMAN SPINRAD, *New Tomorrows*

'If the Marx Brothers had been literary fantasists they would have been Robert Sheckley.' *Harlan Ellison*

Harlan Ellison on Roger Zelazny '. . . we are led inexorably to the conclusion that Roger Zelazny is a reincarnation of Geoffrey Chaucer.' Mr Zelazny was born in London in 1340 and served King Edward on secret missions in Flanders, 1376–7. He also lived under the name of Cyril Torner for 20 years. He is married and now lives in Baltimore.

ROGER ZELAZNY, *Damnation Alley*

THE SCIENCE-FICTION PEOPLE

'As children, all science-fiction writers were toads.'

DAMON KNIGHT

And from the earliest science-fiction writers on they have been slagging each other off. They *sometimes* say nice things about each other. They always say nice things about themselves:

I sent my characters to the Moon with gunpowder, a thing one may see every day. Where does M. Wells find his cavorite? Let him show it to me!

JULES VERNE

. . . conveniently ignoring the fact that his gunpowder-propelled bullet would have splattered its passengers on take-off.

Forrest J. Ackerman is the most important fan/collector/ human being in the history of science fiction.

RAY BRADBURY

In my opinion, Ackerman is a bloated ageing queen.

EDITOR, *The Sleazoid Express*

(**On Asimov's Foundation series.**) The ideas in it are captivating, but the *writing* . . .! I wouldn't employ Asimov to write junk mail!

DOUGLAS ADAMS, *Fantasy Empire*

Poul Anderson doesn't know shit from wild honey.

KEITH LAUMER, *Dream Makers 2* by CHARLES PLATT

Deep down underneath it all, I have the heart of a small boy. I keep it in a jar, on my desk.

Autobiography, ROBERT BLOCH, *Weird Tales*, Nov 1942

(**Robert Bloch, asked how he felt about receiving the Lifetime Achievement Award at the First World Fantasy Convention.**) I haven't had so much fun since the rats ate my baby sister.

(**On Ray Bradbury.**) Everyone that knew him wanted to strangle him because he was so boisterous and sure of himself. Nobody could stand him!

FORREST J. ACKERMAN

'Arthur C. Clarke,' Pop told her. 'Great man – too bad he was liquidated in the purge.'

ROBERT A. HEINLEIN, *The Number of the Beast* –

(**Arthur C. Clarke mentioned to Robert Bloch that he'd be having an audience with the Pope.**)

Robert Bloch: That's nice. I wonder what kind of advice he wants from you.'

It's a full-time job just trying to decide how to spend all this money.

ARTHUR C. CLARKE, *Dream Makers 2* by CHARLES PLATT

Clarke is undoubtedly a firm believer in the Freudian dictum that adult happiness lies in the fulfilment of unfulfiled childhood aspirations.

STANLEY KUBRIK

Avram Davidson writes well but spells badly. He has been a professional writer since 1946, and if you were as rich and famous as he is no one will have heard of you, nor give you credit of a commercial nature, either.

AVRAM DAVIDSON, autobiographical note

Harlan Ellison speaks fifteen different languages, all of them English.

MICHAEL MOORCOCK, from intro to *The Fantasies of Harlan Ellison*

A lot of those great old science-fiction writers had some incredibly good ideas . . . Men like Jules Verne, H. G. Wells, John E. Muller, Karl Zeigfreid, Fanthorpe and their contemporaries . . .

LEO BRETT (AKA JOHN E. MULLER, AKA KARL ZEIGFRIED, AKA LIONEL FANTHORPE), *Power Sphere*

(**Re his brain surgery.**) I feel I have proved one of two things: either I have fully recovered . . . or a hole in the head is no handicap to a science fiction writer.

ROBERT A. HEINLEIN, *Expanded Universe*

Heinlein was booed at the World SF Convention for saying something to the effect that War was not only inevitable but desirable because it gave a man an opportunity to be a real Man and protect his wife, children and property.

FORREST J. ACKERMAN

I find Heinlein totally unreadable.

IAN WATSON, *Who Writes Science Fiction* by CHARLES PLATT

Gee, if Hitler hadn't become what he did he could have easily become a sword and sorcery writer.

NORMAN SPINRAD, *SF Voices*

In her preface to her third sci-fi novel, the sputtering *Sirian Experiments*, Doris Lessing even wishes she were a physicist. Myself, I wish she were an artist, a job I consider at least as admirable as designing nuclear bombs or torturing laboratory animals.

ARNOLD KLEIN, *Harpers* magazine

Moorcock is the Old Inextinguishable, and makes most other British writers seem pale and constipated by comparison.

BRIAN ALDISS, *This World and Nearer Ones*

Tom Disch: I'm writing a book about what everyone wants most.
Moorcock: Really? Is it about elephants?
Disch: Elephants? No, it's about becoming more intelligent.
Moorcock: Oh, what I've always wanted most is to be an elephant.
Quoted in *Who Writes Science Fiction* by CHARLES PLATT

(Larry Niven, asked at a convention 'What is the best advice you have ever been given?') On my 21st birthday my father said, 'Son, here's a million dollars. Don't lose it.'

The Penguin Dictionary of Modern Quotations

I think my wife would not even be civil to John Norman if she were to meet him at a cocktail party.

JERRY POURNELLE, *Dream Makers 2* by CHARLES PLATT

Norman is both ethically horrifying and *dull.*

(*ibid.*)

When the SF best-seller list consisted of the latest Thongor book by Lin Carter or the latest bondage and sadist fantasy by John Norman or fifteen moronic Star Trek adaptions, then it was pretty hard for me not to know that what I was writing was . . . definitely superior to this kind of garbage . . . But that's not saying a lot. It's like saying 'I'm a nicer fellow than Hitler.'

RICHARD LUPOFF, *SF Voices 3*

Jerry Pournelle's still doing it (**writing hard SF**) but he can't write.

HARRY HARRISON, *Knave*

Tolstoy and Celine are Mary Poppins compared to Bob Silverberg when he gets a good grump on.

FREDERIK POHL, *The Way the Future Was*

It has been suggested that Tiptree is female, a theory I find absurd, for there is to me something ineluctably masculine about Tiptree's writing. I don't think the novels of Jane Austen could have been written by a man, nor the stories of Ernest Hemingway by a woman, and in the same way I believe the author of the James Tiptree stories is male.

ROBERT SILVERBERG, intro to *Warm Worlds and Otherwise*
by James Tiptree Jr

(It should be pointed out that 'James Tiptree Jr' was later revealed to be the pen name for American psychologist and writer Alice B. Sheldon.)

If Jules Verne could really have looked in the future of, say AD 1966, he would have crapped his pants.

PHILIP JOSE FARMER, *Riders of the Purple Sage*

When Ian Watson grows up he wants to be John Brunner.

HARRY HARRISON, *Ansible*

LAWS

The most famous Laws in science fiction are, without doubt, Isaac Asimov's Three Laws of Robotics.

Therefore, they can be found in the section called *Robots.*

Here are some of the rest:

Aldiss' Law of Civilisation:

Civilisation is the distance man has placed between himself and his excreta.

BRIAN ALDISS, Epigraph for *The Dark Light Years*

Anderson's Observation:

I have yet to see any problem, however complicated, which, when you looked at it in the right way, did not become more complicated.

POUL ANDERSON, *New Scientist* 1969

Bloch's Law of the Theatre:

The first rule of the theatre – give the best lines to yourself.

ROBERT BLOCH, *Cold Chills*

Boucher's Law of Mind-Distention:

You can distend a reader's mind with new concepts only so far. Eventually he says 'Phooey!' and goes back to the more homely commonplaces of Joe here, or me, who modestly consider the destruction of a solar system or maybe just a planet as colossal enough, without annihilating galaxies left and right.

ANTHONY BOUCHER, *Rocket to the Morgue*

Chetwynd-Hayes' Rules of Monsterdom:

The Basic rules of Monsterdom: Vampires – sup; Werewolves – hunt; Ghouls – tear; Shaddies – lick; Maddies – yawn; Mocks – blow; Shadmocks – only whistle.

R. CHETWYND-HAYES, *The Monster Club*

Clarke's Laws:

1. When a distinguished but elderly scientist states that something is possible, he is almost certainly right. When he states that something is impossible, he is very probably wrong.
2. The only way to discover the limits of the possible is to go beyond them, to the impossible.
3. Any sufficiently advanced technology is indistinguishable from *magic*.

ARTHUR C. CLARKE, *Profiles of the Future*

Asimov's Corollary to Clarke's First Law:

When the lay public rallies round to an idea that is denounced by distinguished but elderly scientists, and supports that idea with great fervour and emotion, the distinguished but elderly scientists are then, after all, right.

ISAAC ASIMOV, *The Magazine of Fantasy and Science Fiction* 1977

Arthur C. Clarke's Law:

It has yet to be proved that intelligence has any survival value.

Clarke's Law of New Ideas:

Like all revolutionary new ideas, the subject has had to pass through three stages, which may be summed up by these reactions:

1. 'It's crazy – don't waste my time.'
2. 'It's possible, but it's not worth doing.'
3. 'I always said it was a good idea.'

ARTHUR C. CLARKE, *Report on Planet 3*

deCamp's Observation:

It does not pay a prophet to be too specific.

L. SPRAGUE DECAMP

Delany's Law:

Today's technology is tomorrow's handicraft.

SAMUEL DELANY, *The Jewel Hinged Jaw*

Dick's Law of Kipple:

Kipple is useless objects, like junk mail or match folders after you use the last match or gum wrappers or yesterday's homeopape. When nobody's around, kipple reproduces itself . . . the entire universe is moving towards a final state of total, absolute kipplesation.

PHILIP K. DICK, *Do Androids Dream of Electric Sheep?*

Haldane's Law:

The universe is not only stranger than we imagine, it is stranger than we *can* imagine.

J. B. S. HALDANE

Heinlein's Law for Explorers:

Advice to all explorers: Do not roam the universes without a spare can opener.

ROBERT A. HEINLEIN, *The Number of the Beast* –

Pohl's Oldest Laws:

You can't knock up a pregnant woman, and you can't kill someone who is dead already.

FREDERIK POHL, *Heechee Rendezvous*

Eric Frank Russell's Dogs' Laws:

The supreme test of intelligence is the ability to live as one pleases without working.

The art of retribution is that of concealing it beyond all suspicion.

The sharpest, most subtle, most effective weapon in the cosmos is flattery.

If a thing can think it likes to think that it is God – treat it as God and it becomes your willing slave.

ERIC FRANK RUSSELL, *Into Your Tent I'll Creep*

Cordwainer Smith's Laws:

'Never plan too far ahead. Go from one immediate situation to another. Never make a decision if you can put the decision on somebody else and still win for yourself. And most of all . . .'

'Most of all?'

'Most of all, *never get caught winning*. Just win, but don't let it show.'

CORDWAINER SMITH, *The Underpeople*

Theodore Sturgeon's Much-Quoted in a Number of Different Forms and Possibly Apocryphal Law (seen here in it's most commonly-quoted form):

Ninety percent of everything is crap.

THEODORE STURGEON

Oh, and just for the record:

Dear Mr Gaiman,

You may use the three Laws of Robotics and other phrases of mine that strike your fancy in your book of SF quotations (and, in return, please have the publishers send me a copy when it is done).

Unfortunately, I honestly do not have the time to root among my voluminous output for deathless phrases, nor do I imagine I can judge good from bad.

Isaac Asimov

PART TWO
The Movies

For Starters

COMING ATTRACTIONS

'It's called *Dominique,'* **said producer Milton Subotsky of his 1978 mystery,** 'because I want the ads to read: "*Dominique* will make you shriek!" ' **A good publicity package is essential to the success of any film, from** *Seven Brides for Seven Brothers* (1972) **to** *The Rats Are Coming! The Werewolves Are Here!* (1972), **and the least appreciated item in the selling of any movie is the slogan. But would** *Alien* (1979) **have attracted so many soon-to-be-scared people without** 'In space, no one can hear you scream'? **And would there have been round-the-block queues for** *Love Story* **without the memorably meaningless** 'Love means never having to say you're sorry'? **Which leads us to . . .**

The Abominable Dr Phibes (1971): Love means never having to say you're ugly.

The Abominable Snowman (1957): See it with someone brave.

The Amazing Colossal Man (1957): . . . growing! Growing! GROWING! To a GIANT! To a MONSTER! WHEN WILL IT STOP?

The Andromeda Strain (1971): Universal Pictures and Robert Wise wish to deny completely suggestions of official pressure in regard to the withdrawal of the film *The Andromeda Strain* and to take this opportunity to confirm in the light of certain facts it is not the right time to release a film of this nature.

The Animal World (1956): Two billion years in the making!

Atragon (1964):

SEE: the terror swath of the deadly Astral Disks!

SEE: the Exotic Rites and Grotesque Passions of the Kingdom of MU!

SEE: the underwater juggernauts of destruction!

Attack of the 50 Foot Woman (1958): The world's biggest sensation!

Attack of the Killer Tomatoes (1979): Aaargh! . . .

Attack of the Puppet People (1957): Doll Dwarfs versus the Crushing Giant Beasts.

Barbarella (1968): See Barbarella do her thing!

Baron Blood (1972): He sought the ultimate in HUMAN AGONY . . . with instruments of TORTURE ghastly beyond belief!

Baron Blood (1972): SPECIAL NOTICE! The management hereby disclaims any responsibility for patrons who suffer (A) APOPLECTIC STROKES, (B) CEREBRAL HEMORRHAGES, (C) CARDIAC SEIZURES, or (D) FAINTING SPELLS during the shockingly gruesome scenes in this film.

The Bat (1959): When it flies . . . someone dies!

Behemoth the Sea Monster (1959): Two hundred feet of living, burning horror!

The Birds (1963): *The Birds* is coming!

Black Christmas (1975): If this film doesn't make your skin creep . . . it's on *too tight*!

The Black Scorpion (1957): BLACK – so you can't see him until he's ready to get you! BLOODLESS – that's why he wants yours!

The Black Sleep (1956): a horror horde of monster-mutants walks the Earth!

Black Sunday (1960): The undead demons of hell terrorise the world in an orgy of stark horror!

(**Surprisingly,** *Black Sunday,* **which began life in Italy as** *La Maschara del Demonio,* **does its best to live up to the promise of its ad. line.**)

Black Waters (1929): 100% all-talking. They won't need eyes at all to thrill at this startling story of the Frisco docks and Tiger Larrabee's death ship. A beautiful girl and her rival lovers; the gristly midnight fog through which an unseen fiend launches silent, invincible death bolts; a scared-to-death stuttering valet for comedy relief; the hissing creeping black waters that carry the ship and its frantic freight down-bay until . . .

(**Gristly midnight fog?**)

Blade (1975): A psycho-karate killer brutalises his victims *And Your Emotions*.

Blood and Black Lace (1964): Guaranteed! The Eight Greatest Shocks Ever Filmed!

Blood Beach (1980): Just when you thought it was safe to go back in the water – you can't get to it.

Blood Feast (1964): A weird, grisly ancient rite horrendously brought to life in blood colour.

The Blood Suckers/The Liver Eaters: So shocking it will SLIVER YOUR LIVER . . . so shocking we can't advertise what's in it.

(So obscure we couldn't find out the release dates.)

The Bloodsuckers (1966): Death stalking vegetation devours human blood!

Bloodthirsty Butchers (1970)/*Torture Dungeon* (1970): Too sensual to miss if you're *curious*! Too terrifying to see if you're *yellow*!

(Note how entrepreneur Andy Milligan, the master of quiet good taste, manages to make a totally spurious connection between his grindhouse massacre double bill and the arty, commercially successful 1967 dirty movie *I Am Curious – Yellow* through subtle wording.)

The Body Snatcher (1945): Cemeteries raided, children slain for bodies to dissect! Unthinkable realities and unbelievable FACTS of the dark days of early surgical research EXPOSED IN THE MOST DARING SHRIEK-AND-SHUDDER SHOCK SENSATION EVER BROUGHT TO THE SCREEN!

The Boogie Man Will Get You (1942): You'll be tickled to death . . . with this gay chiller-diller of a mayhem-and-merriment show!

The Boy Who Cried Werewolf (1973): Possible in this day and age? Those who didn't believe ARE DEAD!

The Brain From Planet Arous (1958): It Came From Another World WITH AN INSATIABLE LUST FOR EARTH WOMEN!

Brain of Blood (1971): A Blood-Dripping Brain Transplant Turns a Maniac into a Monster.

Bride of Frankenstein (1935): The Monster demands a mate.

Buck Rogers in the 25th Century (1979): Buck Rogers swings back to Earth and lays it on the 25th Century.

Cage of Evil (1957): Blonde Bait . . . in a murder trap!!

Carrie (1976): If you've got a taste for terror . . . take Carrie to the prom.

(Almost tame, isn't it? Presumably Brian DePalma knew that word-of-mouth would be enough to get shock-lovers into the cinemas, and decided against a really lurid publicity campaign.)

Cat People (1942): She was marked with the curse of those who slink and court and kill by night.

Circus of Horrors (1960): One man's lust . . . made men into beasts, stripped women of their souls.

Close Encounters of the Third Kind (1977): We are not alone.

Color Me Blood Red (1966): Not for the eyes and ears of anyone under sixteen years.

Conquest of Space (1954): See how it will happen . . . in your lifetime.

(Some of us are still waiting for NASA to put an unbalanced religious fanatic in charge of their first Martian expedition.)

Corruption (1968): *Corruption* is a super shock film! Therefore: No woman will be admitted to see it alone!

Crash! (1977): AN OCCULT OBJECT takes possession of a driverless car and causes one spectacular crash after another until five hundred cars are pounded into a mass of twisted metal.

Crazed Vampire (1973): . . . two young girls . . . trapped with no escape! . . . forced to submit to the Horrors of the Pit! . . . their innocence violated beyond description in an endless nightmare of terror.

The Crazies (1973): Man becomes an endangered species.

The Creature From the Black Lagoon (1954): Centuries of passion pent up in his savage heart!

Creepshow (1982): The most fun you'll ever have being scared.

Crescendo (1972): The night the loving ended and the killing began!

The Crooked Circle (1932): Everything from spooks to nuts.

Curse of the Cat People (1944): Cursed with the dread of changing into a fang and claw killer!

(Any resemblance between the title/slogan and the actual motion picture is coincidental and should not be construed as deliberate.)

Curse of the Crimson Altar (1968): WHAT OBSCENE PRAYER or HUMAN SACRIFICE can SATISFY THE DEVIL-GOD?

Curse of the Faceless Man (1958): Entombed for eons . . . turned to stone . . . seeking women, women, women!

Curse of the Fly (1965): What made them half-human creatures from the fourth dimension?

Curse of the Mummy's Tomb (1964): Half-bone, half-bandage, and all blood-curdling terror.

The Cyclops (1957): Nature gone mad! A world of terror—it was a monster, yet it was a man! You'll hardly believe what your own eyes see! The strangest monster the world has ever seen!

Damien: Omen II (1978): The first time was only a warning.

Dark Star (1975): Bombed out in space with a spaced-out bomb.

Dawn of the Dead (1979): When there's no more room in HELL, the Dead will walk the Earth.

The Day the Earth Stood Still (1951): From out of space . . . a warning and an ultimatum.

The Day the World Ended (1955): A new High in NAKED SHRIEKING TERROR!

The Dead Zone (1983): From the mind of Stephen King . . .

(Readers of the novel, who knew that the title refers to a fatal brain tumour, might have been given cause to fear for the health of the writer by this one.)

The Death Dealer (1975): He tortured, killed, and loved it!

Death Ship (1980): Those who survive the ghost ship are better off dead.

Death Trap (1976): Meet the maniac and his friend. Together they make the greatest team in the history of mass slaughter.

Death Weekend (1977): They were going to rape her . . . one by one. She was going to kill them . . . one by one.

Deluge (1933): THOUSANDS EXPECT IT TO HAPPEN! The Destruction of Our Modern World! Continents are swept away! Half a hundred men . . . half a dozen women . . . survive the great flood to 'start over'. Ten men for every woman and no law known except desire! Raw passion rules the naked waste of civilization in this astounding imaginative drama.

Demon (1977): Who were Jesus and Moses really?

(In the film, they turn out to be hermaphrodites from outer space.)

Devil Bat (1941): Your blood will freeze in your veins as these bloodthirsty monsters bring death in the dead of night! . . . Beware of these vampires of the night, this scourge of mankind . . . he lets loose a horrible monster to satisfy his thirst for human blood! . . . fangs of flying doom sink into the bare throats of those marked for death!

Dick Tracy vs Cueball (1946): Dick the Dauntless Dares Death to Deliver Diamonds.

Dr Butcher, M.D. (1982): He is a depraved, sadistic rapist; a bloodthirsty, homicidal killer . . . and he makes house calls.

Dr G and the Bikini Machine (1966): Dr Goldfoot, the mad inventor of instant girls . . . he's *mad*?

Dr Jekyll and Sister Hyde (1971): WARNING: The Sexual Transformation of a Man into a Woman will actually take place before your very eyes! PARENTS: Be sure your children are sufficiently mature to witness the intimate details of this frank and revealing film.

Dr Jekyll's Dungeon of Death (1979): Dr Jekyll is a sadistic, evil, terrifying madman – you'll love him!

Don't Look Now (1973): Pass the warning.

Dracula (1930): The Strangest Love a Man Has Ever Known.

Dracula (1958): The terrifying lover who died, yet lived. Who will be his bride tonight?

Dracula Has Risen From the Grave (1968): When we last saw him . . . Dracula was dead with a stake through his heart – but you just can't keep a good man down.

Dracula's Dog (1978): There's more to the legend than meets . . . the throat.

The Driller Killer (1979): . . . The blood runs in rivers, and the drill keeps tearing through flesh and bone.

The Dunwich Horror (1970): A few years ago in Dunwich a half-witted girl bore illegitimate twins. One of them was almost human!

The End of the World (1979): There is everything to look forward to . . . except tomorrow!

The Erotic Adventures of Pinocchio (1976): It's not his nose that grows!

E.T.: The Extra-Terrestrial (1982): He is afraid. He is totally alone. He is three million light years from home.

The Evil Dead (1982): The ultimate experience in gruelling terror!

The Fear Chamber (1968): Don't panic . . . only your life is in danger.

Fiend Without a Face (1958): SCIENCE GONE WILD! Will men of the future become fiends?

The Final Program (1971): The future is cancelled!

The Flesh Eaters (1964): The only people who will not be STERILISED with FEAR are those among you who are already DEAD!

(STERILISED WITH FEAR? Surely they mean . . . oh well . . .)

The Fly (1958): The first time Atomic Mutation on humans has been shown on the screen.

(a: what about earlier after-the-bomb films like *The Day the World Ended, Captive Women,* etc.? b: *The Fly* is about a teleportation mishap that rearranges the hero's atoms, and so will not be of much interest to the A-bomb buffs this slogan is aimed at.)

The Fly/Return of the Fly: See them together, but don't see them alone.

Forbidden Planet (1956): The amazing flight to one hundred years hence – by spaceship!

The Four Skulls of Jonathan Drake (1959): He was custodian of the icebox that kept the skulls crisp and fresh!

Frankenstein (1931): YOU'LL BE AMAZED at Universal's uncanny picturisation of Mary Shelley's famous thriller of The Man Who Made a MONSTER!

Frankenstein Meets the Space Monster (1965): FREE! The management will supply you FREE space shield eye protectors to prevent your abduction into outer space!!

Frankenstein's Bloody Terror (1971): NEW – Sickening Horror to Make Your Stomach Turn and Flesh Crawl!

SEE – The 'Wolf Monster' attack – Lusting, Slashing, Ripping in a Gory, Flesh-Hungry, Blood-Mad Massacre!

(**We'd go on, but our typewriter is beginning to slobber.**)

Friday the 13th (1980): Come! Watch them die.

Friday the 13th, Part Two (1981): The Body Count Continues . . .

Frogs (1972): Today the pond, tomorrow the world!

Gabriel Over the White House (1933): The picture that will make 1933 famous!

Godzilla, King of the Monsters (1954): . . . makes *King Kong* look like a midget!

Godzilla, King of the Monsters (1954): Incredible, unstoppable titan of terror! It's Alive! *Civilization crumbles* as its death rays blast a city of six million from the face of the Earth.

Grave of the Vampire (1972): Father and son . . . related by blood . . . everyone's blood!

Grizzly (1976): Fourteen feet of gut-crunching terror!

The Gruesome Twosome (1969): Think you've seen blood and gore? Think you've seen stomach-retching mutilation? You ain't seen nothin' yet.

Halloween (1978): The Night HE Came Home.

Halloween II (1981): More of the Night HE Came Home.

Halloween III: Season of the Witch (1982): The Night NOBODY Came Home.

Happy Birthday to Me (1981): The six most bizarre murders you will ever see. John will never eat shish-kebab again. Pray you're not invited!

The Haunting (1963): You may not believe in ghosts, but you cannot deny terror.

The Hills Have Eyes (1977): A nice American family. They didn't want to kill. But they didn't want to die.

(However, they work out a nice compromise which involved some of the most bloodthirsty violence seen on the screen in the 1970s. Even the family dog does his bit, by ripping out the throat of a homicidal maniac mutant.)

Hit and Run (1957): I can't give you anything but love and murder, baby.

The Horrible Dr Hitchcock (1962): The candle of his lust burnt brightest in the shadow of the grave! His secret was a coffin named DESIRE!

House of Mystery (1934): Out of the Mystic Temples of Old India crept this terrible Monster . . . to wreak vengeance of the Hindu Gods . . . One by one its victims fell with not a trace of the bloody assassin. WHAT WAS THIS PHANTOM MURDERER? WHAT WAS THIS MIDNIGHT MENACE? AND WHY DID ITS VICTIMS DIE A HORRIBLE DEATH?

House of Wax (1954): You've never been scared 'til you've been scared in 3-D.

The Howling (1981): Imagine your worst fear a reality.

The Hunger (1982): Nothing human loves forever.

The Hypnotic Eye (1960): Stare if you dare at the screen! You're drawn into the power of the amazing new audience thrill—HYPNOMAGIC!

TWO GREAT BLOOD-HORRORS TO RIP OUT YOUR GUTS! WARNING! Community standards do not permit printing the titles, but these are two of the most HORRIFYING HORROR SHOWS ever presented in this area. Take our word for it! Call theatre or drive-in for titles.

(If you had the nerve to call, an embarrassed cashier was supposed to admit that they were showing the unforgettable double-bill of *I Drink Your Blood* (1971) and *I Eat Your Skin* (1964). Sadly, no mere films could live up to this sort of slobbering publicity, and so most patrons left the cinema with their guts still intact.)

I Spit On Your Grave (1980): This woman has just CUT, CHOPPED, BROKEN and BURNED FIVE MEN BEYOND RECOGNITION . . . but no jury in America would ever convict her!

I Spit On Your Grave (1980): Hunted, captured, stripped, and raped by a gang of grungy guys, Jennifer slashes, gashes and mashes her attackers to a bloody, palpitating pulp.

(A gang of *grungy* guys? No wonder the heroine is upset enough to slash, gash and mash them to bloody, palpitating pulp.)

I Was A Teenage Frankenstein (1957): Body of a Boy . . . Mind of a Monster . . . Soul of an Unearthly THING!

The Incredible Torture Show (1979): *See*: the flesh-eating cannibal women! *See*: the iron tourniquet that screws your brain! *See*: the living dart board! *See*: the orgy of screaming virgins! *See*: the sickness that will make you retch!

Invasion of the Bee Girls (1973): They'll love the very life out of your body! Ordinary housewives turn into ravishing creatures!

Invasion of the Body Snatchers (1956): The world as they knew it was slipping away from them. Time was running out for the human race. And there was nothing to hold on to—except each other.

Invasion U.S.A. (1953): Hedda Hopper says: 'It will scare the pants off you.'

Island of Lost Souls (1932): Pig men . . . wolf women . . . thoughtful human apes . . . and his masterpiece—the panther woman . . . throbbing to the hot flush of newfound love!

It Conquered the World (1956): Every man its prisoner . . . every woman its slave!

There's something wrong with the Davis baby . . . *It's Alive* (1975).

(A rare and welcome instance of understatement. The Davis baby turns out to be a green, fanged, clawed, killer mutant that slaughters the obstetrics unit moments after birth and escapes through a hospital skylight to spread terror.)

Jaws of the Jungle (1936): A Hissing, Snarling, Screeching, Challenge to Man!

Jaws 2 (1978): Just when you thought it was safe to go back in the water.

Jennifer (1978): She's got the power . . . and you haven't got a prayer.

Wherever there was a girl in trouble, there was *Johnny Trouble!* (1957).

King Kong (1933): The strangest story ever conceived by man.

King Kong (1976): . . . the most original screen spectacle of all time.

Kronos (1957): Planet Robber Tramples The Earth!

Lady Frankenstein (1972): Only the monster she made could satisfy her strange desires!

Last House on the Left (1972): Can a movie go too far? To avoid fainting, keep repeating, it's only a movie . . . only a movie . . . only a movie . . . only a movie . . . only a movie . . . only a movie . . . only a movie. WARNING! Not recommended for persons over thirty!

The Last Woman on Earth (1960): They fought for the ultimate prize.

Late Night Trains (1975): Seal of Consumer Awareness: The price of admission to this motion picture is only a down payment; the balance will be extracted from your nerves minute by minute.

Let No Man Write My Epitaph (1960): Ripped Raw and Roaring from Real Life!

Life Without Soul (1915): 'I Have Challenged the Almighty and am Paying the Penalty!' Transcending anything heretofore attempted in motion pictures, it will live in the minds of the public for years to come. An extraordinary five-part feature of intense dramatics, deep pathos, pulsating heart-interest, and a love theme that brings you back to youthful tears.

Liquid Sky (1983): The funniest, dirtiest science fiction film ever.

(**Since** ***Liquid Sky*** **turns out to be solemn and resolutely un-sexy, not to mention pretentious and trendy, you might care to count the lies in this statement.**)

Logan's Run (1976): The 21st Century, and everything is perfect. There's just one catch . . .

(**'It's a rotten movie,' added graffitists.**)

The Lost Missile (1958): The Thing that came from Outer Hell . . . to burn the world alive!

Love Exorcist (1975): WARNING! If the abnormal love of a Sex-Psycho frightens you . . . STAY AWAY!

Macabre (1958): See it with someone who can carry you home.

The Mad Butcher (1972): What's the secret ingredient used by the mad butcher for his superb sausages? Sausage lovers don't see this movie.

Mad Max (1979): He's the only law in a world gone mad. You'd better pray he's out there.

Mad Max 2 (1981): Pray he's still out there.

The Man Who Turned to Stone (1957): Human or inhuman! No woman is safe!

The Man With X-Ray Eyes (1963): He stripped souls as bare as bodies.

Mark of the Devil (1970): Due to horrifying scenes no one admitted without a 'stomach distress' bag.

Masque of the Red Death (1964): Stare into this face and count if you can the orgies of evil.

Master of the World (1961): The fabulous adventures of the man who conquered the Earth to save it.

The Mine With the Iron Door (1936): Behind the iron door was the girl he loved . . . alone in the arms of the living dead . . . guardians of the lost TREASURE!

Monster a Go-Go (1965): 'This picture could set our space program back at least fifty years!'—N.A.S.A. The picture that comes complete with a ten-feet-tall monster to give you the wim-wams. An astronaut went up—a 'guess what' came down! How did a ten-foot-tall monster get into that little bitty space capsule?

The Monster From Green Hell (1957)/*Half Human* (1957): Meet the Monsters Face-to-Face . . . twin terrifying terrors in one towering thrill show! The mammoth monster that terrorized the earth. Too awesome to describe. Too terrifying to escape from. Too powerful to stop! 1400 pounds of frozen fury that moves like a man. Half-man, half-beast, but all monster.

Monster on the Campus (1958): Maniacal monster on bloody trail of destruction . . . every co-ed beauty prey to his fang-slashing passions.

The Monster that Challenged the World (1957): A GIANT MASS OF DESTRUCTION. It's real. It's alive.

Mortuary (1982): Before your funeral . . . before you are buried . . . before you are covered with the last shovelful of dirt . . . be sure you are really dead.

Motel Hell (1980): It takes all kinds of critters to make Farmer Vincent's fritters!

Mothra (1962): Mightiest Monster in All Creation – Ravishing a Universe for Love!

The Mummy's Curse (1945): Hands creeping like cobras . . . eyes crawling with madness.

The Mummy's Ghost (1944): Nameless! Fleshless! Deathless!

(Since the mummy's ghost was called Kharis, played by tubby Lon Chaney jr, and winds up drowned in a swamp, this blurb contains three lies in as many words.)

The Mummy's Shroud (1967): Beware the beat of the cloth-wrapped feet.

Murder at Midnight (1931): FINGERS OF SUSPICION MOVING LIKE THE HANDS OF A CLOCK! Sixteen-cylinder action that will spin you spellbound through avenues of tingling thrills and by-ways of baffling mystery!

Myra Breckinridge (1970): The Book That Couldn't Be Written Is Now a Movie That Couldn't Be Filmed.

The Mysterians (1959): Electronic war erupts from outer space . . . from behind the moon they come . . . to invade the Earth! Abduct its women! Level its cities! Who can say it will not happen?

Never Love a Stranger (1958): The Bullets The Booze The Blood The Blondes of the Roaring Twenties!

The New York Ripper (1982): Fulvia Film proudly announces Slashing Up Women Was His Pleasure!

Night of the Eagle (1962): DON'T SEE THIS PICTURE . . . unless you can withstand the emotional shock of a lifetime!

Night of the Eagle (1962): You must see it from the beginning to feel the SHOCK-IMPACT of the end!

(Variations on this are common, and always seem stupid. Try to think of a few films in which it doesn't matter whether or not you miss the first half hour.)

Night of the Hunter (1954): The scenes . . . the story . . . the stars. But Above All – THE SUSPENSE!

Night of the Quarter Moon (1959): 'I don't care *what* she is . . . she's *mine*!'

Night of a Thousand Cats (1974): Alone, only a harmless pet . . . one thousand strong, they became a man-eating machine.

Night Tide (1963): Was she human . . . or was she a beautiful temptress from the sea, intent upon loving, consuming and killing.

The Night the World Exploded (1957): The most explosive fiction ever filmed!

1984 (1956): Will ecstasy be a crime . . . in the terrifying world of the future?

Somewhere in this world stalks a thing that is . . . *Not of This Earth!* (1956):

The Omen (1975): **Although only a fair-to-middling movie, *The Omen* had a terrific publicity campaign, spearheaded by black on white one-sheet posters sporting a 666 logo and one of three neat slogans:** (a) Good Morning. You Are One Day Closer to the End of the World. (b) If Something Frightening Happens to You Today, Think About It. It May Be *The Omen*. (c) Remember . . . You Have Been Warned.

On The Threshold of Space (1956): The most dangerous frontier of all lies seventeen miles beyond your doorstep – straight up!

One Frightened Night (1935): You'll gasp with terror . . . as you laugh with glee! While you're wondering who killed the first Doris Waverly in the swellest 'Who-Done-It' ever filmed . . . A picture that plays the whole scale of emotions from the highest notes of terror to the lowest guffaws of laughter.

One Million Years B.C. (1967): Travel back through time and space to the edge of man's beginnings . . . discover a savage world whose only law was lust!

Outland (1981): Even in space, the ultimate enemy is man.

Peeping Tom (1960): Do you know what the most FRIGHTENING thing in the world is?

Phantasm (1979): If this one doesn't scare you, you're already dead!

The Pit (1982): Pray to God it only kills you.

Playgirls and the Vampire (1960): She knew . . . when she felt his lips on her, that there was no other man for her . . . *if this was a man*!

Polyester (1981): It'll blow your nose!

(Audiences were given scratch 'n' sniff cards to augment the experience of this movie.)

The Prey (1983): It's not human . . . and it's got an axe!

Psycho (1960): Please don't give away the ending, it's the only one we have.

Psycho Killer (1971): A shocking story . . . a more shocking ending!

Race With the Devil (1975): God help you when the Devil wants you.

Rat Pfink and Boo Boo (1966): Filmed in RegularScope Black and White!

Return of the Fly (1959): All New And More Horrific Than Before! Scream at – The Human Terror Created by Atoms Gone Wild! Scream at – The Ghastly Fly-Monster as He Keeps a Love Tryst! Scream at – The

Desperate Search for the Fly With the Head of a Man! Blood-Curdling Giant Fly-Creature Runs Amuck!

The Returning (1983): He lived before, now he must die again.

Revenge of Frankenstein (1958): We dare you to see it! We double dare you to forget it.

The Rocky Horror Picture Show (1975): A different set of Jaws.

Rodan (1956): More startling than Jules Verne!

Rosemary's Baby (1968): Pray for Rosemary's Baby.

Le Sadique aux Dents Rouges (1970): Un Film de Sex-Horreur!

Satan's Cheerleaders (1976): Funnier than *The Omen* . . . Scarier than *Silent Movie*.

Satan's Slaves (1976): A devilish combination of women and hell.

Savage Gold (1933): Through the green hell of trackless jungles! Battling the blood-lust headhunters of the Amazon.

Scanners (1981): 10 seconds—the pain begins. 15 seconds—you can't breathe. 20 seconds—you explode.

Scanners (1981): MIND YOUR HEAD. The Scanners are about!

Schizo (1976): Schizophrenia . . . when the left hand doesn't know who the right hand is killing.

Scream and Scream Again (1970): Triple distilled nightmare . . . as powerful as a vat of boiling acid!

Scream Bloody Murder (1972): So horrifying you need a blindfold to see it. Blindfold free with admission.

Screamers (1978): Be Warned: You Will Actually See a Man Turned Inside Out!

The Screaming Mimi (1958): Suspense around every curve . . .
(The picture, and the poster, prominently features Anita Ekberg.)

Scum of the Earth (1962): The Motion Picture Your Cashier Will Never Forget.

One bite on her flesh and then . . . *Sex and the Vampire* (1970).

Shadow of Chinatown (1936): Thrills and Chills and Shivering Shocks as a Crazed Scientist Terrorizes the Underworld!

Shock Treatment (1981): Not a sequel, but an equal.

Slaughter Hotel (1979): Carved Out of Today's Headlines!

Finally nature unleashes its revenge! From the pollution of our nuclear waste came the killer we couldn't destroy. HELL HATH NO FURY . . . LIKE . . . *Slithis* (1978).

The Slumber Party Massacre (1982): The guy with the drill is a real party killer.

Snuff (1972–1980): The film that could only be made in South America . . . where life is CHEAP!

(Actually, the scene to which this slogan refers was made in New York, where the cast and crew are visibly unable to refrain from laughing during one of the screen's most ludicrous disembowelments. This gory five minutes, shot in 1980, was tacked onto the end of an unbelievably tedious 1972 Argentine murder movie called *Slaughter*, and the resultant mess was then foisted off on splatter lovers as the real thing.)

Something Wicked This Way Comes (1983): What would you give a man who could make your deepest dream come true?

Squirm (1976): An avalanche of killer worms . . . writhing across the land in a tidal wave of terror.

Star Wars (1977): A long time ago in a galaxy far, far away . . .

(After George Lucas had turned down 'We have seen the epic adventure of the past. We are about to see the epic adventure of the future', 'Where your imagination ends, *Star Wars* begins' and 'It is an adventure that is not only more than you can imagine, *it is more than you can imagine*!', 20th Century-Fox were forced to take their ad line from the film itself.)

Strait Jacket (1964): WARNING! *Strait-Jacket* vividly depicts axe murders!

Strange Invaders (1983): Of all the worlds, in all the galaxies, in all the universe . . . why did they have to pick this one?

The Strange World of Planet X (1959): Every second your pulse pounds they grow foot by incredible foot

. . . shock by incredible shock this ravaging death over-runs the Earth . . . Menacing mankind with over-whelming chaos . . . When men of different planets unite to combat the most loathsome peril the Universe has ever known.

Sugar Hill (1974): The Mob didn't expect Sugar Hill and her *zombie hit men*!

Superman: the Movie (1978): You will believe a man can fly.

(This represents a clever attempt on the part of the publicists to neutralize pre-release rumours that the special effects wizards had not been able to bring off the Superman-in-flight sequences. They hadn't, but the film has enough else going for it to make up for a few matte fringes.)

Supervixens (1978): WARNING: Sex and Violence Can Be Dangerous To Your Health.

Tarantula (1955): Giant Spider Strikes! . . . crawling terror 100 feet high.

A Taste of Blood (1967): Only a stake through her heart could appease his appalling passion.

Taste the Blood of Dracula (1969): Drink a pint of blood a day.

Teenage Monster (1957): Teenage Titan of Terror on a Lustful Binge!

Teenagers From Outer Space (1958): Hoodlums from another world on a ray-gun rampage!

The Texas Chain Saw Massacre (1973): Who will survive and what will be left of them? America's most bizarre and brutal crimes! What has happened is true, now the film that's just as real!

Them! (1954): A Horror Horde of Crawl-and-Crush Giants Clawing Out of the Earth from Mile-Deep Catacombs.

The Thing (1982): Man is the warmest place to hide.

The Thing From Another World (1951): Where did it come from? How did it get here? What is it?

The Thing That Couldn't Die (1958): The grave can't hold it . . . nothing human can stop it!

The Thing With Two Heads (1972): They transplanted a white bigot's head on a soul brother's body!
(. . . **With predictable results. Ray Milland and Rosey Grier are involved.**)

Thirteen Ghosts (1960): WARNING! If you should only count twelve ghosts on the screen, don't feel cheated – one of them likes to mingle with the audience.

This Island Earth (1955): Blood Lust in Outer Space!

The Tingler (1959): Do you have the guts to sit in this chair? Can you take PERCEPTO? Can you take it when The Tingler breaks loose?

Tobor the Great (1954): Man-made monster with EVERY human emotion.

Tomb of Ligea (1965): Even on her wedding night she must share the man she loved with the 'Female Thing' that lived in the Tomb of the Cat!

Twins of Evil (1972): They use the satanic power of their bodies to turn men and women into their blood slaves.

2001: A Space Odyssey (1968): The Ultimate Trip.

(After the film had opened to general mystification, MGM turned it into a hit by aiming their advertising at an audience who got through the epic with the aid of various drugs.)

Two Thousand Maniacs (1964): A Town of Madmen . . . Crazed for Carnage . . . Brutal . . . Evil . . . Ghastly Beyond Belief!

Valley of the Dragons (1962): They go a million years back in time . . . and land a million miles out in space!

The Vampire (1957): A new kind of HORROR! It claws! It drains blood! It feeds on the blood of beautiful women!

Vampire Hookers (1979): Warm blood isn't all they suck.

The Vampire Lovers (1970): A whisper of warm desire becomes a SHRIEK OF CHILLING TERROR in the embrace of the BLOOD-NYMPHS!

The Velvet Vampire (1971): She's waiting to love you . . . to death!

Videodrome (1982): First it controlled her mind. Then it destroyed her body.

Virgin Witch (1972): She's the girl with the Power . . . to turn you on! . . . to turn you off!

Virgic Witch (1972): Her lust was innocence – her desires: evil!

Virus (1980): 863 people were not so lucky . . . they survived!

Visiting Hours (1982): The movie America's dying to see.

Wacko! (1983): At last! A picture made by, for, and › about people . . . just like you.

(*Wacko* should not be confused with *Whacko,* the Jimmy Edwards comedy series from the prehistory of British television.)

The Walking Dead (1935): HE DIED A MAN with a hunger to love AND RETURNED A MONSTER with a lust to kill!

War of the Monsters (1966): Monsters from Space – come to destroy the world.

The Watcher in the Woods (1980): It's not a fairy tale.

The Werewolf of Washington (1973): A biting satire.

Westworld (1973): Where nothing can possibly go wo
r
n
g.

Wham-Bam-Thank You Space Man (1978): He's a UFO Romeo.

When Dinosaurs Ruled the Earth (1970): Enter an age of unknown terrors, pagan worship and virgin sacrifice . . .

White Zombie (1932): He brought her back to life . . . and made her his slave! . . . so fierce was his love for this beautiful creature . . . she was not human . . . she was not an animal . . . she was not a ghost . . . she was not dead . . . she was not alive . . . What Was She? A weird love story, the strangest in 2000 years. A Zombie bride whose soul and heart were dead, performing every wish of he who held her by his magic!

Wild in the Streets (1968): If you're thirty, you're *through.*

Wizards (1976): An epic fantasy of peace and magic.

World Without End (1956): CinemaScope hurls you into the year 2508!

Zombie Creeping Flesh (1981): When the Creeping Dead devour the living flesh.

Zombie Flesh Eaters (1980): We are going to EAT YOU!

Zombies of Mora Tau (1957): His own wife turned killer-zombie!

Zombies of the Stratosphere (1952): You'll say . . . amazing! startling! unbelievable! . . . yet how far is it from the TRUTH?

Zombies on Broadway (1945): They're Alive! . . . They're Dead! . . . They're Not! . . . They're NUTS!

TRAILERS

'HAVE YOU EVER SEEN A LIVING NIGHTMARE?' **runs the trailer for** *The Alligator People* (1959), 'YOU WILL SEE ONE SOON!' **After the splash title, we get a few misleading clips from the film and a breathless narration,** 'Inside this strange, forbidding plantation on the edge of the deadly swamp, there is horror beyond belief. A scientist turns his cobalt rays on the revolting, scaly monarchs of the swamps to transform men into hideous monsters, whose faces must be forever hidden from human sight . . . Suspense that will hold you like quicksand, pulling you down into bottomless depths of suffocating horror!' **Then it's back to the captions, in regulation dripping letters,** 'IT'S THE BIG SHOCKER IN SCREAMING HORRORSCOPE!' **They don't trail 'em like that any more.**

Narrator: We will not let you see this terror creature alone, unless you sign a legal waiver in our lobby. Can your body take it? Are you really not afraid to see

The Fly? (1958)

Narrator: Listen! Do you hear? It's coming back, turning the screen into a buzzing, crawling nightmare of terror.

Return of the Fly (1959)

EVERY MOMENT GRIPPING WITH EXCITEMENT AND SUSPENSE! AS NOTHING CAN STOP THE EVIL INJECTED INTO A WOMAN'S HEART.

She Devil (1957)

SEE: The frogmen battle the mammoth squid!

SEE: Barbara Eden dance to Frankie Avalon's music!

Voyage to the Bottom of the Sea (1961)

PREFACES: NARRATIONS AND CAPTIONS

ACKNOWLEDGEMENT: We wish to express our gratitude to the enemies of crime, and crusaders against crime throughout the world for their inspirational example.

(*Batman*, 1966)

Narrator: What you are about to see can be called truly a fantasy of the future. But one day, maybe not too far distant, audiences will be able to look back on it in the same spirit with which we view pictures about the first covered wagons crossing the plains . . . In the fear-ridden years following the great atomic war, the Earth and its people had been reduced to a state of death and destruction . . .

(*Battle Beyond the Sun*, 1963)

'That which does not kill us makes us stronger –' Nietzsche

(The ideologically apt, but otherwise ludicrous epigraph for *Conan the Barbarian*, 1982. Only John Milius could bridge the gulf between Robert E. Howard and great literature with such grim insouciance.)

Narrator: What you are about to see may never happen . . . but to this anxious age in which we live, it presents a fearsome warning . . . our story begins with . . . THE END!

(*The Day the World Ended*, 1955)

And the Prophet said:
' . . . and lo, the Beast looked
Upon the face of Beauty,
And it stayed its hand
From killing, and from that
Day, it was as one dead.'

(An old Arab proverb made up especially for *King Kong*, 1933)

Narrator: This is the Universe . . . Big, isn't it?

(*A Matter of Life and Death*, 1946)

Narrator: . . . in brooding beauty whose parallel one would have far to seek stand California's high sierras . . .

(*The Neanderthal Man*, 1953)

Narrator: Greetings, my friends. We are all interested in the future, for that is where you and I are going to spend the rest of our lives. And remember, my friends, future events such as these will affect you in the future. You are interested in the unknown, the mysterious, the unexplainable – that is why you are here. And now for the first time we are bringing to you the full story of what happened on that fateful day. We are giving you all the evidence based only on the secret testimony of the miserable souls who survived this terrifying ordeal. The incidents, the places, my friend, we cannot keep this a secret any longer. Let us punish the guilty, let us reward the innocent. My friends, can your hearts stand the shocking facts about *grave robbers from outer space*?

(*Plan Nine From Outer Space*, 1956)

Narrator: In the year nineteen hundred and forty seven, man broke through the sound barrier . . . In the year nineteen hundred and fifty eight, man launched the first satellite and pierced the space barrier . . . Now, in an isolated area, in central Florida, man struggles to penetrate the most imposing barrier of all. The Time Barrier. Here Professor Howard Erling, nuclear physicist, probes relentlessly into the future, only to unleash upon the world . . .

(*Terror From the Year 5000*, 1958)

Expectations

EVIL OMENS

Early on, the movie will have to establish that something horrible is due to happen. Often this entails the use of perfectly innocent snatches of dialogue which tip off the audience as to what's going on, but leave the on-screen characters blithely unaware of the horrendous (heh heh heh) fates in store for them. . .

Local Lurker: . . . you ever been in the bayou country before?
Heroine: . . . it's so wild . . . so primitive . . .
Local Lurker: Yeah . . . and deadly.

(*The Alligator People, 1959*)

While you're our guest for one night only, I must insist on one thing . . . under no circumstances will you leave your room.

(*ibid.*)

. . . and another thing, who was playing the piano in the house last night? In the dark? Someone who left wet footprints on the carpet?

(*ibid.*)

I couldn't rid myself of the premonition that each step was taking me closer to the true secret contained in the shadowy house.

(*ibid.*)

The controls and timing must be precise. When you're dealing with radioactivity and millions of volts of energy, the slightest deviation from standard – even a few seconds of excess time – and anything might happen.

(*ibid.*)

(As the five above quotes indicate, *The Alligator People* is a dead ominous film.)

Dave Walker wasn't the kind of man to hang himself, not even with two murder charges against him. I talked with Dave less than an hour before he killed himself. That man was in a state of shock. I've seen frightened men, terrified men, but I've never seen anything to compare with the horror and the fear in Walker's eyes.

(*Attack of the Giant Leeches*, 1959)

Don Pedro: That swamp is a very mysterious and sinister place.
Sceptical Gringo: I don't buy those superstitions.
Don Pedro: Steers don't jump in a swamp.

(*The Beast of Hollow Mountain*, 1956)

Farmer: It all started since this plane flew over yesterday. Carol, suppose it wasn't a plane in our sense of the word. Suppose it landed out there in the desert somewhere. For a reason.
Wife: You mean . . . a plane from *somewhere else*?
Farmer: Can you imagine anything human in all this?
Wife: A plane from another world. Oh, Allen, what's it trying to do? What kind of a trap are we in?
Farmer: I wish I knew . . .

(*Beast With a Million Eyes*, 1958)

. . . having someone special for dinner?

(*Cannibal Girls*, 1972)

Overconfident Monster Hunter: A few well-placed 375 slugs will turn him into a rug.

(*Claws*, 1977)

First Mourner: Honey, who is Count Yorga?
Second Mourner: He was my mother's boyfriend.
First Mourner: How come I never met him before?
Second Mourner: Because she only knew him for three weeks before she died.

(*Count Yorga – Vampire*, 1970)

Narrator: Dr Paul Mallen began to feel a deep concern for his fiancée, for he was wondering now if the faceless apparition she had painted was an impossibility. . .

(*Curse of the Faceless Man*, 1958)

Mom tried to call the maintenance man, but there's something wrong with the phone.

(*The Day Mars Invaded Earth*, 1962)

Frankenstein was actually murdered many times, and yet science found that, surprisingly enough, his body always came to life again. His heart, however, has never died.

(*Frankenstein Conquers the World*, 1966)

Doomed Teenager: . . . where's that fancy corkscrew?

(*Friday the 13th – The Final Chapter*, 1984)

Leave now, it's not going to get any better.

(*Geek Maggot Bingo,*1982)

(The caption is all too apt.)

Philosophical Teenager: I have a heavy feeling about this. We shouldn't tamper with the unknown, the imponderble.

(*The Ghost of Dragstrip Hollow*, 1959)

Naive Scientist: May I propose a toast on behalf of all of us? To Professor Frankenstein, a true servant of science.

(*I Was a Teenage Frankenstein*, 1957)

Mad Doctor: You'll be the first to see his new face.
Assistant: New face? But how . . . where did you get it?
Mad Doctor: Oh come now, doctor. Why burden yourself with unnecessary details?

(*ibid.*)

Mr Wiles, you are going to tangle with the wrong woman one day, and she is going to give you your head for a going away present.

(*Macumba Love*, 1960)

. . . but don't speak his name above a whisper, or else the disfigured maniac will return to answer whoever has called him.

(*Madman*, 1982)

Always she walk like she's asleep. Swamp pretty bad for people like that.

(*The Mummy's Curse*, 1945)

It's all too preposterous for serious thought! Phantom marine mutations! Death rays! Utter nonsense! I'm afraid, doctor, that you are the victim of an overwhelming imagination.

(*Phantom From 10,000 Leagues*, 1955)

She is singing to bring down the chandelier.

(*Phantom of the Opera*, 1925)

. . . beneath your dancing feet are the tombs of tortured men.

(*ibid.*)

First Archaeologist: (translating hieroglyphs) . . . let ye who seek to disturb the eternal peace and sleep of the high priest beware. Flesh of thy flesh shall creep into thy body and eat of thy flesh and of thy spirit until such time as ye shall return into the pit of everlasting darkness whence we lived before life.
Second Archaeologist: All right, let's cut it open.
First Archaeologist: Robert, I'm not a superstitious man, but, er, I feel a wee bit strange about desecrating this tomb.

(*Pharoah's Curse*, 1957)

Minion: . . . the fish, sir. They're eating the guests.
(*Piranha*, 1978)

Transylvanian Peasant: There's nowhere else for miles around except the castle.
Doomed But Jaunty Stranger: Do they do bed and breakfast?
Peasant: Oh you can't go there! You mustn't!
Stranger: Why not?
Peasant: Well, I don't know, I'm new here. But you mustn't go there. Not at night.

(*Scars of Dracula*, 1970)

It certainly isn't like Paul to disappear like this.

(*ibid.*)

First Concerned Citizen: Where's Dorothy?
Second Concerned Citizen: She went for a walk with Ted. I wish she hadn't.
First Concerned Citizen: Why?
Second Concerned Citizen: Well, Dr Lombardi said something terrible is going to happen along this part of the coast tonight . . . some visitation from the occult world.

(*The She Creature*, 1956)

I may be old-fashioned and conventional, but somehow I feel there's something unnatural, perhaps even dangerous, about this.

(*She Devil*, 1957)

Mad Doctor: Now, Martha, it's no use carrying on like this. So let's get this over with . . . but Martha, we've administered this dozens of times before.
Nervous Patient: But all that snake poison in my blood? You don't know, nobody knows, what it will do!
Mad Doctor: Of course I know what it will do. You were hopelessly insane. Others have used snake venom in treating haemophilia, epilepsy, rheumatism, hypertension, even cancer. But it's Horace Adderson, your husband, who will cure a sick mind with snake venom.
Nervous Patient: . . . but what about the baby?

(*The Snake Woman*, 1961)

Looking for Sarah? She disappeared.

(*Suspiria*, 1977)

Doomed Teenager: Saturn is in retrograde . . . Saturn is malefic, and that means it's going to be a bad day.

(*The Texas Chainsaw Massacre*, 1974)

I know I've never completely freed myself of the suspicion that there are some extremely odd things about this mission.

(*2001: A Space Odyssey*, 1968)

First Scientist: You know, this is odd. Campbell's pills were a control serum extracted from bats.
Second Scientist: That's hard to believe.
First Scientist: Yes, especially when you consider they were vampire bats.

(*The Vampire*, 1957)

Ilona, there's something about your smile right now that reminds me of Jack the Ripper.

(*Weird Woman*, 1944)

Bar room Cassandra: When they start eatin' on ya, don't come to me for help.
Ordinary Joe: C'mon Sarge, lighten up.

(*Without Warning*, 1980)

First Worried Teen: Where are those guys? They've been gone over an hour. They knew we'd be worried about 'em.
Second Worried Teen: Yeah, I'm worried.

(*ibid.*)

BAD NEWS

After the properly ominous mood of impending doom has been established, the film feels the need to tip its hand a little, and let on that not only is something horrible about to happen, but that it has already started. . . . Favourite devices for this include the public service announcement (. . . we interrupt this broadcast . . .) *à la* Orson Welles memorable radio *War of the Worlds*, the (now rather outmoded) newspaper headline spinning up to the camera, and the scientific summing-up ('I pray that my theories are wrong, but. . .').

Every human being left has become mutant or sterile, or a combination of both.

(*Beyond the Time Barrier*, 1960)

Misfortune follows misfortune! Another innocent victim has been done away with! We have killed your coachman. Terribly sorry. Terribly, terribly sorry.

(*Blood of Dr Jekyll*, 1980)

Dad's gonna become a werewolf again, we gotta do something.

(*The Boy Who Cried Werewolf*, 1973)

Cop: It can't be alive!
Hero: . . . not the way we know life.
Doc: . . . and it is not dead, not as we know death.

(*Curse of the Faceless Man*, 1958)

This whole town is infested with killer cockroaches.

(*Damnation Alley,* 1977)

Newsreader: All reports confirm that the world is witnessing an unprecedented shower of meteorites. There is no record of a display such as this in recorded history.

(*Day of the Triffids*, 1963)

There are two forms of life fighting for survival here in this valley, and only one of them can win. It's got to be us.

(*The Day the World Ended*, 1955)

Andrew McGee and his daughter constitute the greatest threat that has ever confronted this nation.

(*Firestarter*, 1984)

(Considering that the USA has been confronted by the Civil War, the Depression, Watergate, Ronald Reagan, and The Osmonds one can understand the shudder of horror that runs through audiences after this line.)

Attention! The monster is somewhere in the vicinity, and is liable to attack without warning.

(*Frankenstein Conquers the World*, 1966)

I believe that Frankenstein isn't the only monster around here. There's another monster in the area. (*ibid.*)

Look out there! It's a giant monster egg.

(*Godzilla vs. the Thing*, 1964)

Jesus! That's all we need, a killer bear on the loose.

(*Grizzly*, 1976)

PROMINENT SOCIALITE DECAPITATED – HEAD STILL MISSING (**newspaper headline**).

(*I Love a Mystery*, 1945)

Oh my God, it's his ear!

(*The Incredible Melting Man*, 1978)

What a situation is now confronting the world!

(*Invasion of the Neptune Men*, 1961)

(**Oh, the joys of dubbing English dialogue over Japanese lip movements!**)

CHARGES OF SPACE ATTACK BRANDED RIDICULOUS (**newspaper headline**)

(*Invisible Invaders*, 1959)

Newsreader: It is impossible to estimate the death toll, since many of our news headquarters in other nations have been destroyed. (*ibid.*)

I can't explain what happened tonight, I'm not going to try to. All I know is that we're all just twenty-four hours away from destruction. (*ibid.*)

How can we anticipate what a bizarre and fantastic organism might or might not do.

(*The Man From Planet X*, 1951)

I don't want to alarm you unduly, but if just one of those creatures lived and got through the patrols into the canal system and multiplied, the species would threaten the entire world, first devouring all life in the ocean, and then foraging on land.

(*The Monster that Challenged the World*, 1957)

Dr Mirakle of the Rue Morgue is guilty of four murders so far this week.

(*Murders in the Rue Morgue*, 1932)

Attention! There's a herd of killer rabbits heading this way.

(*Night of the Lepus*, 1972)

Our big problem is that he's still alive.

(*Pyro*, 1964)

Newsreader: . . . and Mrs Claus has positively identified the kidnappers as Martians.

(*Santa Claus Conquers the Martians*, 1964)

They came at him from the sewers.

(*The Slime People*, 1963)

The light bothers Henry's eyes. He suffered a trauma in early childhood. His mother was killed by a gas heater. He hasn't adjusted to society yet.

(*The Vampire*, 1957)

No one can doubt that civilisation as we know it will disintegrate if the temperature should rise to 175 degrees.

(*Voyage to the Bottom of the Sea*, 1961)

RHUBARBING LOCALS

In the background, there are any number of rhubarbing locals. Their function is threefold: a) they can get messily slaughtered by the menace early on in the film and leave a mutilated corpse whose presence will alert the quick-thinking hero to the fact that something horrible is happening; b) they can sit around in the tavern or on the porch muttering darkly, and filling in vital plot details; or c) they can cringe when the hero asks for directions to Castle Dracula on Walpurgis Night, and be ignored when they warn the unbelieving strangers of the horrors to come.

This is a trouble house . . . real, deep, big trouble. Like the ol' conjure woman in Big Bayou says . . . Miz Hawthorne she deal with the Evil One . . . she got big sorrow. Jus' like you get if you stay here. Go, child . . . please go!

(*The Alligator People*, 1959)

First Good Ol' Boy: Like I'm sayin', I put five slugs into that critter before it went under. Had regular arms on it like a man, only they was sorta different lookin', had like suckers on 'em, like one o' them octopus things. Ah, it was plumb awful.

Second Good Ol' Boy: Lem, you sure that critter weren't pink?

First Good Ol' Boy: I told you before it was sorta gray lookin'. Well, laugh if you want, but that thing weren't no freak 'gator neither. I been poachin' this country for forty years and I ain't never seen nothin' like it.

(*Attack of the Giant Leeches*, 1959)

Man in the Street noting that the Dynamic Duo are rushing to Gotham City Police Headquarters: Oh, it gives a feller a good feelin' to know they're up there doin' their job.

(*Batman*, 1966)

It's a lovely day outside. Much too nice for all these crazy animal revolutions.

(*Beast With a Million Eyes*, 1958)

First Peasant: I heard a woman screaming, just as if she had seen the Devil himself. I'm no coward, but her shrieks chilled my blood. I came flying here to be among human kind.
Second Peasant: Come, come. We're sitting here like children listening to stories about hobgoblins. I don't believe in things supernatural.
First Peasant: You would if you'd been at that castle for the past three months.

(*Beauty and the Beast*, 1963)

Aren't you going to do anything about the green men? It may be a whole invasion!

(*Invasion of the Saucer Men*, 1957)

Peasant: I say let's all go up there. Put a stake through their evil hearts!
Landlord: Calm down, Hans.

(*Lust for a Vampire*, 1971)

People on other planets! I don't believe it. It'd 'ave been in the papers, and me 'usband would 'ave told me about it.

(*The Terrornauts*, 1967)

Somebody killed Carrie Dietz! It's the most frightening thing that ever happened.

(*The Vampire*, 1957)

Troubled Teenager: My friends are dead!
Phlegmatic Barfly: Give the kid a beer lady.

(*Without Warning*, 1980)

NUKES

Recent research suggests that the world after a global thermonuclear war is unlikely to have much room for square-jawed heroes, troublemaking three-eyed mutants, and leather 'n' chrome clad wasteland warriors. These are, however, the vital ingredients of the Post-Apocalypse Exploitation movie.

Glory be to the Bomb, and to the Holy Fall-Out.

(*Beneath the Planet of the Apes*, 1970)

Odd Things To Say After WW III No. 1: You've got pretty good taste in sports shirts, mister.

(*The Day the World Ended*, 1955)

First Survivor: That's all we need. A cheeky kid and a pregnant girl.
Second Survivor: They're probably the most important people on Earth right now.

(*The Earth Dies Screaming*, 1964)

All of a sudden, people mean something again.

(*ibid.*)

Narrator: After Pearl Harbour, it took us months to get ready for war. Against attack by missiles, we have only minutes. There may be no tomorrow. There may be no this afternoon.

(*The Lost Missile*, 1958)

Hero: There must be at least two million children in New York. I wonder how many will get out alive.
Heroine: Under martial law, no car is leaving Manhattan unless it's carrying children. They must have planned it that way. (*ibid.*)

('Wishful thinking' view of civil defence measures.)

Odd Things To Say After WWIII No. 2: Books! That's what started this whole Apocalypse!

(*The New Barbarians*, 1982)

Hardboiled Survivor: Look, sweetheart, two and two doesn't make four any more. At the moment, it adds up to exactly nothing. For the next few weeks, survival is going to have to be on an individual basis. At the moment, we have to have food, a way to protect it, and a way to get more when it's gone.
Softboiled Survivor: What do you wanna do, write off the rest of the world?
Hardboiled Survivor: When civilization gets civilized again, I'll rejoin.

(*Panic in the Year Zero*, 1962)

Hardboiled Survivor: Every footpath will be crawling with men saying 'no matter what, I'm going to live'. That's what I'm saying too. My family must survive.
Softboiled Survivor: Intelligent people don't just turn their backs on the rest of the world.
Hardboiled Survivor: Under these conditions, intelligent people will be the first to try.

(*ibid.*)

I want you to use that gun if you have to, but I want you to hate it. A big piece of civilization is gone, and your mother wants to save what's left.

(*ibid.*)

Odd Things To Say After WWIII No. 3: Nothing like eating under an open sky . . . even if it is radioactive.

(*ibid.*)

KIDS

One of the incidental delights afforded by a study of cheap horror and science-fiction films is the insight given into teenage sociology by middle-aged film-makers trying to slant their movies to the high-school drive-in crowd. The first of these figures is Herman Cohen, the man who realized that most cinema-goers were between the ages of twelve and twenty-five, discovered their predilections for monsters and rock 'n' roll, and began a series with *I Was a Teenage Werewolf* (1957). Since then, werewolves and vampires have been chasing teeny-boppers, bobby-soxers, beatniks, rockers, mods, hippies, punks, preppies, and whoever else happened to be buying records that year.

Honest, Roxie, I believe you. I swear on my Elvis Presley LP.

(*Eegah!*, 1962)

Cop: Did you ever hear of such a cock and bull story? Spacemen, spaceships. . .
Doc: In my day we were content with pink elephants. But kids these days. . .
Cop: And tough! The gal says to me, 'You don't call him human, do you?' Think about that.
Doc: Well, what can you expect with all these bad books bein' written nowadays.

(*The Eye Creatures*, 1965)

Teen: This is a double do daddy. After the cats go home, the she-cats nap.
Hopeless Square: What?
Teen: A slumber party.

(*Ghost of Dragstrip Hollow*, 1959)

–Plug the cork, york.
–He's got static in his attic.
–Holy mackerel, you just ain't a-mouthin' syllables!
–My draggin' wagon's laggin'.
–Well, it's PMing. I better peel out.
–Take your flippers off me, seal!

(**A selection of the teen talk from** *ibid.*)

We'll get all the hep kids we know and stage a party on Mount Fuji.

(*Godzilla vs. the Smog Monster*, 1972)

Post-Holocaust Teen: Somebody dropped a bomb, dad. Crazy kick, huh?

(*Panic in the Year Zero*, 1962)

I'm all for integration, but not with my cat.

(*Toomorrow*, 1970)

Bravery isn't my bag, man.

(*Tower of Evil*, 1973)

SPACEMEN

From *Flash Gordon* (1936) to *The Right Stuff* (1983), the movies have had a commitment to the exploration of outer space. In addition to the scientific and technical qualifications required of real astronauts, movie spacemen should have a down-to-Earth sense of humour, the ability to organize a revolution against a corrupt extra-terrestrial dictatorship, some left over smooth talk for romancing curvy aliens, and a fishbowl to wear during asteroid storms.

Spacewoman: Where's Earth?
Spaceman: You should know, Lambert. You're the navigator.

Alien (1979)

First Spaceman: Something's wrong! Our course is changing!
Second Spaceman: Hah! It couldn't be! Our angle is perfect!
First Spaceman: Can't you understand? I said it was changing.
Second Spaceman: What's wrong? Check it again.
First Spaceman: I have, twice. We're being pulled away by a powerful magnetic field. It's the Sun!

(*Battle Beyond the Sun*, 1962)

First Spaceman: Let's relax and celebrate. We have two reasons. Craig's forthcoming marriage to the nicest girl I know, and the rocket bringing fuel.
Second Spaceman: It's strange. Any other time, a fuel rocket couldn't compare to Nancy, but now I'm not so sure.

(*ibid.*)

Inexperienced Spaceman, donning helmet: I won't be able to breathe in this thing!
More Scientific Type: You won't be able to breathe without it. There's no air out there.
Inexperienced Spaceman, contemplating the vastness of the Universe: There's enough room for it!

(*Destination Moon*, 1950)

First Spaceman: The emergency air lock in C compartment has been left open. What gives?
Second Spaceman: Sorry sir, that was me. I was dumping some empty crates overboard a while ago.

(*It! The Terror From Beyond Space*, 1958)

Spaceman: What kind of a planet is this?

(*The New Planet of the Apes*, 1974)

Spaceman's Sweetheart: Oh Larry, the spaceship is so dangerous.

(*Queen of Outer Space*, 1958)

The automatic landing controls must've worked perfectly, or we'd have been splattered over a hundred acres.

(*ibid.*)

Zero-X calling. We are under attack from a form of life we don't understand.

(*Thunderbirds Are Go*, 1966)

IN THE JUNGLE

Although unfashionable in recent years, except in Italian cannibal movies and German art films, the jungle is an ideal setting for tribal tortures, pagan worship, heroic white hunters, unethical experiments, unscrupulous treasure-seekers and headstrong heroines in jodhpurs.

White Hunter: The bearers are becoming uneasy.
Overconfident Heroine: They would not dare lay hands on a Goddess of the Golden Bat.

(*Darkest Africa*, 1936)

White Hunter: I know the jungle. You don't. Every sign tells us to go back.
Overconfident Heroine: Well, now you're acting like you believe in superstitions.

(*The Flame Barrier*, 1957)

This isn't gorilla territory.

(*Mark of the Gorilla*, 1950)

We haven't come this far to be turned back by a primitive tree carving.

(*Prehistoric Women*, 1968)

Your presence has disturbed the spirit of the rhinoceros.

(*ibid.*)

The jungle is no place for a woman.

(*Prisoners of the Cannibal God*, 1979)

These mountains can make you rich beyond your wildest dreams.

(*ibid.*)

From here on, we'll be in voodoo country. They won't like us there.

(*Voodoo Woman*, 1957)

Old Jungle Hand: One of you killed a native girl last night. He must be punished at once. Otherwise, you will all die.
Murderous Coward: It was him!
Upright Hero: If I remember right, I was tied up all night.

(*ibid.*)

The Nasties

PSYCHOS

Judging from the movies, homicidal mania is more common than the measles. In order to turn psycho, you merely need a solid flashback trauma (seeing your mother murder your father in a gruesomely inventive way is popular), an offbeat *modus operandi* (doing away with your victims with the aid of a pneumatic drill, a cigarette lighter, a lawnmower, a pressure cooker, etc.), and a variety of facial tics and stuttering mannerisms to give you away.

I wanted to devote my life to the healing of mankind. I wanted to be a doctor. But they got together, those narrow-minded, prejudiced medical men, to see how they could ruin me. Brilliant, but unbalanced! That was the verdict.

(*Dark Eyes of London*, 1939)

Don't drive me crazy! I can't control myself when I drink. You know that.

(*The Dead Are Alive*, 1972)

The end will come quickly, my love. There is a pain beyond pain, an agony so intense it shocks the mind into instant beauty. We will find immortality together. They will remember me through you.

(*House of Wax*, 1953)

First Psychopath: Who was the greatest sex killer of the century?
Second Psychopath: Frood ... Sigmund Frood. I remember when a cigar was just a cigar.

(*Last House on the Left*, 1972)

My child, why are you crouched there so pitifully afraid? Immortality has been the dream, the inspiration of our kind, and I am going to give you the only guarantee of immortality you have ever had ... you will always be beautiful. Think, my child. In a thousand years you will be as lovely as you are now.

(*Mystery of the Wax Museum*, 1933)

That's right. I'm EVIL!

(*New Year's Evil*, 1980)

M-my mother, uh, what is the phrase? She isn't quite herself today.

(*Psycho*, 1960)

It-it-it's not as if she were ... a maniac ... a raving thing. She just goes a little mad sometimes. We all go a little mad sometimes. Haven't you?

(ibid.)

I think that we're all in our private traps, clamped in them, and none of us can ever get out. We scratch and claw, but ... only at the air, only at each other. And for all of it, we never budge an inch.

(ibid.)

It's sad when a mother has to speak the words that condemn her own son. I can't allow them to think I would commit murder. Put him away now as I should have years ago. He was always bad and in the end he intended to tell them I killed those girls and that man, as if I could do anything but just sit here and stare like one of his stuffed birds. They know I can't move a finger and I want just to sit here and be quiet just in case they suspect me. They are probably watching me . . . well, let them. Let them see what kind of person I am. Not even going to swat that fly. I hope they are watching. They will see and they will say . . . why, she wouldn't even harm a fly.

(*ibid.*)

You smell like the toasted cheese sandwiches my mother used to make.

(*Psycho 2*, 1983)

Little pigs, little pigs, let me come in!

(*The Shining*, 1980)

I want a couple of hamburgers, and I'd like them raw!

(*Stranger on the Third Floor*, 1940)

My family's always been in meat.

(*The Texas Chainsaw Massacre*, 1973)

Granpaw was the best killer of 'em all, never took more than one lick.

(*ibid.*)

I can't take no pleasure in killin'. There's just some things you gotta do. Don't mean you gotta like it.

(*ibid.*)

You give Hermann apple, Hermann give you nice soft bat.

(*The Vampire Bat*, 1933)

ALIENS

They come from outer space, and they get most of the snappiest dialogue.

We have learned patience in two hundred million years.

(*The Brain Eaters*, 1958)

Hate and malice are the keys to power in my world.

(*The Beast With a Million Eyes*, 1955)

We feed on brains. Unfortunately, they don't last very long, so we've been reduced to seeking a new world.

(ibid.)

Braineating is obviously a recurring theme in 1950s American International Pictures.

There is life on Mars, Dr Fields. Oh, not as you know it. Your organisms couldn't exist in our environment. Instead we have intelligence in the abstract, much like your electricity here.

(*The Day Mars Invaded Earth*, 1962)

I have come to visit you in peace and goodwill.

(*The Day the Earth Stood Still*, 1951)

(Of course, he is immediately shot.)

Soon one of your nations will apply atomic power to rockets. Up to now we have not cared how you solved your petty squabbles. But if you threaten to extend your violence, this Earth of yours will be reduced to a burnt-out cinder. Your choice is simple. Join us and live in peace. Or pursue your present course and face obliteration.

(ibid.)

Anthropophagus Alien: I'll check to see if the boys are poisonous. If not, they'll be our rations.

(*Gamera vs. Guiron*, 1969)

We come from the sixth planet of the black hole in space.

(*Godzilla vs. the Cosmic Monsters*, 1974)

This is the corpse of the earthling who was once known as Karol Noymann.

(*Invisible Invaders*, 1958)

People of Earth, this is your last warning. Unless the nations of your planet surrender immediately all human life will be destroyed in a war you cannot win.

(ibid.)

Invaders of my universe, your destiny is to die.

(*Journey to the Seventh Planet*, 1962)

Shabbily-Treated Alien, to Apologetic Earthling: Don't worry about it. We'd probably have done the same to you if you'd have come to our place.

(*The Man Who Fell to Earth*, 1976)

These ties serve no functional purpose. Red planet abandoned the use of ties fifty years ago, as useless male vanity. It simply reveals the environmental naïveté of Earthmen.

(*Mars Needs Women*, 1966)

First Martian, observing poolside teen party: I say, let's call the whole invasion off. What do we need with a crazy planet?

Second Martian: That's not it. We owe it to the universe. If those are Earth teenagers, they've got to cause intergalactic trouble when they grow up.

(*Pajama Party*, 1964)

A transducer is what you Earth people call a ray gun.

(ibid.)

. . . in the name of the people of the planet where I was born, a once-proud race facing defeat by a vicious and detestable enemy, greetings!

(*The Terrornauts*, 1967)

Martian: My mission here is to plant an H–bomb explosion sufficiently strong enough to send Earth spinning into space and leave room for my own planet.
Earth Quisling: But that would mean the destruction of the world and everyone on it!
Martian: That need not concern you if you are safe with us on Mars.

(*Zombies of the Stratosphere*, 1952)

MONSTERS

Monsters don't usually get to say much more than 'RRRRRGGHHH!', but there are articulate, even chatty, exceptions.

Alligator Person: Why didn't he just let me die?

(*The Alligator People*, 1959)

Amazing Colossal Man: What sin can a man commit in a single lifetime that would bring this upon himself.

(*The Amazing Colossal Man*, 1957)

Philosophical Monster: Bread – good. Friend – good. Fire – bad! (*Bride of Frankenstein, 1935)*

Number One Head: Shut up! I'm running this monster!

(*The Incredible Two-Headed Transplant*, 1970)

Teenage Monster: I keep thinking of the day when I'll have my new face.

(*I Was a Teenage Frankenstein*, 1957)

Rabid Rose: I need blood to live, but I'm still *me*!

(*Rabid*, 1977)

HAL: Look, Dave, I can see you're really upset about this. I honestly think you should sit down calmly, take a stress pill, and think things over.

(*2001: A Space Odyssey*, 1968)

VAMPIRES

In direct contrast to most ill-spoken monsters, vampires, being of aristocratic extraction, have a positive fondness for the well-turned phrase, the curiously accented syllable, and the blackly humorous remark.

Count Dracula, upon being asked by an African ambassador to sign a petition against the slave trade: I will place a curse of suffering on you that will doom you to a living hell! A hunger, a wild, gnawing animal hunger, will grow in you – a hunger for human blood!

(*Blacula*, 1972)

Carmilla Karnstein: I live in you; and you would die for me . . . You must come with me, loving me, to death. (*Blood and Roses*, 1960)

Jewish Vampire, faced with a crucifix-waving peasant girl: Oy yoy . . . have you got the wrong vampire!

(*Dance of the Vampires*, 1967)

Countess Elisabeth Bathory, revealing the secret of the beauty treatments that have kept her chic for four hundred years: Diet . . . and lots of sleep.

(*Daughters of Darkness*, 1971)

Count Dracula: Children of the night . . . what music they make.

(*Dracula*, 1930)

I never drink . . . wine.

(*ibid.*)

To die, to be really dead, that must be glorious. (*ibid.*)

For a man who has not lived even one lifetime, you are wise, Van Helsing. (*ibid.*)

Vampish Vampire: Sandor, what do you see in my eyes?
Cloddish Servant: Death!

(*Dracula's Daughter*, 1936)

Count Dracula: Children of the night . . . shut up!

(*Love at First Bite*, 1979)

How would you like to spend a thousand years dressed like a headwaiter! (*ibid.*)

I have a horror of bloodshed . . . it's such a waste!

(*Mother Riley Meets the Vampire*, 1952)

Graf von Orlok: Is this your wife? What a lovely throat!

(*Nosferatu*, 1922)

Party guest: Where are your fangs?
Caped Aristocrat: Where are your manners?

(*Return of Count Yorga*, 1972)

Frank, isn't eternity better than a few years of ordinary life?

(*Son of Dracula*, 1943)

Carmilla Karnstein, observing funeral: What a fuss! Why you must die, everyone must die. And all are happier when they do.

(*The Vampire Lovers*, 1970)

SF Style

WISECRACKS

Obviously, the endless rounds of murder, monstrosity, massacre, mutilation and mean-mindedness served up by the average horror movie needs a certain leavening of humour in order to make it all palatable. Hence the inclusion of characters who, while everyone around them is being torn to shreds by the Flying Purple People Eater, continue to make smartass remarks.

Werewolf: You don't understand. Every night when the moon is full, I turn into a wolf.
Comedian: Yeah, you and fifty million other guys.

(*Abbott and Costello Meet Frankenstein*, 1948)

Sherlock Holmes: You've a magnificent brain, Moriarty. I admire it. I'd like to present it pickled in alcohol to the London Medical Society.

(*The Adventures of Sherlock Holmes*, 1939)

Have you ever talked to a corpse? It's *boring*!

(*An American Werewolf in London*, 1981)

Terrorized Heir: Don't these empty old houses frighten you?
Comedian: Not me, I was in Vaudeville.

(*The Cat and the Canary*, 1939)

Hero, upon being informed that he is the sole descendant of the infamous vampire count: If what you say is true, I'm gonna make a lot of money. I'm gonna sue all those people who have been making Dracula pictures without my permission.

(*Dracula's Dog*, 1976)

The line between food and sex has completely disappeared.

(*Eating Raoul*, 1982)

Terrorized Haitian: It's worse than horrible because a zombie has no will of his own. You see them sometimes, walking around blindly, with dead eyes, following orders, not knowing what they do, not caring . . .
Comedian: You mean like Democrats.

(*The Ghost Breakers*, 1940)

Werewolves? They're worse than cockroaches!

(*The Howling*, 1981)

You're from California! The wildest thing you ever heard was Wolfman Jack!

(*ibid.*)

Werewolf, digging a bullet out of his brain and offering the resultant mess to a terrified onlooker: I'm gonna give you a piece of my mind!

(*ibid.*)

Rejected Swain: You can find more ways of saying no than the government.

(*Macumba Love*, 1960)

Minion: Master, I'm curious to know why you always sleep in your evening clothes?
Vampire: I was buried in them.

(*Mother Riley Meets the Vampire*, 1952)

Hardboiled Editor: Have a pleasant vacation?
Hardboiled Lady Journalist: Charming. More delightful people crippled.

(*Mystery of the Wax Museum*, 1933)

Hardboiled Lady Journalist: Did you ever hear of such a thing as a death mask?
Hardboiled Editor: I used to be married to one.

(*ibid.*)

Softboiled Gold-Digger: Rich men love you and leave you.
Hardboiled Gold-Digger: Yeah, but they leave you plenty.

(*ibid.*)

Host: My wife's body is buried in a crypt beneath the house.
Guest: Where else?

(*The Raven*, 1933)

Tortured Romantic: Will I ever see again the rare and radiant maiden whom the angels name Lenore?
Raven: How the hell should I know? What am I, a fortune teller?

(*ibid.*)

Guest, entering cobwebbed crypt: Gee, hard place to keep clean, huh?

(*ibid.*)

Anyone who calls a psychiatrist a head-shrinker needs a pyschiatrist. Or a head-shrinker.

(*The Vengeance of She*, 1968)

PAUSE FOR THOUGHT

Never let it be said that science fiction, fantasy and horror films are purely escapist. Tucked in among the flesh-eating zombies and the costumed crime fighters are often philosophical tid-bits, seriously-argued political positions, and deep meditations upon the burning issues of the day.

Philosophical Psycho: It's not just us crazy ones who kill when we must.

(*Alone in the Dark*, 1982)

There is a man who has unlocked every door. Except the one to his own soul. Now he has the key.

(*The Amazing Transparent Man*, 1960)

Teenage Sidekick: When you think, Batman, with people in weird outfits like the four supercriminals running around here, it's amazing someone hasn't already reported this to the police.
Stern Superhero: It's a low neighbourhood, full of rum-pots. They're used to curious sights, which they attribute to alcoholic delusions.
Teenage Sidekick: Gosh, drink sure is a filthy thing, isn't it? I'd rather be dead than unable to trust my own eyes.

(*Batman*, 1966)

There will always be death when men seek to take what ain't their'n.

(*Before Dawn*, 1933)

Wise Old Woman: There is a power greater than science that rules the earth, and those who lust and pervert knowledge for evil only work out their own destruction. I'll call the police.

(*Blood of Dracula*, 1957)

Gosh Lord, sometimes your ways are downright incomprehensible.

(*The Cars That Ate Paris*, 1974)

When man meets man, you never know which one will die. When an animal meets a man, it's always the animal that dies. I'm on the animal's side.

(*Conquest*, 1983)

When the dead walk, we must stop killing or we lose the war.

(*Dawn of the Dead*, 1979)

To know death, one must first fuck life in the gall bladder.

(*Flesh for Frankenstein*, 1974)

Sakai: It's so desolate. It's hard to believe it's inhabited.
Junko: . . . and this is the result of atomic tests?
Mura: At one time, this was a beautiful green island. As a scientist, I feel partly responsible for this. This island alone is a good enough reason to end nuclear testing. Those who think of war should come and see this, eh?

(*Godzilla vs. the Thing*, 1964)

Philosophical Madman: Creation is almost a sacred thing. All creation. The Good Lord created saints and also he created sinners. He created the lamb and the faun, but He also created the wolf and the jackal. Now, who can judge which is the most praiseworthy?
Ordinary Joe: Well, that's one way to look at it.

(*How to Make a Monster*, 1958)

Simple Soldier: Do you still feel the same way about the testing of nuclear weapons?
Dissident Scientist: Yes, Major, I think I do. If the Lord wills it, we'll come out of this alive . . . then perhaps the nations of the world will realize it's possible to work together, as they're doing now, instead of trying to destroy each other with nuclear bombs.

(*Invisible Invaders*, 1959)

The Devil doesn't wait until we die to punish us.

(*Macumba Love*, 1960)

Good and Evil . . . that's the classic struggle.

(*Midnight Offerings*, 1981)

I wonder if Einstein meant his theory of relativity to encompass the relativity of beauty?

(*The Neptune Factor*, 1973)

Wise Indian: She speaks you the truth. She knows it from the university, I know it from my ancestors.

(*Orca – Killer Whale*, 1977)

I can't help thinking that somewhere in the Universe there has to be something better than man.

(*Planet of the Apes*, 1968)

Hero: He hates you. Why?

Long-Suffering Slave: The man he used to hate died last week. He needs someone new. They all hate. It keeps them alive.

(*Prehistoric Women*, 1968)

Memory's a mirror. It brings back only the things that hurt.

(*Pyro*, 1964)

Deep Thinker: The man who invented the wheel, invented the world. That doesn't make much sense, does it?

Shallow Woman: Nothing you've been saying makes much sense.

Deep Thinker: Well, if the man who invented the wheel copied the world . . .

Shallow Woman: Well, when the wheel was invented, the world was thought to be flat . . .

Deep Thinker: Yes, of course, but that's what made him so extraordinary, don't you see? He copied a flat world and it came out round. That's what I like so much about ferris wheels.

(*ibid.*)

Hideous Killer: Maybe if a man looks ugly he does ugly things.

Suave Psycho: You are saying something profound.

(*The Raven*, 1935)

Frankensteinian Scientist: Man is God now; as a matter of fact, he always was.

(*Scream and Scream Again*, 1969)

I'm not a mystic, Linda, but there are things beyond us . . . things perhaps we're not to understand . . . if what's happened has made us all think, why then . . . perhaps it makes sense after all . . . have faith, Linda. Have faith in the good that's still in Larry, and in all men.

(*The Split*, 1962)

Bad luck isn't brought by broken mirrors but by broken minds.

(*Suspiria*, 1977)

Mutated Woman of the Future, to Complacent Woman of the Present: Our history clearly records how the women of the twentieth century stood idly by while the atmosphere was contaminated and the children of the future doomed.

(*Terror From the Year 5000*, 1958)

Our true size is the size of our God.

(*This Island Earth*, 1955)

Is it what men do that darkens the sky? Or do skies blacken the souls of men?

(*Tower of London*, 1962)

Let the dead . . . stay dead.

(*The Walking Dead*, 1936)

PURPLE PROSE

The movies are self-evidently a visual medium. Perhaps certain screen-writers should be appraised of the fact. Imagine how it feels to be an actor required to rattle off the following speeches in a conversational style . . .

Post-Holocaust Cassandra: Now the shadow of death darkens the halls of our citadel. Our bright ray of hope is gone. It is the end of us.

Square-Jawed Hero: No, no, it's not the end. As long as we believe, there is always hope. I'll return to my time and my people. We will prevent the plague. You will not live in a world of darkness.

(*Beyond the Time Barrier*, 1960)

The agony of a soul mutilated in manhood will continue long after the body has ceased to bleed.

(*Bizarre*, 1969)

Narrator: For Tina Enright, time had ceased to exist, as she was suspended in the vague twilight between the past and the present.

(*Curse of the Faceless Man*, 1958)

Even the ears of corn are deaf to the torments of the damned.

(*The Devil's Cleavage*, 1975)

Do you want to be left as you are, or do you want your eyes and your soul to be blasted by a sight that would stagger the devil himself?

(*Dr Jekyll and Mr Hyde*, 1932)

I made it possible for you to come here. I welcomed you to Earth, and you made it a charnel house!

(*It Conquered the World*, 1956)

There is no more foul and relentless enemy of man in the occult world than this dead-alive creature spewed up from the grave!

(*Mark of the Vampire*, 1935)

Sceptical Scientist: Do I understand you correctly, Professor Graves? Are you advancing the astonishing concept that the mentality of primitive man compares favourably with that organ which a million years of evolutionary progress has developed in his modern counterpart?

(*The Neanderthal Man*, 1953)

Can your soul ever forgive mine?

(*The Oblong Box*, 1969)

Feast your eyes, gloat your soul, upon my accursed ugliness!

(*Phantom of the Opera*, 1925)

The Phantom of the Opera, explaining why he sleeps in a tomb: It reminds me of that other, dreamless, sleep that cures all ills forever.

(*ibid.*)

I've learned now that one second can turn a normal life, a fine life, a wonderful human, to something monstrous, evil, until it destroys itself . . . and I've tried to forget it.

(*Pyro*, 1964)

I heard this voice, and then I didn't hear any more, because the beating of my blood was louder.

(*Secret Beyond the Door*, 1948)

I like to bask in the reflected glory of a young biochemist whose brilliance approaches genius.

(*She Devil*, 1957)

Vengeance-Crazed Spaceborne Ubermensch, unwisely quoting Captain Ahab as his starship explodes: From Hell's heart I stab at thee . . .

(*Star Trek II: The Wrath of Khan*, 1982)

You will never find a wretched hive of more scum and villainy . . . we must be cautious.

(*Star Wars*, 1977)

RHYMES, RITUALS, AND SCRAPS OF LORE

Apart from Edgar Allan Poe's *The Raven*, few poems have been turned into horror films, but there has always been a streak of poetry in the genre. *Cat People* (1942) ends with a bit of John Donne, and *The Sentinel* (1976) hinges on a scrap of *Paradise Lost*. Otherwise, there is a great proliferation of Transylvanian gypsy sayings, ancient necromantic rituals, and the odd venture into free verse.

Max Brock: A master sculptor is in our midst. He is none other than Walter Paisley, our very own busboy, whose hands of genius have been carrying away the empty cups of your frustrations. His is the silent voice of creation within the dark, rich soil of humility, he blossoms as the hope of our nearly sterile century . . . Bring me an *espresso*, Walter.

The bird that flies now pays later through the nose of ambidextrous apathy.
Necrophiles may dance upon the place mats in an orgy of togetherness.
The highway of life cuts sharply through all the shady ghettos and the ivy-covered tombs.
And laughter rings from every time capsule in the star-spangled firmament.
And in the deep-freeze, it is the children's hour.
And no one knows that Duncan is murdered.
And no one knows that Walter Paisley is born.
Duncan knows.

The early sunrise knows.
Alley cats and garbage cans and steaming pavement and you and I and the nude descending the staircase and such things with souls: we know that Walter Paisley is born.
Ring rubber bells.
Beat cotton gongs.
Strike silken cymbals.
Play leathern flutes.
The cats and you and I and all such things with souls: we should hear Walter Paisley is born.
And the souls become flesh.
Walter Paisley is born.

(**Beat poetry by Charles Griffith for** *A Bucket of Blood*, 1959)

O Amon-Ra. O, God of Gods. Death is but the doorway to new life. We live today. We shall live again. In many forms shall we return, oh Mystic One.

(**The incantation that revives Boris Karloff from the dead in** *The Mummy*, 1932)

If the house is filled with dread
Place the beds at head to head.

(**Peasant superstition from** *Son of Frankenstein*, 1939)

Somehow I smell death in this room. My grandmother was Irish, you know.

(*Spaceways*, 1953)

If you break the law again, the people will give you death. I shouldn't give you my voice 'til you've been born again after the rites of manhood.

(*Teenage Cavemen*, 1958)

Sing a song of graveyards
An acre full of germs
Four and twenty landlords
Dinner for the worms
And when the box was planted
The worms began to sing
Wasn't that a danty dish to set before the Thing?

(Charles Griffith again, a merry ditty sung by the half-witted gravedigger in *The Undead*, 1957)

When stars are bright
On a frosty night
Beware the bane
In the rocky lane.

(The family curse in *The Undying Monster*, 1942)

The werewolf instinctively seeks to kill the thing it loves best.

(*The Werewolf of London*, 1935)

Even a man who is pure in heart
And says his prayers by night
May become a wolf
When the wolfbane blooms
And the autumn moon is bright.

(The old gypsy rhyme made up by Curt Siodmak for *The Wolf Man*, 1941, **and repeated, with slight variations, in a pack of sequels.**)

SONGS

While the renditions of 'Daisy, Daisy', 'Somewhere Over the Rainbow' and 'Puttin' on the Ritz' provided by HAL 9000, Vincent Price and the Frankenstein Monster in *2001: A Space Odyssey* (1968), *The Abominable Dr Phibes* (1971) and *Young Frankenstein*

(1974), not to mention Cameron Mitchell's heart-rending version of 'L.O.L.L.I.P.O.P. Spells Lollipop' in *The Toolbox Murders* (1979), prove that horror and fantasy films have not been averse to the occasional song, the genre has been somewhat backward in contributing to the hit parade. Aside from David Bowie's dirge for *Cat People* (1982) and Michael Jackson's nauseating hymn to a rat for *Ben* (1972), monsters, in the accepted sense of the term, have made little impression on the pop charts. However, there have been a number of also-rans.

I know I'm going to miss her,
A tomato ate my sister.

(Theme from *Attack of the Killer Tomatoes*, 1979)

Benson, Arizona
Blew all winds through your hair
My body flies the galaxies
My heart wants to be there.

('Benson, Arizona', theme from *Dark Star*, 1974)

You've got me tongue-tied
A tic a tac a talka like this
And be ba boppa, be ba boppa baby
Means bows a how's a little kiss?

('You've Got Me Tongue-Tied', the song everyone was humming as they walked out of *Ghost of Dragstrip Hollow*, 1959)

Save the Earth!
Save the Earth!
There's one solution,
Stop the pollution.

('Save the Earth', from *Godzilla vs. the Smog Monster*, 1971)

Well, some call it glamour
And some call it class,
But when they call it Ee-Ooo
You're cookin' with gas.

(**'You've Got to Have Ee-Ooo to Go with Your Smile' from** *How to Make a Monster*, 1958)

Journey to the seventh planet, come to me
Let your dreams become reality
I wait for you
Somewhere on the seventh planet out in space
You and I will find a magic place
Like lovers do.
And while we're up above
We'll touch the stars that we have wished upon
There our love will take wings and go on and on.

(**Theme from** *Journey to the Seventh Planet*, 1962)

My son the vampire, he'll make you a wreck
Every time he kisses you, he leaves two holes in the neck.

(**'My Son the Vampire' from the American release of** *Mother Riley Meets the Vampire*, 1952)

Tomorrow is the answer I will give
If you ask me where do I live.

(**Title song from** *Toomorrow*, 1970)

There's a new sun rising up angry in the sky
There's a new voice cryin' we're not afraid to die.
Let the old world make believe it's blind and deaf and dumb.
But nothing can change the shape of things to come.

(**'The Shape of Things to Come', from** *Wild in the Streets*, 1968)

CLICHÉS

. . . you've heard them before, and you'll hear them again . . .

Heroine: Why is this terrible thing happening? I've looked everywhere for the answer, and I can't find it. All night, I lie awake thinking . . . why . . . why . . . why? Why does this thing have to happen? You're a smart man, Dr Linton. You're a doctor. Tell me . . .
Avuncular Scientist: I wish I knew, Carol. I wish I knew.

(*The Amazing Colossal Man*, 1957)

First Astronaut: Craig, you haven't given up hope?
Second Astronaut: No.
First Astronaut: We're alive, and that's what's important.
Second Astronaut: You're right.

(*Battle Beyond the Sun*, 1962)

There's only one thing to do. We've got to track this thing down, and find out what it is. And destroy it.

(*Behemoth, the Sea Monster*, 1959)

We have a problem. It's never been tested on a human subject.

(*Blind Date*, 1983)

Get away from that lever or you'll blow us to atoms.

(*Bride of Frankenstein*, 1935)

I think your English police are wonderful.

(*Dark Eyes of London*, 1939)

Heroine: Whatever it is, I have the feeling it's going to harm us.
Hero: Pah, Claire, you have no way of knowing that.

(*The Day Mars Invaded Earth*, 1962)

You've got to remember, I'm just a simple private detective. I deal in facts. All you've given me is demons and devils.

(*The Devil's Men*, 1977)

Darling – really! This is the twentieth century.

(*Devils of Darkness*, 1964)

Minion: Sire, we must put plan epsilon into action.
King: But the epsilon plan is untried, it needs further tests.
Minion: We may have to use it anyway.

(*Escape from Galaxy 3*, 1982)

Witness: Who could forget the look on that dead man's face?
Sceptic: It's probably some simple explanation.

(*Fiend Without a Face*, 1958)

Earthling: Who are you?
Alien: I am from another planet, Dr Bryant. The one you call Mars.
Earthling: Mars! And you know my name!
Alien: I have recognized your voice. We have been listening to you Earth people ever since you developed radio. So we have learned your languages and a great deal about you.
Earthling: But this is astonishing!

(*Flying Disc Man From Mars*, 1951)

Mad Doctor's Sane Daughter: You've just got to stop these experiments!

(*The Four Skulls of Jonathan Drake*, 1959)

Doomed but Conscience-Stricken Assistant: You can't do that. It's too inhuman! I can't be party to such a fiendish plan.

(*I Was a Teenage Frankenstein*, 1957)

I meddled in things that man must leave alone.

(*The Invisible Man*, 1932)

The natives are restless tonight.

(*Island of Lost Souls*, 1932)

The oxygen, sir. We've only got one third left. We'd better be getting back.

(*Journey to the Seventh Planet*, 1962)

There'll be no women on my expedition.

(*The Lost World*, 1960)

Mama Loi: If you want to write a book about voodoo, go back to where you are safe. Here, you are surrounded by evil.
Unbeliever: How can you say such things? This is the twentieth century, the age of science and enlightenment. There should be no corner of the world where such things are permitted to exist.

(*Macumba Love*, 1960)

Bullets cannot harm the Serpent Goddess.

(*ibid.*)

High priest, you were great, just great.

(*Magic Curse*, 1977)

You can fight known things, but I don't know how to fight the Unknown.

(*Pharoah's Curse*, 1957)

Let's take it easy. There must be some explanation. A logical one.

(*Planet of the Vampires*, 1965)

Your program is precisely what I need to make those fools in the halls of sicence take my work seriously.

(*Prisoners of the Lost Universe*, 1983)

We may not have a chance to talk later, we may not even live through the day. I just want to say . . . I love you.

(*Queen of Outer Space*, 1958)

I told you never to open that door after dark.

(*Scars of Dracula*, 1970)

Oh God, Carl. I beg of you, don't try to bring back the dead!

(*Twice Told Tales*, 1983)

Hero: You don't believe in this superstitious rot do you?
Less Scientific Colleague: There's usually some basis for this sort of thing.

(*The Undying Monster*, 1942)

Perhaps there are still some things in the world science hasn't found out about.

(*ibid.*)

Mad Doctor: We'll shatter the very foundation of science!
Intolerant Wife: You're . . . you're . . . *insane*!
Mad Doctor: Don't ever say that to me again.

(*Voodoo Woman*, 1957)

Aww, honey. You're gonna drive us both mad with these foolish superstitions of yours.

(*Weird Woman*, 1944)

Hold it, you're scarin' the women.

(*Without Warning*, 1980)

The Cast

OUR SIDE I: THE MILITARY

The purpose of the military in SF films is to provide the firepower. Of course, since 'bullets can't hurt it', the civilian hero will have to come up with a super-weapon to do away with the monsters, but it will be the military who use it. There are two types of military men—officers, who stand around holding binoculars and making doomy pronouncements; and enlisted men, who, as in real life, spend most of their time getting spectacularly killed.

It shouldn't be too difficult to spot a sixty foot man.

(*The Amazing Colossal Man*, 1957)

When a powerful and threatening force lands on our nation's doorstep, we don't meet it with milk and cookies.

(*Earth vs. The Flying Saucers*, 1956)

Minion: I don't need to remind you of the need for absolute security on this, general.
General: No . . . I realize that civilization itself may depend on it.

(*The Eye Creatures*, 1965)

Lieutenant: I don't believe anybody is in that thing. It's probably under remote control.
Colonel: Would you like to take a walk out there in the open and test your theory?
Lieutenant: Well, no, sir, not especially.
Colonel: Then shut up and start thinking of a way to explain this thing without terrorizing the whole nation into a complete panic.
Lieutenant: Yes sir.
Private: I beg your pardon, sir, but maybe if we fired a few rounds at them, we'd get someone out. Anyhow, get some reaction.

(*ibid.*)

Colonel: Think of it, nobody but this special unit and the President of the United States know what really happened here tonight.
Lieutenant: You mean you think we know what happened?
Colonel: Well, of course we do . . . I think.

(*ibid.*)

First Soldier: It's weird. Why don't we see anyone here? What's happened to anybody who was hurt or killed?
Second Soldier: I think I know what happened. Frankenstein got hungry and they were just available, that's all.

(*Frankenstein Conquers the World*, 1966)

We'll have the situation under control soon. We've spotted that creation of yours. If he gives us trouble, we'll bring you back the pieces.

(*Frankenstein Meets the Space Monster*, 1964)

Colonel: Makes you proud, doesn't it, lieutenant?
Lieutenant: What sir?
Colonel: Being part of a show like this. Protecting your country from alien invaders.

(*Invasion of the Saucer Man*, 1957)

Lieutenant: Do you think it could have been from another world?
Colonel: Lieutenant, when you've been in the army as long as I have, you learn you don't have to think.

(*ibid.*)

Science is your business, protecting this country is mine.

(*Invisible Invaders*, 1959)

Hawkish Hero: You hate my guts, don't you?
Peacenik Heroine: You killed a man in cold blood this morning. I keep seeing his face.
Hawkish (but Inwardly Sensitive) Hero: So do I . . . I fought all through Korea, and I probably killed a *lot* of men. But I never saw their faces. Dropping bombs from a plane isn't quite so personal.
Peacenik (But Melting) Heroine: Can I fix you some coffee?

(*ibid.*)

If you know any special prayers for a job like this, you'd better say them. Fast.

(*ibid.*)

Gentlemen, these are seconds of utter emergency.

(*The Lost Missile*, 1958)

Ace Newshound: This is the biggest story of all time. Think what it means for the world.
Military Hero: I'm not working for the world, but the Air Force.

(*The Thing From Another World*, 1951)

OUR SIDE II: COPS

The police are more versatile than the military – in addition to turning out in force with pump shotguns in the event of a large-scale monstrosity, they can wander around the site of incredibly gory murders looking puzzled and asking penetrating questions. In recent years, cops have been getting more embittered, as witness Eli Wallach in *The Sentinel* (1976) explains: 'If we didn't stack the evidence once in a while, *all* the crooks would get off – instead of just ninety-eight percent!'

I've never seen a look like that on the face of a living woman before.

(*Before Dawn*, 1933)

With a killer loose, I do not take chances.

(*Curse of the Faceless Man*, 1958)

I've got your mangler cornered in the old monastery on Twenty-Fourth Street.

(*The Dark*, 1979)

If you ask me, it's clear. A sex maniac. But a rather unusual maniac, with a strange sideline, a hobby . . . Etruscology.

(*The Dead Are Alive*, 1972)

One thing is established, the criminal had wings.

(*The Flying Serpent*, 1946)

Cop: Miss Alison Drake told me that the dead man worried about a . . . shrunken head?

Witness: Roger found one hanging outside the window one night.

(*The Four Skulls of Jonathan Drake*, 1959)

Curses have nothing to do with facts. When somebody mutilates a corpse, that's a fact.

(*ibid.*)

Heroine: Are you sure it was something human?
Cop: Only human beings wear sandals.

(*ibid.*)

First Cop: A large dog was found dead in the Okayama district.
Second Cop: How does that concern us?
First Cop: The dog wasn't just killed, it was eaten.
Second Cop: Then the only thing this can mean is that Frankenstein is in Okayama.

(*Frankenstein Conquers the World*, 1966)

Bullets don't hurt it. The only thing I've got to stop him here is a traffic light.

(*The Giant Spider Invasion*, 1975)

Cop: What's that gizmo?
Scientist: It's a geiger counter.
Cop: Geiger counter? What's the use of that? We don't have any geigers around here.

(*ibid.*)

There's a killer bear out there, and I'm sitting around here crushing ice cubes in my mouth.

(*Grizzly*, 1977)

It doesn't take the finished product to commit a murder.

(*How to Make a Monster*, 1958)

We won't take up much of your time. It's about this fiend that's operating in this neighbourhood . . .

(*I Was a Teenage Frankenstein*, 1957)

(Note the studied nonchalance that guarantees no undue panic will be spread among the populace.)

I wish the dead could come back to life, you bastard, because then I could kill you again!

(*The Living Dead at the Manchester Morgue*, 1974)

Witness: Is anything wrong?
Cop: I'm afraid she met her death in strange circumstances.
Witness: Who did it?
Cop: We don't know. The evidence is hard to believe.

(*Naked Exorcism*, 1975)

Dang it, man! Don't treat me like a harmless crackpot! I'm a state officer and I aim to be listened to with consideration!

(*The Neanderthal Man*, 1953)

Tell me, doctor, could this severed body here have been caused by that chainsaw over there?

(*Pieces*, 1982)

Inspector Clay is dead. Murdered. *And somebody is responsible*!

(*Plan Nine From Outer Space*, 1956)

Cop: Well, doctor?
Expert: The blood's been drained out of her body.
Cop: I know that, but where is it?

(*Return of Dr X*, 1939)

I'm dealing with half a dozen murders a day, and you're busting my chops on a maybe?

(*Schizoid*, 1980)

Believe me, this guy don't want to kill, he wants to communicate.

(*ibid.*)

You can only hang a man once, Crenshaw. In your case, it's a pity.

(*Spaceways*, 1953)

The President's gonna be real grateful to you kids.

(*Teenage Zombies*, 1960)

The way the law protects those maggots you'd think they were an endangered species!

(*Ten to Midnight*, 1982)

Ah hah! The old head in a fish tank bit!

(*Terror Eyes*, 1980)

The only thing left to account for now is the woman's hair going white overnight.

(*The Vulture*, 1967)

OUR SIDE III: DOCS

When the town doctor is not (as in *The Vampire*, 1958) turning into the monster, his job is to examine the ghastly mess left after the latest multiple murder and enumerate the incredible symptoms before saying 'I've never seen anything like it.'

First Psychiatrist: This girl has lived through a horrible experience, true or not, but she made a satisfactory adjustment. She lives a normal, useful, happy life by completely suppressing it.
Second Psychiatrist: It's obvious. Anxiety neurosis and amnesia suppression. You didn't need me to tell you that.

(*The Alligator People*, 1959)

Doc: She's gonna be all right. I'm sorry about the baby.
Husband: You did your best, doctor.
Doc: It'll be a shock, losing the baby. She may not be herself for a few days.

(*Back From the Dead*, 1957)

Coroner: Two punctures of the external jugular vein, right side.
Cop: Blood?
Coroner: That's the strange part. No external symptoms of blood. And what's even stranger, not much left inside.

(*Blood of Dracula*, 1957)

Anything is possible in deep shock.

(*Curse of the Faceless Man*, 1959)

Doc: I made a complete autopsy. On examination of the skull of Mr Adams, I noticed two small holes in the base of the occipital region here. They penetrate to the *medulla oblongata*, where the spinal cord meets the brain. I opened the skull to investigate and found this . . .
Ordinary Joe: The brain! It's gone!
Doc: Yes. Sucked out like an egg through two holes. That's not all. The entire spinal cord is missing.
Colonel: But it . . . it's incredible!

Hero: It's as if some mental vampire were at work.
Colonel: Where's the brain and the spinal cord gone?
Doc: I'm a doctor, colonel, not a detective. There's nothing like this in the books.

(*Fiend Without a Face*, 1958)

Heroine: How is he, doctor?
Doc: Organically, perfectly sound.

(*The Four Skulls of Jonathan Drake*, 1959)

The heart lives on as if it forgot to die, feeding only on protein.

(*Frankenstein Conquers the World*, 1966)

Don't worry. She's only in a coma.

(*Green Hell*, 1939)

Ranger: There's more than enough food and fish for them up there.
Doc: Guess maybe she had enough fish.
Ranger: Hang on to your sick humour, doc.
Doc: It's not sick. She was hungry enough to eat two women.
Ranger: But bears don't eat people.
Doc: This one did.

(*Grizzly*, 1977)

Every bone in his body must be broken, but I'm not sure that's what killed him.

(*It! The Terror From Beyond Space*, 1958)

I never thought I'd live to see the day when I'd declare the great W. H. Donovan dead.

(*The Lady and the Monster*, 1943)

The score – four murders in two days. Cause of death – the element was hungry.

(*Magnetic Monster*, 1953)

(Yep, the villain of *Magnetic Monster* is a ravenous and growing speck of a hitherto unknown radioactive element.)

In death he seems so calm, and yet what a conflagration of horrible desires burns within this uncoffined thing.

(*Mark of the Vampire*, 1935)

The shock was about as great as any *woman* could be asked to bear, but with rest, she'll be all right.

(*The Neanderthal Man*, 1953)

The person that killed those two men used a set of false teeth.

(*The Rogue's Tavern*, 1936)

Doc: She's in a kind of somnambulistic state.
Ordinary Joe: Aw, c'mon doc, don't give me them ten-dollar words.

(*Ruby*, 1977)

Patient: Doctor, don't you think I'm well enough to walk?
Doc: The way the sun strikes you . . . you look too ethereal to move at all.
Older Doc: Well, now there's a scientific opinion if ever I heard one.

(*She Devil*, 1957)

Patient: Are you trying to say I'm insane?
Doc: No, no. It's just that the treatment may have unbalanced your glandular functions temporarily.

(*ibid.*)

Cop: When you get him to town, make out a coroner's report. Put down Jack Flynn for the name, and for the cause of death . . .
Doc: He was eaten by a spider.
Cop: Just write in 'unknown' and let the coroner figure it out for himself. That's the trouble with you eggheads, you jump to conclusions.

(*The Spider*, 1958)

There's a couple of little marks on his throat. Maybe insect bites?

(*The Vampire*, 1957)

I've never seen such cellular destruction.

(*ibid.*)

HEROINES

When there's a two-hundred-mile trek through hostile jungle to be made, she twists her ankle. When there's a two-hundred-foot ape rampaging through the city, she gets abducted by it. When there are two hundred giant cockroaches to be faced, she screams a lot. She's a horror movie heroine. To some, she's a pain in the neck the hero would be better off without. But she is absolutely essential to the film—if only because she is called upon to appear on the poster with suitably torn clothes, fleeing from the monster. There has recently been a trend, pioneered by *Halloween* (1978), *Coma* (1978) and *Alien* (1979), to replace the screaming nuisance-style heroine with a two-fisted, gutsy feminist who is more than a match for any psycho, conspiracy, or thing from another world. However there are still plenty of shrieking, cringing traditionalists about.

Don't hand me that weaker sex picture, I'm going.

(*The Amazing Captain Nemo*, 1978)

Don't worry father, I'm sure we'll overcome the forces of evil.

(*Escape from Galaxy 3*, 1982)

(They did, but father was past caring since he, and his entire planet, got blown up in the first scene.)

Father, I'm sure our planet will come through in the end.

(*ibid.*)

Sensitive heroine, taking pity on monster: Your dinner is here. The chain hurts you? The chain is too small isn't it? I'll get you a larger one.

(*Frankenstein Conquers the World*, 1966)

Barbarian Heroine: If I go there among the noise of their perversion, I will leave among the silence of their death.

(*Hundra*, 1983)

('They' are the male barbarians who had massacred Hundra's separatist sisters. After she gets her own back, the narrator declares: 'The seed of Hundra is in all women, so let all men beware!')

You are as I knew you would be – ugly, horrible, unfit to live on this or any other world. No wonder your race is dying. I'm proud to hurry the process.

(*It Conquered the World*, 1956)

We decided to miss lunch and get married, but all you can think of is a hydrogen warhead.

(*The Lost Missile*, 1958)

There's lipstick on your nose, very undignified for a man of science.

(*Magnetic Monster*, 1953)

Wet Heroine: Father! Father! That crash of glass! It awakened me! What happened?

(*The Neanderthal Man*, 1953)

Holy cow, of everyone in the world to fall in love with, I have to pick a Martian!

(*Pajama Party*, 1964)

What am I supposed to do with a mad scientist for an hour? . . . I'll pretend you didn't say that.

(*Prisoners of the Lost Universe*, 1983)

Don't give me that macho revenge John Wayne stuff!

(*Without Warning*, 1980)

ROMANCE

Aside from screaming and looking cute in the publicity, the heroine can be relied on to introduce the supposedly vital 'love stuff' to the film. Generations of audiences have hissed heroes who take time off from their monster-killing activities to go all mushy over a girl, but . . . gosh darn it . . . a guy can't spend *all* his time driving stakes through vampires. If nothing else, the science fiction and horror film allows for some bizarre twists on formula romantic situations.

You're cute when you slobber.

(*Basket Case*, 1982)

Pretty Medium: I'm sorry I couldn't locate your Aunt Minnie. Have you any other relatives who've passed on?

Smart Aleck: No, but I might kill off a couple and come back tomorrow.

(*Before Dawn*, 1933)

You know, you're lovely. I keep forgetting that you can read my thoughts. I wish you couldn't.

(*Beyond the Time Barrier*, 1960)

Alien Lovely: Do you have a special Earth girl?

(*Cat Women of the Moon*, 1954)

If you love me, please kill me.

(*Daughter of Dr Jekyll*, 1957)

Post-Holocaust Hero: Well, I think I'm beginning to want to live again. It's taken seven weeks, and you.

(*The Day the World Ended*, 1955)

I want to talk to you . . . and I want to make love to you. Right now. Right here. Doesn't the idea of an Etruscan burial ground turn you on?

(*The Dead Are Alive*, 1972)

Heroine, while besieged with the hero during an attack by giant rats: This may be a bad time, but there's something on my mind . . . I want you to make love to me.

(*Food of the Gods, 1976*)

Heroine: Oh Ken, you must never return to Canada. I couldn't bear it.
Hero: . . . unless you leave with me as my wife.
Heroine: But that won't be for years, not until you've completed your studies. Psychological medicine seems such a big thing.
Hero: Darling, it's new. When I win my diploma, think of the prospect – a new idea, and a new country. With you at my side, nobody can stop me.
Heroine: I can't wait.

(*Grip of the Strangler*, 1958)

Bewildered Heroine: He never seemed to be *that* terribly interested in cactus derivatives before.
Older Scientist: Well . . . he's isolated some remarkable alkaloids already.
Bewildered Heroine: Maybe I just don't want to admit that I can't compete with a cactus plant.

(*Hand of Death*, 1961)

Heroine: I never spent the night with an invisible man before.
Hero: With the lights out, you'll never know the difference.

(*The Invisible Man*, 1975)

Every time Van sees you he floats. Even though the ship is equipped with artificial gravity.

(*It! The Terror From Beyond Space*, 1958)

When this night is over Leyland, and the curse of the vampires is taken from here, I will cook sweet noodles for you.

(*Legend of the Seven Golden Vampires*, 1973)

Amorous Martian: The word 'love' went out of our vocabulary a hundred years ago, but whatever love is, I know it must be what I feel for you.

(*Mars Needs Women*, 1966)

Katsura, you're a cyborg but I still love you.

(*Monsters From an Unknown Planet*, 1975)

Heroine: You ought to do that more often.
Hero: Do what?
Heroine: Smile. I like it.

(*Phantom From 10,000 Leagues*, 1958)

No longer like a toad in these foul cellars shall I secrete the venom of hatred – for you shall bring me love.

(*Phantom of the Opera*, 1925)

Downtrodden Slave: That woman, she is your special woman?
Hero: Yes.
Downtrodden Slave: I had forgotten about such things.

(*Prehistoric Women*, 1968)

Laura, don't spoil everything. My house has always been too peaceful. Home sweet home. You are war. As long as we keep peace at home, I'll be needing violence.

(*Pyro*, 1964)

You know, there's a certain irony in the fact that our lives, and perhaps the lives of everyone on Earth, may depend on Captain Patterson's sex appeal.

(*Queen of Outer Space*, 1958)

Rich Heroine: You're a million miles away, Ted. And just when I thought I was beginning to get through to you.
Poor But Honest Hero: Look, Dorothy, I'm out of my element in a place like this. This preoccupation with triviality. This talk about money. I'm what you might call a 'square', I guess.
Rich Heroine: I'm real, aren't I?
Poor But Honest Hero: I don't know. Sometimes I think you are, and then I see you as part of this elegant design.
Rich Heroine: Well, that sounds like a high-class brush-off!

(*The She Creature*, 1956)

Naïve Hero: Your hair is simply beautiful. It fascinates me.
Vamp: It fascinates me too.

(*She Devil*, 1957)

Heroine: Beauty is only skin deep.
Hero: Well, it's deep enough, isn't it? What do you want, a lovely liver?

(*The Time Travelers*, 1964)

Girl: This place is really made for lovers.
Guy: These stones have been stoically defying the elements for centuries.
Girl: I wish human relationships were strong like that, but they usually end up crumbling and destroying themselves. It's ironic.

(*Tintorera*, 1977)

HEROES

They can have smooth-shaven square jaws or a week's-worth of five o'clock shadow. They can dress in silver foil underwear or a grubby trench coat. They can be career army officers or unemployed lab assistants. But they've all got one thing in common – they're movie heroes. Whether gung-ho like Flash Gordon or world-weary like Darren McGavin in *The Night Stalker* (1972), youthfully impetuous like Luke Skywalker or an elderly expert like Dr Van Helsing, they all have that underlying integrity and determination to rid the world of whatever menace is confronting it, enabling them to qualify unreservedly as the representative of Our Side. Their job is to kill the monster. Their reward is that they get the girl.

Superhero: Tell me, commissioner, what known super-criminals are at large just now?

(*Batman*, 1966)

. . . give me an oscillator and a fast boat!

(*The Beginning of the End*, 1957)

Lesser Mortal: You will never leave the citadel alive.
Hero: That's a chance I have to take.

(*Beyond the Time Barrier*, 1960)

. . . and I don't think he'll conquer the world. It's been tried!

(*The Black Widow*, 1947)

That Count Dracula – he's no good to anyone, and he never was!

(*Blood for Dracula*, 1974)

Hero, chancing upon a monster snapping a little old lady's leg bones: I'll thank you to stop that!

(*Blood of Dr Jekyll*, 1980)

What kind of religion tells children to murder their parents? . . . answer me that, buddy?

(*Children of the Corn*, 1983)

First Barbarian Hero: Who are you?
Second Barbarian Hero: My enemies call me Mace.
First Barbarian Hero: . . . and what do your friends call you?
Second Barbarian Hero: I don't have any friends.

(*Conquest*, 1983)

Vampire Expert: How would you feel about driving a stake through somebody's heart?
Hero: Marvellous.

(*Count Yorga – Vampire*, 1970)

In this situation, weapons are useless. I have some wooden stakes in the car.

(*Dracula's Dog*, 1977)

Porky Pig: Take that, you Thing From Another World you!

(*Duck Dodgers in the 24½ Century*, 1953)

The American people don't scare easily.

(*Flying Disc Man from Mars*, 1951)

Heroine, upon the destruction of an alien arsenal: It's just as well, those weapons were too dangerous anyway.
Hero: Maybe, but I'd sure like to've tried them out!

(*ibid.*)

Heroine: I shouldn't talk to you when you're doing your thing.
Hero: What's my thing?
Heroine: Facing danger.

(*Food of the Gods*, 1976)

First Gosh-Wow Hero: That giant octopus must be a machine!
Second Gosh-Wow Hero: The magnetic gun's still working, but it won't do!
First Gosh-Wow Hero: Well, aim it at the octopus' computer! It'll throw the magnetic data off balance!

(*The Ghost Clipper*, 1969)

First Scientific Hero: Looks like our Black Hole has turned into an open door from hell.
Second Scientific Hero: And we're gonna have to find a way to close it.

(*The Giant Spider Invasion*, 1975)

Hedorah's only sludge. He can be dried!

(*Godzilla vs. the Smog Monster*, 1972)

I've got two girls, ages nineteen to twenty, both eaten to the bone. So don't give me any bullshit about regulations.

(*Grizzly*, 1976)

Millionaire Big-game hunting hero: This forty-foot monster with a brain the size of a dried pea has just destroyed a man with one of the great minds of the century. I will hunt this thing down, and I will kill it.

(*The Last Dinosaur*, 1977)

Stooge: A Voodoo Queen does not see a disbeliever.
Hero: She'd see me.
Stooge: It is customary to be invited.
Hero: I have a reputation for party crashing.

(*Macumba Love*, 1960)

I like this world. Let's keep it in one piece. At least, let's try.

(*Magnetic Monster*, 1953)

Sassy Heroine: So you refuse to quit?
Salty Hero: That's not my style. Especially when a pretty and intelligent girl like you tells me that I'm dumber than a fish.

(*Orca – Killer Whale*, 1977)

Don't tell me how you created it, tell me how to destroy it.

(*Phantom From 10,000 Leagues*, 1955)

It wouldn't be the first time in history a monster was mistaken for a god. I guess that's why I have to kill it. If you can kill it, it's not a god, just a good old-fashioned monster.

(*Q – The Winged Serpent*, 1982)

Underling: His High Exaltedness, the great Jabba the Hutt, has decreed that you are to be terminated immediately.
Hero: Good, I hate long waits.
Underling: You will therefore be taken to the Dune Sea and cast into the Pit of Carkoon, the nesting place of the all-powerful Sarlacc.
Hero: Doesn't sound so bad.
Underling: In his belly, you will find a new definition of pain and suffering, as you are slowly digested over a thousand years.
Hero: On second thoughts, let's pass on that, huh?

(*Return of the Jedi*, 1982)

We've got to find their trail – footprints, slime, *anything*!

(*The Slime People*, 1963)

I'm not gonna catch it, I'm gonna kill it.

(*Spasms*, 1982)

(**'It' is a twenty-foot snake god from South Asia that our hero had imported to the USA only to see it accidentally get loose.**)

Sherlock Holmes: Directing these 'pajama suicides' is one of the most fiendishly clever minds in all Europe today. I suspect a woman.
Dr Watson: You amaze me, Holmes. Why a woman?
Sherlock Holmes: Because the method, whatever it is, is peculiarly subtle and cruel. Feline, not canine.

Inspector Lestrade: Poppycock. When a bloke does himself in, that's suicide.
Sherlock Holmes: Unless a bloke is driven to suicide; in that case, it's murder.
Dr Watson: Driven? That sounds like a woman, doesn't it?
Sherlock Holmes: Definitely – a female Moriarty. Clever. Ruthless. And above all, cautious.

(*The Spider Woman*, 1944)

Travellin' through hyperspace ain't like dustin' crops, boy.

(*Star Wars*, 1977)

Mycroft Holmes, of his brother's musical ability: What I cannot understand is why, since you've had that violin with you so long, you have never learned to play.

(*A Study in Terror*, 1965)

Heroine: Dad, that sounded like a woman screaming!
Old Hero: Yes.
Young Hero: You got a gun in the house?
Old Hero: Only my twenty-gauge shotgun I use for ducks.
Old Hero: Let's take it with us, just in case.
Old Hero: All right. Better put on our anti-radiation suits.

(*Terror From the Year 5000*, 1958)

Sensitive Hero: I'm afraid the world doesn't think of a sixty-foot man the way a sister does.

(*War of the Colossal Beast*, 1958)

Quick-Thinking Vampire Hunter: Start checking casket companies in the morning.

(*Vampire*, 1979)

Absent-Minded Professor: Carnivorous coelacanths. They're supposed to be extinct.
Pragmatic Hero: So will we be if you don't get out of here.

(*Warlords of Atlantis*, 1978)

VILLAINS

Villains, don't you just hate 'em? Well . . . no. In the movies, at least, villains always seem to come off better than the heroes. Whereas Good Guys from Buster Crabbe through John Agar to Mark Hamill are so blandly dedicated to purity and decency that you inevitably suspect them of covering up their minor transgressions, Bela Lugosi, Boris Karloff or Vincent Price seem at least to have an honest enjoyment of their foulness. What's more, they're usually better actors than the heroes, and consequently tend to cop all the best lines.

You're bitter, Faust. Mean and bitter. You trust no one, and you hate everyone. You're the kind of man that I need and understand.

(*The Amazing Transparent Man*, 1960)

Do you know what one of these bullets will do, son? It'll rip out your spine and roll it up like a ball of string.

(*ibid.*)

Dastard: Doctor, I'm not concerned with the welfare of one man. I must know the full potential of your invention. Because my aim is to make an entire army invisible. Do you understand? An entire army!
Conscience-stricken Scientist: I did not agree to kill a man by deliberate radiation poisoning.

Dastard: You're too old-fashioned to be a genius. It's you scientists that brought the world to what it is today. You can hardly blame me for taking advantage of your discoveries.

(*ibid.*)

Riddler: You and your trainee exploding shark!
Penguin: Faugh! Quack! How should I know they'd have a can of shark repellent batspray handy?

(*Batman*, 1966)

The pain when I am going through the layers of your skin will not be unendurable. It is only when I begin to cut on the inside that you will realize you are having an experience.

(*Behind the Mask*, 1932)

I'm going to tear the skin from your body . . . bit by bit!

(*The Black Cat*, 1934)

Betray that trust and I'll feed your entrails to the pigs!

(*Crimes at the Dark House*, 1940)

You're blind. And you can't speak. But you can hear, and that will never do.

(*Dark Eyes of London*, 1939)

If there's two men and one gun, I like to have it.

(*The Day the World Ended*, 1955)

It'll take more than one bullet to destroy the beauty of fascism!

(*Desperate Living*, 1977)

Enough of this playing around, destroy the whole planet!

(*Escape From Galaxy 3*, 1982)

The Antichrist: Have our people liquidate the Nazarene . . . fail, and you will be condemned to a numbing eternity in the flaccid bosom of Christ.

(*The Final Conflict*, 1981)

I want so badly to see you die slowly and painfully!

(*Four Flies on Grey Velvet*, 1972)

(Sad to report, Mimsy Farmer does not get her wish, since the hero is promptly saved by his best friend. The villainess then has the misfortune to be decapitated in a slow-motion car accident.)

Enough, Nadir! This is a clear case of failure. If the fugitive was able to inflict this damage, he may be capable of escape!

(*Frankenstein meets the Space Monster*, 1965)

I'm going to give that brain of yours a new home.

(*House of Frankenstein*, 1944)

If you're bored by it, pretend it's real; but, if you're excited by it, pretend it's fake.

(**Introduction to** *The Incredible Torture Show*, 1978)

(The Great Sardu, introducing his Incredible Torture Show, here sums up the philosophy of the hard-gore porn film. For what it's worth, it's fake.)

Megalomaniac: It's impossible for me to make an enemy of anyone any more, darling. The word 'enemy' is about to disappear from the human vocabulary.
Long-Suffering Wife: How about the word 'tact'?

(*It Conquered the World*, 1956)

Victim: You're a monster!
Villain: No, I'm a genius.

(*Latitude Zero*, 1969)

(He is both.)

Convince your father to cooperate, or I'll turn you into a creature like that.

(*ibid.*)

Decadent but Philosophical Villain: Kill! Then love! When you have known that, you have known everything.

(*The Most Dangerous Game*, 1932)

A few hours with the rats will make him speak the truth!

(*The Mysterious Mr Wong*, 1935)

I'm going to blow up the *entire* world!

(*The Phantom Creeps*, 1939)

(Flying above New York harbour in his private plane, clutching a sample of 'the most destructive explosive ever devised', Bela Lugosi here comes up with the most ambitious piece of evil-doing even he ever attempted. He also forgets that, should he be successful, he might in some small way be inconvenienced himself.)

Victim: What's that thing?
Villain: A knife.
Victim: What's it doing?
Villain: Descending.
Victim: What are you trying to do to me?
Villain: Torture you.

(*The Raven*, 1935)

Minion: An assassination televised live coast-to-coast. Why?
Villain: That's entertainment.

(*Phantom of the Paradise*, 1974)

Villain: I can make you grovel in the dust . . . but I can't make you love me.
Lady Victim: Some day, I'm going to kill you.
Villain: I should kill you, but the artist is vain. He can't destroy the beauty he has created.

(*The She Creature*, 1956)

You don't know how hard I found it signing the order to terminate your life.

(*Star Wars*, 1977)

Do you fear me, sorceress? Why, Gobbo's the gentlest jailer ever to gouge a prisoner's eye.

(*The Undead*, 1957)

For this one, father, I would suggest a slower death.

(*The Vengeance of Fu Manchu*, 1968)

Hero: Have you forgotten that the Nobel Prize Committee once considered you the foremost contender for their top award—The Scientist Who Had Done The Most To Benefit Mankind?
Villain: I *am* benefiting mankind, by ridding the world of all the people who would stand in the way of communism. When I press this button, thc force of the explosion will scatter germs for hundreds of miles . . . communism will rule throughout the world.

(*The Whip Hand*, 1951)

Science

GOOD SCIENCE

Science, in the movies, is often a matter of flashing lights, bubbling retorts, strange noises, and bits of half-understood information cribbed by unscientific screen-writers from an out-of-date encyclopedia. But who cares? Those crashing explosions in the airless deep space of *Star Wars* (1977) may be impossible, but the film would be the poorer without them. Also, it's nice sometimes for audiences who failed science subjects at school to feel superior to the perpetrators of pseudo-scientific double talk who populate the cinema.

As you can see, it's pretty hard to describe.

(*Alien*, 1979)

When he comes to, give him some additional hydro-spray therapy.

(*The Alligator People*, 1959)

(Translation: throw a bucket of water over him.)

Here's something intriguing. Two similar muscular charts. You might take them for the same animal, but, as you know, this is a man . . . and this is an alligator.

(*ibid.*)

First Scientist: The answer is in the bone marrow. The bone marrow! We were so close we couldn't see it!
Second Scientist: Sulphydryl! Inject sulphydryl compounds into the bone marrow!
First Scientist: Exactly! The secret is in the degree of the expanse.
Second Scientist: Then injections of sulphydryl could correct the body's regenerative balance!

(*The Amazing Colossal Man*, 1957)

Ground Control: All personnel clear the flight deck without delay!
Supposedly Experienced Spaceman: What is the reason for doing that?
Ground Control: Someone could get hurt in the blast-off.

(*Battle Beyond the Sun*, 1962)

It's almost impossible to think of intelligence existing without a brain. Yet – let's face it – any organic brain we're familiar with couldn't exist on Mars.

(*The Day Mars Invaded Earth*, 1962)

Cop: . . . Don't seem to be any reason for a thing like that to happen.
Meticulous Scientist: That's why we call them 'accidents'.

(*ibid.*)

I was hoping we could get back to dissecting that stingray this evening.

(*Day of the Triffids*, 1963)

It must be the sulphur in the walls of his cave that has kept this creature alive for all these years.

(*Eegah!*, 1962)

We're facing a new form of life that nobody understands. I believe it feeds on the radiation from your atomic plant, and that it's evil.

(*Fiend Without a Face*, 1958)

I've been lucky enough to stumble on the most important discovery since man sawed off the end of a tree trunk and found the wheel. The disintegrator-integrator will completely change life as we know it.

(*The Fly*, 1958)

They sewed Frankenstein together and activated it. They stimulated his heart with electricity, and this palpitating thing is it.

(*Frankenstein Conquers the World*, 1966)

When you return to Japan, there is a way to find out if the creature is truly Frankenstein. Cut off the monster's arms and legs. If he is Frankenstein, new arms and legs will grow, and the severed limbs also will remain alive. Have I helped you any?

(*ibid.*)

First Scientist: Here's the way I look at it. The creatures vanished that were here during the Mesozoic era. They disappeared when the Earth cooled off, didn't they? I believe they burrowed underground for warmth, and when they escaped the cold of the surface, they may have continued to live on.

Second Scientist: No one can say for certain that your theory is absolutely impossible, but I think your idea is utterly ridiculous.

(*ibid.*)

We continue to hear a modulated hydrogen frequency of twenty-one centimetres, princess.

(*Frankenstein Meets the Space Monster*, 1965)

We did it! We've proven again that science and the military can accomplish the impossible!

(*ibid.*)

(**Go tell the North Vietnamese.**)

First Scientist: I've never seen such fouled-up data in my life. It's against every known law of physics. There's only one thing I know of could cause a warp like this.
Second Scientist: A miniature black hole?

(*The Giant Spider Invasion*, 1975)

Well, it all fits . . . Einstein's general theory of relativity!

(*ibid.*)

The radiation level is far too lethal!

(*ibid.*)

Ordinary Joe: Why did you put us in there?
Scientist: You were radioactive.
Ordinary Joe: We were?
Scientist: Yes, So we decontaminated you.

(*Godzilla vs. the Thing*, 1964)

(**And very decent of them too.**)

Eggs can't run. You know that.

(*ibid.*)

First Scientist: All right, let's assume you're right. A superior intelligence has come from Venus—in *my* satellite—established residency, turned off the world's power, and is about to take over the world population. Why aren't you fighting it?
Second Scientist: Because this superior intelligence happens to be a personal friend of mine.

(*It Conquered the World*, 1956)

Ordinary Joe: What exactly has this Okada done?
Scientist: He's invented a serum against radiation.
Ordinary Joe: Wow! No wonder every nation wants him.

(*Latitude Zero*, 1969)

Doubting Scientist: Professor, did you say 'dinosaurs'?
Professor Challenger: Your hearing is excellent.
Doubting Scientist: Were they big dinosaurs, professor?
Professor Challenger: I do not deal in small dinosaurs.

(*The Lost World*, 1960)

I've found that people are always jumping to wild conclusions concerning atomic reactors.

(*The Monster That Challenged the World*, 1957)

Scientist: Everything has a logical explanation in science. I refuse to believe the supernatural. There must be logical cause and effect to this . . . this unholy adventure.
Tactless Stooge: Of course there must. Any ideas?
Scientist: Well, no.

(*The Neanderthal Man*, 1953)

Please, Miss Madison. The matter transmitter is a finely calibrated instrument.

(*Prisoners of the Lost Universe*, 1983)

The gravity's so close to Earth's that the atmosphere must be breathable.

(*Queen of Outer Space*, 1958)

Interesting stuff, blood.

(*The Return of Dr X*, 1939)

All that power you can muster there in your best right is nothing to what you get in your unconscious mind.

(*Ruby*, 1977)

Frivolous Scientist: Can you program him to have a sense of humour?
Stern Robot Builder: That's not an early priority.

(*Saturn 3*, 1979)

I've got something that almost convinces me I'm a genius.

(*She Devil*, 1957)

Somewhere in that hideous carcass are the genes that control organic growth. Man had better find out what made this creature so big, and find out pretty fast, or we'll all be in pretty serious trouble.

(*The Spider*, 1958)

As far as I'm concerned, nothing which sends signals across space is a monster.

(*The Terrornauts*, 1967)

Ace Newshound: Please doctor, I want to ask you. It sounds like you're describing some sort of supercarrot.
Scientist: That's nearly right, Mr Scott. This carrot has constructed an aircraft capable of flying millions of miles through space propelled by a force as yet unknown to us.
Ace Newshound: An intellectual carrot. The mind boggles.

(*The Thing From Another World*, 1951)

With the energy from just one square dance, we could send that meteor back where it came from.

(*War of the Worlds*, 1953)

Concerned Citizen: If that thing's radioactive, we ought to keep people away from it.
Expert: Might be a good idea.

(*ibid.*)

That ray gun you developed. Would one of its shells penetrate the hull of Martin's rocket?

(*Zombies of the Stratosphere*, 1952)

SCIENTISTS ARE PEOPLE TOO

Nobel Prize-winners and high-IQ atom-splitters might be all right when it comes to inventing a time machine or discovering the cure for cancer, but these head-in-the-air, super-technical types would be disastrous as SF movie heroes. It is essential for a hero, no matter how brilliant, to display the kind of human warmth and bar-room wit that stamps him as just another Ordinary Joe underneath his lab. coat. Even as late as *Altered States* (1980), in which the scientists are at last allowed to talk to each other in the impenetrable, high-flown patter used by real life geniuses, the laboratory-dwelling heroes are shown to lead private lives of such soap opera banality that the film seems no more realistic than *It! The Terror From Beyond Space.*

Technician: Say, Astronaut Johnson has just blasted off for Mars.
Witty Ground Control: Call us when you get there.
Wisecracking Astronaut: I will if I can find a telephone.
Witty Ground Control: Don't reverse the charges.

(*Battle Beyond the Sun*, 1962)

Scientist's Adoring Offspring: Dad, did you get to Mars?
Self-Satisfied Parent: We sure did, honey.

(*The Day Mars Invaded Earth*, 1962)

Scientist's Adoring Wife: What are you doing?
Humble Husband: Oh, just looking at the sky. Looking at God, perhaps.
Scientist's Adoring Wife: You're a strange man, André. So precise and practical and yet so . . . I don't quite know how to put it.
Humble Husband: . . . so aware of the Infinite. The more I know, the more sure I am . . . I know so little.

(*The Fly*, 1958)

Scientist: Barbara knows more about genetic systems than anyone alive.
Hero: Sounds like fun.

(*Forbidden World*, 1980)

First Spaceman: The second we hit Earth, I'm gonna jump right through that airlock. All the way to the ground. Then I'm gonna roll around and stretch like a cat in the sun.
Second Spaceman: Oh boy, the sun. We'll be fifty million miles closer to it. You know, even when I was a kid, I could never stand being cold.
First Spaceman: How'd you ever win the Ardmore Fellowship in Low Temperature Physics?
Second Spaceman: I wore long underwear.

(*It! The Terror From Beyond Space*, 1958)

So I decided after one bad marriage to bury myself in science.

(*ibid.*)

Lady Scientist: We've known one another for less than five hours . . .
Smooth-Talking Martian: According to Dr Einstein's calculations, time is relative.

(*Mars Needs Women*, 1966)

Happy? That's a very inexact word for a higher mathematician, Lisa.

(*Spaceways*, 1953)

Lady Scientist, introducing Laboratory Cat: We call him 'Neutron', because he's so positive.

(*This Island Earth*, 1955)

MAD SCIENCE

When a scientist develops a bomb that can take humanity back to the Stone Age overnight, he's a patriot. But if he creates a giant globbering monster that terrorizes a postage stamp community in the Mid-West or the Carpathians, then he's a fruitcake. The first guy gets a medal, the second usually gets what's coming to him when the torch-carrying villagers chase the creature back to his lair and burn the place down. Mad Scientists are not obliged to be addicted to chocolate sodas and wisecracks in order to show that they are Ordinary Joes. Instead, they get to indulge in unethical experiments, body-snatching, wild theories, and endless ranting. Dr Frankenstein, Dr Phibes, Dr Fu Manchu, Dr G, Dr X, Dr No, Dr Death, Dr Maniac, even Dr Butcher M.D. – we salute you, and wish you well in your never-ending struggle to bring homicidal psychopaths back from the dead, create armies of radioactive gorilla people, and take over the world.

In the interests of science anything – *anything* – is justified!

(*The Black Sleep*, 1956)

Mad Lady Scientist: We live in a world ruled by men – for men. I can't even get them to consider my theories. They mock at me – at my work – but they're convinced they're on the right track. Before they're proven wrong – and I can do that – they'll wreck the world through reckless experiments. I'm not against progress, but these stubborn fools are searching for atomic power in the wrong place. If they continue . . . do you realize what the people of the future will be? What they'll look like? Monsters! Grotesque, misshapen, frightening fiends. Isotopes and fall-out . . . in our lungs, in our glands, distorting natural growth and proportions. Nobody can calculate the hazards of radiation monsters. What reckless fools! They search in the wrong place when I can demonstrate that a power strong enough to destroy the world is buried in each of us. I can release a destructive power in a human being that would make a split atom bomb look like a blessing.

(*Blood of Dracula*, 1957)

Conscience-Stricken Assistant: You killed him, Callistratus! You murdered this man!
Ruthless Researcher: . . . and you ruined an important experiment. That is infinitely worse.

(*Blood of the Vampire*, 1958)

To a new world of Gods and Monsters.

(*Bride of Frankenstein*, 1935)

The fools! Here we are so close to solving the mystery of life and death, and they worry about their precious lives!

(*Curse of the Faceless Man*, 1958)

I don't care about you! All I want is your brain!

(*Dr Butcher, M.D.*, 1982)

You know, Igor, I'm beginning to regret that I brought you back to life.

(*Dr G and the Bikini Machine*, 1966)

I created you, Super Germ!

(*The Evil Brain From Outer Space*, 1959)

Where are the plans of my radar-controlled atomic guns?

(*Flying Disc Man From Mars*, 1951)

If we are ever to make a start in our campaign of world conquest we must have radium.

(*ibid.*)

My evil self is at that door, and I have no power to stop it.

(*Forbidden Planet*, 1956)

The neck's broken, the brain is useless. We must find another brain.

(*Frankenstein*, 1931)

Frankenstein: I am going to turn that ray on that body and endow it with life.
Sceptical Colleague: . . . and you really believe that you can bring life to the dead?
Frankenstein: That body is not dead, it has never lived. I created it.

(*ibid.*)

Now I know what it feels like to be God.

(*ibid.*)

(This line has often been censored from prints of *Frankenstein* on the grounds of blasphemy.)

Mad Doctor: The scientific mind demands patience. I have discovered you have none.
Sane Assistant: I have a conscience.
Mad Doctor: There is no room in science for such a word.
Sane Assistant: Do you intend to murder me as well?
Mad Doctor: Come now, you lack subtlety.

(*The Gamma People*, 1956)

Frankenstein: Don't dare! You know, I'm sure that someone said those same words and hurled that same challenge at that great ancestor of mine whose name I bear.

(*I Was a Teenage Frankenstein*, 1957)

Do as I say, and you'll share in the greatest experiment science has ever made!

(*ibid.*)

Mad Doctor: What condition is he in?
Assistant: Dead!
Mad Doctor: I know that! That's the way a layman would describe it . . . in this laboratory there is no death until I declare it so!

(*ibid.*)

Dr Karlton, you mustn't be squeamish. I've seen worse. Anyway, the face is a comparatively simple replacement.

(*ibid.*)

Speak! You have a civil tongue in your head. I know you have because I sewed it back myself!

(*ibid.*)

Mankind is on the verge of destroying itself. The only hope for the human race is to hurl it back to its primitive dawn, to start all over again. What's one life compared to such a triumph?

(*I Was a Teenage Werewolf*, 1957)

Hugo, prepare the scopolamine!

(*ibid.*)

Assistant: . . . but you're sacrificing a human life!
Mad Doctor: Do you cry over a guinea pig? This boy's a free police case. We're probably saving him from the gas chamber.
Assistant: . . . but this boy is so young, and the transformation is so horrible.
Mad Doctor: You call yourself a scientist!? That's why you've never been more than an assistant!

(*ibid.*)

I don't like to hear the subject of a world-shaking experiment referred to as a 'victim'.

(*ibid.*)

Suddenly, I realized the power I held – the power to rule, to make the world grovel at my feet. We'll soon put the world to rights now. We'll begin with a reign of terror. A few murders here and there. Murders of great men, murders of little men, just to show we make no distinction. We might even wreck a train or two.

(*The Invisible Man*, 1933)

. . . to send thousands squealing in terror at the touch of my little invisible finger. The whole world's frightened of me, even the *moon*'s frightened of me!

(*ibid.*)

I took a gorilla, and, working with infinite care, I made my first man.

(*Island of Lost Souls*, 1932)

When you try to solve the mysteries of nature, it doesn't matter whether you experiment with guinea pigs or human beings.

(*The Lady and the Monster*, 1943)

Your surgeons are so elated at being able to transplant organs. That's child's play! I'm about to transplant the brain of this woman into a lion's body.

(*Latitude Zero*, 1969)

Hero, impressed at a machine which can turn black men white: Dr Manyus, this is the greatest invention in history.
Benevolent Genius: Science can accomplish *anything*!

(*The Lost City*, 1936)

I, a poor peasant, have conquered science. Why can't I conquer love?

(*Mad Love*, 1935)

The forces of creation – bah!

(*Man Made Monster*, 1942)

Mad Doctor, to Heroine: You know, it's a curious fact, but ever since my earliest experiments with guinea pigs, I've always found that the female of the species was more sensitive to electrical impulses than was the male.

(*ibid.*)

They call me a scientist.

(*The Monster and the Girl*, 1941)

(**Heh heh heh.**)

Mad Doctor: I intend to build 50,000 robots.
Assistant: . . . but how many have you built so far?

Mad Doctor: Er, one. To build the rest, I need an almost unlimited supply of uranium.

(*Mother Riley Meets the Vampire*, 1952)

This is my cross, the penalty of being born into an era of little men who are small even in their spirits. You're creatures of paper, bred from an artificial culture whose dearest possession is your prejudices and important only in the hollowness of your smirking vanities. Hypocrisy is your bible, stupidity is the cornerstone of your existence, and dishonesty your human essence.

(*The Neanderthal Man*, 1953)

Mad Doctor: I won't be laughed at any more.
Devoted Wife: I would never laugh at you darling. Who would ever laugh?
Mad Doctor: They laughed.
Devoted wife: They?
Mad Doctor: That pack of thick-headed egotistic stuffed shirts at the naturalists' club. Lunacy, eh? A lot they know in their stupid obstinacy. In their peevish pettiness of mind and soul. It's here, I tell you, all here. After all this work, I've done it. I know I have.
Devoted Wife: What? Done what? Cliff, what is it?
Mad Doctor: The embodiment of my theories of memory stimulation, the reactivation of dormant cells in the mind of man.

(*ibid.*)

Come, Julio, help me drag the cadaver of the gorilla to the incinerator.

(*Night of the Bloody Apes*, 1971)

The day is coming when man will be able to control blood and when he does, he'll control his destiny.

(*Return of Dr X*, 1939)

It won't really be dying, because you'll be living on in this plant.

(*The Spider Woman Strikes Back*, 1946)

Kenji, get back! You've changed even more, haven't you? Back, Kenji, back! I don't suppose you understand me now. You were my brother. You were an experiment that didn't work out. I am sorry, Kenji.

(*The Split*, 1962)

Mad Doctor, explaining Human/Gorilla Brain Transplant: He's gonna be smart, and you'll be . . . not so smart.

(*The Strange Case of Dr Rx*, 1942)

Mad? I, who have discovered the secret of life! You call me mad?!

(*The Vampire Bat*, 1933)

Funny Bits

ONE-LINERS

Some films are packed to the brim with quotable lines, either through the wit of the screenwriter or the kind of unintentional quirks that slip through when you knock together your scenario over a weekend. Sometimes, a single good line will redeem a totally awful movie, at others, a few laughs will ease the tension enough to make the next scare all the more satisfying.

You don't believe in that giant possum stuff?

(*The Alien Dead*, 1980)

Eeeeh! Dirty stinkin' slimy 'gators! Yuh bit my hand off, didn't yuh? I'm gonna spend the rest of my life killin' 'gators.

(*The Alligator People*, 1959)

You have the cobalt bomb. It arrived today. (*ibid.*)

If you weren't one of the best dermatologists in the country, I'd say you'd been drinking.

(*The Amazing Colossal Man*, 1957)

Doc, what's wrong? Why do I keep appearing and disappearing?

(*The Amazing Transparent Man*, 1960)

We've been together the last three days. We didn't see a trace of anything unusual. Not so much as a suggestion of any form of life unknown to us.

(*Attack of the Giant Leeches*, 1959)

I loved my daughter, despite the evil in her. But she's dead six years. I don't want her back, not this way.

(*Back From the Dead*, 1957)

Decrucify the angel or I'll melt your face off.

(*Barbarella*, 1968)

Do you feel ill at ease being descended from a family of vampires?

(*The Bare Breasted Countess*, 1975)

Seldom have I seen a man more ingenious than Dr Gordon.

(*Battle Beyond the Sun*, 1963)

A date ranch in the off season is the loneliest place in the world. When you've lived through ten years of off seasons, it does things to you. Not very nice things, I'm afraid.

(*Beast with a Million Eyes*, 1958)

Oh, I've encountered her type before in my psychological studies of abnormals.

(*Before Dawn*, 1933)

Time is not affected by the laws of gravity.

(*Beyond the Time Barrier*, 1960)

Telepath: I do not trust him. Especially his thoughts.

(*ibid.*)

Whew! The speed of light! I thought ten thousand miles an hour was fast.

(*ibid.*)

Time has very little meaning here in the catalisphere.

(*ibid.*)

Jeremy, I'm going to let you into a little secret. I've trapped all my lovers' souls into these plants here.

(*Bizarre*, 1970)

Ahh, the perplexities of science!

(*Blood of Dr Jekyll*, 1980)

How often have I told you to stop that cat from desecrating my graves.

(*Bowery at Midnight*, 1972)

It's like Hallowe'en for grown-ups.

(*Close Encounters of the Third Kind*, 1977)

They run rings around us on the moon, but we're light years ahead of them on the highways.

(*ibid.*)

How would you like to wake up knowing you have parts of a cat inside your stomach?

(*Count Yorga – Vampire*, 1970)

How do you apologize to someone for killing them?

(*Creation of the Humanoids*, 1962)

Oh I know she got nailed for pushing heroin in the laundry room at boys' town, but I'm willing to give anyone the benefit of the doubt.

(*Creature from the Haunted Sea*, 1960)

We've been tricked by cleverness!

(*The Crimson Ghost*, 1946)

I'll respect you when you stop making me sick.

(*Crucible of Terror*, 1972)

To think that one man could kill so many with such single-minded cunning.

(*Curse of the Living Corpse*, 1964)

It isn't every day we make a successful landing on Mars.

(*The Day Mars Invaded Earth*, 1962)

There's no sense in getting killed by a plant.

(*Day of the Triffids*, 1963)

That necropolis is fantastic.

(*The Dead are Alive*, 1972)

If the police are not suspicious of a faggot choreographer, I wonder how they feel about a drunken archaeologist.

(*ibid.*)

He wouldn't be the first man to be driven mad by studying the processes of the mind.

(*Dead Man's Eyes*, 1944)

Blindness is a serious thing to have happen to an artist.

(*ibid.*)

Why would a soldier want to kill anybody?

(*Dead of Night*, 1974)

My taste buds got wiped out in the crash of '97.

(*Death Race 2000*, 1975)

This ghost walking is plumb mysterious.

(*Desert Phantom*, 1936)

What man would want to know the secret of enlarging bats?

(*Devil Bat's Daughter*, 1946)

Mr Armstrong'll tell you, Uncle Donald. This girl Diane is definitely a robot. And he ought to know, because he married her.

(*Dr G and the Bikini Machine*, 1966)

Lunar rays will never effect you and me, sir. We're normal people.

(*Dr X*, 1932)

Fearless Vampire hunter: . . . in this part of the country, every tomb interests me.

(*Dracula's Dog*, 1977)

Will you buy me a new frying pan? I don't feel good about cooking in the one we're using to kill people.

(*Eating Raoul*, 1982)

It's amazing when you think of the thousands of years we've wasted.

(*ibid.*)

(A pair of alien immortals have crash-landed on Earth, and been told by the natives that sex can be quite fun.)

To destroy the brain will be difficult. It's indestructible.

(*The Evil Brain From Outer Space*, 1958)

These are Marxist fanatics, not normal people.

(*Fail Safe*, 1964)

Each application of the electrical charge created a shock almost equal to electrocution. It made me ill.

(*Fiend Without a Face*, 1958)

You cannot expect to bring Earth under the control of our Supreme Dictator on Mars without taking risks.

(*Flying Disc Man From Mars*, 1951)

Yeah, the story of Hiroshima is tragic. But it's given us the opportunity to study the cellular tissues of the human body. It's ironic, but science progresses this way.

(*Frankenstein Conquers the World*, 1966)

Oh, he's eaten the cow.

(*ibid.*)

This is really something. He murdered a dog and he took it away with him. I believe he is going to eat it.

(*ibid.*)

Gamera is headed this way with a spaceship in his mouth.

(*Gamera vs. Guiron*, 1969)

What can we do with twenty million volts?

(*The Gamma People*, 1966)

Gammera doesn't mean to step on people. He's just lonely. Even turtles get lonely sometimes.

(*Gammera the Invincible*, 1966)

(Students of Japanese monster movies, and the copy editor of this book, will note that between his first appearance in *Gammera the Invincible* and his heroic follow-up in *Gamera vs. Guiron*, the giant, radioactive, flying turtle that is the hero of this series decided to drop an 'm' from his name in order to create confusion.)

Oh Godzilla, what terrible language!

(*Ghidrah the Three-Headed Monster*, 1965)

I know who to blame for human evaporation!

(*The Ghost Clipper*, 1969)

We saw the skeleton ghost . . . you know, the one from the ghost ship.

(*ibid.*)

Oh Cecily my dear, you're looking lovely, as usual. Hey, wait a minute. You're dead. You've been dead for thirty years.

(*The Ghost in the Invisible Bikini*, 1966)

What good is a brain without eyes?

(*Ghost of Frankenstein*, 1942)

We must have help, or all Japan will get trampled.

(*Godzilla vs. the Thing*, 1964)

What in hell is a million year old grizzly doing here?

(*Grizzly*, 1976)

Doctor, do you realize this could be a weapon so powerful it could conceivably banish nuclear warfare?

(*The Hand of Death*, 1961)

The hunchback will have something to say about this.

(*Hawk the Slayer*, 1982)

To mortals, I am not a pretty sight – a headless body and a bodiless head.

(*Headless Ghost*, 1959)

Is Professor Saxton's fossil still at large?

(*Horror Express*, 1972)

Werewolf . . . meet Frankenstein. Shake hands and come out snarling?

(*How to Make a Monster*, 1958)

How would you like to get a cemetery plot for a wedding gift?

(*I Bury the Living*, 1958)

I'll want you to assemble a small Synchroton, something in the 100,000 volt category.

(*I Was a Teenage Frankenstein*, 1957)

. . . and without the future, there would be no present.

(*Invasion of the Animal People*, 1960)

Hooray for the electro-barrier!

(*Invasion of the Neptune Men*, 1961)

I am using the body of this dead man so I can communicate with you.

(*Invisible Invaders*, 1959)

Dear Lord, I pray that I *am* wrong. I pray that tomorrow the sun will shine again on living things, not on a world where only the dead walk the Earth.

(*ibid.*)

In twenty-four hours, John, you might not be alive to enjoy that precious career of yours.

(*ibid.*)

There's enough radiation out there to kill you. Be careful, please.

(*ibid.*)

Major, there's your weapon. It not only makes the invaders visible, but destroys them as well.

(*ibid.*)

Look! 'e's all eaten away!

(*The Invisible Man*, 1933)

There's breathin' in me barn!

(*ibid.*)

The ultimate scientific achievement of the century has disappeared from the skies. Don't just stand there, find it!

(*It Conquered the World*, 1956)

I'm a strange guy, show me a couple of murders and I'm convinced.

(*It Lives Again*, 1978)

Mars is almost as big as Texas!

(*It! The Terror From Beyond Space*, 1958)

Janice! Look . . . I contacted the brain!

(*The Lady and the Monster*, 1943)

They're dead . . . and they're *eating* me!

(*The Living Dead at the Manchester Morgue*, 1974)

(This line comes from a British bobby, who manfully manages to get his walkie-talkie out during his big death scene in order to give his superiors the bad news.)

It's hard to know that maybe you're going to die within the hour, hard to understand. But it's got to be faced without panic. Possibly with some hope.

(*The Lost Missile*, 1958)

She'd never marry something that looked like a nightmare.

(*The Malpas Mystery*, 1960)

You know it's odd, this head living on your dead assistant's body.

(*Man Without a Body*, 1958)

He's pretty smart for a gorilla.

(*Mark of the Gorilla*, 1950)

He went for a little walk.

(*The Mummy*, 1932, **quoted in** *Mad Love*, 1935)

It's hard to imagine – carnivorous trees that walk on their roots.

(*Navy vs. the Night Monsters*, 1966)

Panic and time are inseperable, doctor.

(*The Neptune Factor*, 1973)

He did seem to be more normal, 'til we took off the chains.

(*The Oblong Box*, 1969)

Have a potato.

(*The Old Dark House*, 1932)

Have some gin, it's my only weakness.

(*ibid.*, **quoted in** *Bride of Frankenstein*, 1935)

(These lines might not read very well, but as enunciated by Ernest Thesiger, they are unforgettable.)

Why the gloom? Dad's just been acquitted of murder!

(*Phantom From 10,000 Leagues*, 1955)

(**The gloom doubtless has something to do with the mutant monster still at large.**)

So far so good, for a house with a curse on it.

(*Phantom of the Opera*, 1925)

I have brought you here, five cellars underground, because I love you.

(*ibid.*)

It's not hard to die. It's the coming back that's hard.

(*The Phantom Speaks*, 1945)

If you ask me, that beautiful mirage is a walking nightmare.

(*Pharoah's Curse*, 1957)

Are you asking me to believe that a man who's been dead three thousand years has the power to transfer his soul into the body of another human being?

(*ibid.*)

No use, Mark. You can't harm me with violence.

(*Planet of the Vampires*, 1965)

Spacewoman: It's sad Mark. Out of eighteen people, there are only three of us that are left.

(*ibid.*)

That's not snow, it's angel hair. We done died and gone to Heaven.

(*Queen of Outer Space*, 1958)

You don't just accidentally land on a planet twenty-six million miles across.

(*ibid.*)

Representative of an Extra-Terrestrial Matriarchy: We know how belligerent and quarrelsome you men are.

Macho Earthling: Why don't you girls knock off all this Gestapo stuff and try to be friendly:

(*ibid.*)

Sexist Earthling observing Venusian Death Ray: How could a bunch of women invent a gizmo like that?

(*ibid.*)

(It's only fair to point out that the writers of *Queen of Outer Space*, Ben Hecht and Charles Beaumont, knew exactly what they were doing. Sadly, few of the audience caught on, and so one of the most devastating send-ups of the cheap SF film was released as just another outer space exploitationer.)

What if Philippe does not have the mind of a human, but the hideous brain of a fly?

(*Return of the Fly*, 1959)

You're putting her in a cataleptic state. That's dangerous.

(*The She Creature*, 1956)

You wouldn't be the first man to fall in love with his own creation.

(*She Devils*, 1957)

Confrontations with evil can be dangerous.

(*Sinbad and the Eye of the Tiger*, 1977)

One doesn't easily forget an arm torn out by the roots.

(*Son of Frankenstein*, 1939)

Monsters live, saints die.

(*The Soul of a Monster*, 1944)

Do you realize that with seven shows a week and two on Friday and Saturday, I'll be biting the heads off nine snakes a week?

(*Stanley*, 1972)

Do you question the Keeper-of-the-Gifts often?

(*Teenage Cavemen*, 1958)

Ahh, the Law's strange and hard to know about.

(*ibid.*)

He looked like a man, but how do we know that he was? Evil gods take strange shapes.

(*ibid.*)

Maybe I've been seeing too much, but has it ever occurred to you that if you suddenly dropped dead, you'd be the victim of an almost perfect crime.

(*Terror From the Year 5000*, 1958)

You don't understand, officer, we are not tourists. We come from another planet. We've just saved the world.

(*The Terrornauts*, 1967)

We might become famous. Few people can boast of having lost a flying saucer and a man from Mars.

(*The Thing From Another World*, 1951)

Decadence is the mother of invention.
(*Torture Dungeon*, 1969)

It's strange, seeing that flowers weren't meant to kill.
(*Twice Told Tales*, 1963)

There are no midgets in the United States Air Force.
(*Twilight's Last Gleaming*, 1977)

Open the pod bay door, HAL.
(*2001: A Space Odyssey*, 1968)

Suppose you confess to that killing last night. You'll never be able to pick up your work here again. It's a small town. People don't forget.
(*The Vampire*, 1957)

How do you reason with a sixty-foot giant?
(*War of the Colossal Beast*, 1958)

Senator, I'm sure my son has a very good reason for paralysing the country.
(*Wild in the Streets*, 1968)

My God, it's eating the windshield.
(*Without Warning*, 1980)

Aliens ain't human.
(*ibid.*)

Look! He's a vampire. No, now he's a mummy again.
(*Wrestling Women vs. the Aztec Mummy* (1964)

Isn't it great having the only working tape deck in the world?
(*Zontar, the Thing From Venus*, 1968)

DOUBLE-ACTS

Among the great horror, fantasy and science fiction double-acts are Abbott and Costello, Dracula and Frankenstein, King Kong and Godzilla, Dr Jekyll and Mr Hyde, Batman and Robin, the Mad Scientist and his Hunchbacked Assistant, and, of course, the authors of this book. For future reference, Neil Gaiman is the one who says 'Yes Master' a lot, and slobbers.

Well-Intentioned Mad Doctor: I'll never be able to tell you how sorry I am.
Alligator Person: Don't blame yourself. I certainly don't. Who could know anything? You're not God, Mark.
Well-Intentioned Mad Scientist: I feel as if I've been playing at it, and been punished.
Alligator Person: Forget it.

(*The Alligator People*, 1959)

Upstanding Type: Don't you care what Krenner's doing to your country?
Embittered Hero: Why should I care? What did my country ever do for me but try and bury me in a concrete tomb for the rest of my life.

(*The Amazing Transparent Man*, 1960)

First Bystander: She'll tear up the whole town until she finds Harry.
Second Bystander: Yeah, then she'll tear up Harry.

(*Attack of the 50 Foot Woman*, 1958)

Concerned Type: What's the matter, Larry? What happened to you?
Battered Type: That looney of yours has gone mad.

(*Beast With a Million Eyes*, 1955)

Official: Mr Lacombe is the highest authority.
No-Nonsense Hero: He isn't even American.

(*Close Encounters of the Third Kind*, 1978)

Official: On Earth, there are forces of Good and Evil, and we are the forces of Good.
Alien: I'm not interested in such foolishness.

(*The Day the Earth Stood Still*, 1951)

Magistrate: He tried to kill me!
Jailer: I warned you. Murderers – they're all the same. Humanity is much better off without them.

(*Diary of a Madman*, 1963)

Official: You were right. Definitely a vampire tomb.
Professor: I know these villagers. If word of this gets around, the whole country will be terrorized.

(*Dracula's Dog*, 1977)

Alien Princess: Father, Captain Lithin has reported that our radar has picked up an unidentified spaceship that shouldn't be in our galaxy.
Alien King: I feared this.

(*Escape From Galaxy 3*, 1982)

Good Guy: Oraclon, powerful king of the night, I am ready to give myself up to you.
Bad Guy: A very wise decision, you have no other choice.

(*ibid.*)

First Alien: What is that stuff?
Second Alien: It's water. I once saw it in my father's collection of intergalactic minerals.

(*ibid.*)

Heroine: Francois, I've killed André. I need your help.
Brother-in-Law: Oh, now look, Helene, it's past midnight. I've had a hard day.

(*The Fly*, 1958)

Doc: Some of our strongest cultures were based on the taking of heads.
Cop: But there are better ways to kill somebody than hacking off his head.

(*The Four Skulls of Jonathan Drake*, 1959)

Reporter: They feel they have to become adults quickly. They're not sure there'll be a tomorrow.
Adult: That's a depressing thought.

(*Ghost of Dragstrip Hollow*, 1959)

Mortal: I guess even a ghost's life isn't all it's cracked up to be.
Ghost: You try it for six or seven hundred years, gliding about waiting for strangers or adventurers to save your soul, and put your head back on your own shoulders.

(*Headless Ghost*, 1960)

Aristocrat: This food is revolting, Alys.
Maidservant: They're hanging your cook tomorrow, remember.

(*Horror of Frankenstein*, 1970)

Establishment Scientist: Professor Frankenstein, how can you ask us to believe such a preposterous theory?
Mad Scientist: You cling to your scepticism . . . I'll hold to my beliefs.

(*I Was a Teenage Frankenstein*, 1957)

Mad Scientist: You're standing in the way of progress.

Sane Scientist: Progress? You call it progress to hurl the human race back to its savage beginnings?

(*I was a Teenage Werewolf*, 1957)

Alien Invader: More then seven thousand years ago, my planet invaded the moon and destroyed the life that existed there. We have controlled the moon since then and made it an impregnable base for our spaceship.
Earthling: We'd have seen signs of life there!
Alien Invader: You would see nothing . . . we are invisible.

(*Invisible Invaders*, 1958)

Distressed Citizen: Officer, my husband. He's in an iron lung. It stopped!
Harassed Cop: Then what are you doing out here? Get back inside and operate it manually.

(*It Conquered the World*, 1956)

Voodoo Priestess: A reptile is a holy thing.
Ordinary Joe: Not where I come from.

(*Macumba Love*, 1960)

Establishment Scientist: I suppose you have some scientific proof for your egotistic theory, professor?
Mad Scientist: No, merely an awareness of the comic-strip mentality which now debates with me.

(*The Neanderthal Man*, 1953)

Minor Villain: I'm a lawyer, not a businessman.
Major Villain: You're a forger and an embezzler, and now you're going to become a bodysnatcher.

(*The Oblong Box*, 1969)

Mad Scientist: Knowledge sometimes has steel jaws . . . like a trap . . . and it can destroy either the hunter or the hunted.

Mad Scientist's Beautiful (but dumb) Daughter: You frighten me when you talk like that.

(*Phantom From 10,000 Leagues*, 1955)

Fat Transvestite: Someone has sent me a bowel movement.
Loyal Son: Momma, no one sends you a turd and expects to live.

(*Pink Flamingoes*, 1973)

Vampish Villainess: You refuse me?
Hero: What can you expect? Your heartless cruelty is sickening.
Vampish Villainess: You would have me otherwise?

(*Prehistoric Women*, 1968)

Space Psycho: You have a beautiful body, may I use it?
Satellite Sweetie: No.
Space Psycho: That would be considered penally unsocial back on Earth.

(*Saturn 3*, 1980)

Hardboiled Hero: It's not wise to upset a wookiee.
Pain-in-the-ass Comic Relief Robot: Nobody minds about upsetting a 'droid.
Hardboiled Hero: That's because 'droids aren't liable to tear people's arms out of their sockets.

(*Star Wars*, 1977)

First Occultist: So you've come back, eh? After seven years, you've come back.
Second Occultist: Time has little meaning in Tibet.

(*The Undead*, 1956)

Doc: Blood? That's a strange request.
Vampire: I'm a strange man.

(*Valley of the Zombies*, 1946)

Heroine: If I stay here, he'll kill me. You can help if you want to.
Native servant: I know I help. I bring you cup nice hot tea.

(*Voodoo Woman*, 1957)

Sleuth: The foot that made the print is about ten times the size of a normal man's. That would make him about sixty feet tall.
Grieving Relative: Glen was sixty feet tall!

(*War of the Colossal Beast*, 1958)

Awestruck Tourist: They're . . . floating!
Smug Atlantean: Levitation is not so difficult.

(*Warlords of Atlantis*, 1978)

Heroine: Beautiful, isn't it?
Hero: In its own alien way, I guess it is. It's another world all right.

(*The Wizard of Mars*, 1964)

Countdown

'NOTHING CAN STOP IT, EXCEPT. . .'

In order to make room for a Happy Ending, the unkillable monster has to be killed. In a big budget film, this can involve spectacularly destructive weapons developed in a race against time by a hard-working scientist, his beautiful daughter, and a handsome lab assistant. In a low budget film, something as simple as a blowtorch (*It Conquered the World*) or hot-rod headlights (*Invasion of the Saucer Men*) will see the monsters off. Also popular are those God-given natural weaknesses, like the vulnerability of the monsters to sea water (*Day of the Triffids*), germs (*War of the Worlds*), or rock music (*Attack of the Killer Tomatoes*), which can be usefully exploited to get Our Side off the hook in the last reel.

First Scientist: I wonder. If we introduced, say, ten centigrams of pure radium into this disingtegrating mass . . . wouldn't it precipitate the process, destroy the creature, burn it up from inside?
Second Scientist: Yes, that's quite possible.

(*Behemoth the Sea Monster*, 1959)

First Scientist: First things first. We've gotta find some way to kill that monster.

Second Scientist: We could shower it with neutrons . . .
First Scientist: A neutron instigator! It just might work!

(*The Giant Spider Invasion*, 1975)

Tanamura: Junka, what's going on?
Junka: We're discussing what to do with Godzilla.
Tanamura: There is the Thing. It might defeat Godzilla.
Masuta: That's silly . . . wait, go on . . .
Tanamura: My idea is to ask it for assistance against Godzilla.
Masuta: That's it! You're a genius!
Tanamura: That's what I think. Do you think I should get a raise?

(*Godzilla vs. the Thing*, 1964)

Scientist: The sound is low key to our ears, but the device must have used sonic rays, sound vibrations that created resonance on the basic molecular structure of the metal ore and that resonance caused *visibility*.
Soldier: Sounds good, I just hope it's not too late.

(*Invisible Invaders*, 1959)

Grenades, gas and bullets have failed to stop the beast, but perhaps it can be electrocuted. There's enough voltage in these lines to kill three human beings. The only drawback is, the thing isn't human.

(*It! The Terror From Beyond Space*, 1958)

Maybe bullets and electricity won't stop him, but gas might.

(*The Most Dangerous Man Alive*, 1961)

My contention is that in an obvious case of devil possession, we should try exorcism.

(*Naked Exorcism*, 1975)

Minion: Nothing seems to hurt it!
Hero: What do you do with a vegetable?
Heroine: Boil it! Boil it, stew it, bake it, fry it.

(*The Thing From Another World*, 1951)

EPITAPHS

Hard-Bitten Hero, as Villain falls in a trash grinder: He died a fitting death for the garbage he was.

(*Blood Feast*, 1964)

Telepathic Dog to Hero, after they have eaten Heroine: She certainly had marvellous judgement, if not particularly good taste.

(*A Boy and His Dog*, 1975)

Suicidal Monster: We belong dead.

(*Bride of Frankenstein*, 1935)

Hero, of Recently Dead Mad Doctor: He tampered in God's domain.

(*Bride of the Monster*, 1955)

Hard-Bitten Hero, gunning down unarmed psycho: Adios, Creep!

(*Don't Answer the Phone*, 1979)

Dr Van Helsing, on Lady Vampire: She was beautiful when she died, one hundred years ago.

(*Dracula's Daughter, 1936*)

Man-Headed Fly: Help meeeee!

(*The Fly*, 1958)

Horrified Heroine: Was he the bogey man?
Loopy Psychiatrist: As a matter of fact, he was.

(*Halloweeen*, 1978)

Little Girl: He was quite a nice monster really.

(*Horror of Frankenstein*, 1970)

Showman, of Giant Gorilla: It wasn't the airplanes, 'twas beauty killed the beast.

(*King Kong*, 1933)

Hero, of Human Frog: For over two centuries, he endured the torment of knowing he was a monster and feeling he was a man.

(*The Maze*, 1953)

Hero: For months, Professor Graves was labouring to perfect his discovery. He experimented on himself. Here lies the result. We mustn't think of him too harshly. The things he did, and they were terrible, all of us are capable of doing when we give free play to the baseness which is part of everyone. He tampered with things beyond his province, beyond that which man should do, and if it was madness, well, those whom the gods destroy, then, they first make mad.
Philosophical Professor: It is better this way.

(*The Neanderthal Man*, 1953)

Dead Doctor's Daughter: If only I'd known in time, perhaps I could have stopped him. I knew he meant this power to be used to help humanity . . . not destroy it.
Hero: I'm sure he did, and he paid for his mistake. Nature has many secrets that man mustn't disturb . . . and this is one of them.

(*Phantom From 10,000 Leagues*, 1955)

Old Gypsy Woman: The way you walk is thorny through no fault of your own. For as the rain enters the soil, and evil enters the sea, so tears run to their predestined end. Your suffering is over. Now find peace for eternity, my son.

(*The Wolf Man*, 1941)

THE END

Pragmatic Heroine: Allen, what killed the creature in the ship?
Philosophical Hero: Where did the eagle come from? Why do men have souls?
Pragmatic Heroine, catching on: If I could answer that I'd be more than human, I'd be . . .
Philosophical Hero, *looking skyward*: . . . yes.

(*Beast With a Million Eyes*, 1958)

Cop: He's dissolving! He's turning to powder!
Heroine: Paul?
Hero: It's all right, honey. Everything's okay now.
Heroine: What are we doing on the beach?
Hero: You mean you don't know why you're here?
Heroine: I can't seem to remember anything.
Hero: Ahh . . . just as well. Let's go home, honey.
Stentorian Narrator: The strange narrative of Quintillus Aurelius ended here, in the quiet waters of the Bay of Naples. The story is finished and perhaps Quintillus Aurelius has found the true Lucilla Helena, where mortal men don't walk and time is eternal . . .

(*Curse of the Faceless Man*, 1958)

Heroine: Russ, will they ever come back?
Hero: Not on such a pretty day, and to such a pretty world.

(*Earth vs. the Flying Saucer*, 1956)

Narrator: Scientists say that beyond the Earth, the perfect vacuum exists. Poets say there is eternal night. Dreamers say there is life. Perhaps tomorrow, we should know the answer . . .

(*The Flame Barrier*, 1957)

I was continuing to shrink, to become . . . what? . . . the Infinitesimal? What was I? Still a human being? Or was I the Man of the Future? If there were other clouds of radiation, other clouds drifting across seas and continents, would other beings follow me into this vast new world? So close, the Infinitesimal and the Infinite. But I suddenly knew they were really the two ends of the same concept. The unbelievably small and the unbelievably vast eventually meet, like the closing of a gigantic circle. I looked up, as if somehow I would grasp the heavens, the Universe, worlds without number, God's silver tapestry spread across the night, and in that moment I knew the answer to the riddle of the Infinite. I had thought in terms of Man's own limited dimension. I had presumed upon Nature. That Existence begins and ends, is Man's conception, not Nature's. And I felt my body dwindling, melting, becoming nothing. My fears melted away, and in their place came . . . Acceptance. All this vast majesty of creation, it had to mean something, and then I meant something, too. Yes, smaller than the smallest, I meant something, too. To God there is no zero. I still exist.

(*The Incredible Shrinking Man*,
script by Richard Matheson, 1957)

Cop: We know as little as we did a month ago, and we understand less. Something has died, someone has lived . . . but why? What has really happened? What have we accomplished?

Hero: That's your question, not mine.

(*Macumba Love*, 1960)

Homicidal Maniac, to Audience: Please don't reveal the ending, or I'll tear you limb from limb.

(*Night of Terror*, 1933)

Narrator: My friends, you have seen this incident based on sworn testimony. Can you prove that it didn't happen? Perhaps on your way home someone will pass you in the dark and you will never know it because they will be from outer space! Many scientists believe that another world is watching us at this moment. We once laughed at the horseless carriage, the telephone, electric light, vitamins, radio, and even television. And even some of us laugh at outer space! *God help us in the future . . .*

(*Plan Nine From Outer Space*, 1956)

He forced her to come out of her will. He should have left her alone. There are a lot of dark corners we weren't meant to pry into, I guess.

(*The She Creature*, 1956)

Fatherly Old Scientist: She was meant to die, but we wouldn't accept the fate that had been decreed for her, as though she was dutied to die.

Heroic Young Scientist: As doctors, it was our duty to save her.

Fatherly Old Scientist: So it was. So we thought. But we pitted our puny powers against the Supernatural Power that had marked Kyra Zelas for death and we won . . . or did we win? Did we save the life of a human being? Or did we perhaps only create an *inhuman* being. An inhuman being that had no place in the human world, who exists only by destroying everybody human that it encounters in its struggle for survival . . . Whether she is to live a normal life again will not be decided by science, Dan, not even by

nature, but by a far greater and higher power. (**She dies.**) It is best this way, Dan. You know that.
Heroic Young Scientist: She was so beautiful.

(*She Devil*, 1957)

Ace Newshound: . . . one of the world's greatest battles was won today by the human race. A handful of men met the first invasion from another planet. Noah once saved our world with an Ark of wood, here at the north pole it was done with an arc of electricity . . . I bring you a warning . . . tell the world . . . tell this to everybody wherever they are . . . watch the skies! *Keep watching the skies*!

(*The Thing From Another World*, 1951)

Long live the New Flesh!

(*Videodrome*, 1982)

Dissatisfied Youth: We're gonna put everybody over ten out of business.

(*Wild in the Streets*, 1968)

(**The film is about the take-over of the U.S.A. by the under-thirty generation. A pop singer becomes President and has his mother put in a concentration camp where she is force-fed LSD. In a chilling finale, the under-tens become restless with the new oppression.**)

Radio announcer: The zombies are at the door . . . they're coming in . . . aargh!

(*Zombie Flesh Eaters*, 1980)

End Titles

Some films just aren't content to go out with a dignified 'The End' title, and feel that their way-out subject matter warrants some variation on the formula.

IS THIS THE END?
(*Curse of the Fly*, 1965)

THIS IS THE END OF THE BEGINNING
(*Destination Moon*, 1950)

THE ENDEST, MAN
(*The Ghost of Dragstrip Hollow, 1959)*

The End. OR IS IT?
(Grave of the Vampire, 1972)

THERE MUST BE NO END – ONLY A NEW BEGINNING.
(*Panic in the Year Zero*, 1962)

THIS MAY NOT BE THE END.
(*Voodoo Woman*, 1957)

'HOORAY FOR HOLLYWOOD'

THE MEN (AND WOMEN) WHO MAKE THE MOVIES

'What we're trying to do here,' **claims Erich von Leppe (Paul Bartel), the skid-row SF film director in Joe Dante and Allan Arkush's lovably cheapskate in-joke *Hollywood Boulevard* (1976) when quizzed on the set of *Atomic War Brides* by an earnest reporter,** 'is combine the legend of Romeo and Juliet with high-speed car action and a sincere plea for international atomic controls in our time.' **Von Leppe then takes time off from impressing the public with his artistic integrity, and instructs a Godzilla-suited extra to** 'step on as many people as possible'. **It is this mixture of art, pretension, humour and lurid glee that makes Hollywood's horror and fantasy film-makers such an entertaining lot.**

DARIO ARGENTO

'I like women, especially beautiful ones. If they have a good face and figure, I would much prefer to watch them being murdered than an ugly girl or man. I certainly don't have to justify myself to anyone about this. I don't care what anybody thinks or reads into it. I have often had journalists walk out of interviews when I say what I feel about this subject.'

ISAAC ASIMOV

The noted SF author has stayed away from the cinema, although he did deign to write a novelization of *Fantastic Voyage* (1966), the story of a miniaturized submarine exploring the human body. Asimov recounts the difficulty his daughter Robyn had with the film's ending, in which the crew escape from the body before they resume their original sizes, leaving the submarine inside the test subject.

' "Won't the ship now expand and kill the man, Daddy?"

' "Yes, Robyn," I explained, "but you see that because you're smarter than the average Hollywood producer. After all, you're eleven." '

JOHN BOORMAN

In explaining the commercial failure of *Exorcist II: The Heretic* (1978), the ambitious, uneven, highly mystical sequel to the 1973 violence-filled crowd-pleaser, *The Exorcist*, Boorman summed up the appeal of too many horror films with 'I guess I didn't throw enough Christians to the lions.'

Herman Cohen

Interviewer: 'Why, in *Konga* (1960), did you have the girl eaten by the plants when she had done nothing to make the audience relish such a grisly death?'

Producer Cohen: 'I wanted to use my carnivorous plants. She was a very pretty girl, and very sexy, and I thought the audience would get a big kick out of seeing her killed rather than Michael Gough.'

Roger Corman

'We live in a compromised society, and I would think of myself as something of a compromised artist.'

On *It Conquered the World* (1956), he learned an important lesson while designing the monster that would later be described by Frank Zappa as 'an upended ice-cream cone with teeth'. **Corman's reasoning was that a creature from Venus, which has a higher gravity than Earth, would be short and squat.**

Corman: 'The first day we were shooting, Beverly Garland, the leading lady, went over and looked at the creature. Standing *over* it, she said, "So you've come to conquer the world, eh? Take that!" and she kicked it . . . I had discovered a general axiom for science fiction films. In movies, *the monster should always be bigger than the leading lady*!'

Francis Ford Coppola's first job for Corman was to supervise the dubbing of *Battle Beyond the Sun* (1962), a propagandist Soviet outer space epic, into English.

Coppola: 'We were watching this film together and, at one point, a Russian astronaut saw what was presumably a symbol of hope, a golden astronaut standing on a hilltop holding a flare. It was lovely. Then Roger leaned over to me and said "We've got to put two monsters up on that hill". And we did.'

Despite hs insistence on monsters rather than symbols, Corman generally lets his dicoveries make the films they want to, within certain limits.

Interviewer: 'Did Corman have any direct influence on *Piranha* (1978)?'

Producer Jon Davison: 'Yeah, he cut the budget two hundred thousand dollars.'

Interviewer: 'Artistically speaking, that is . . .'

Davison: 'Yeah, he cut the budget two hundred thousand dollars.'

LUIGI COZZI

'In Italy, when you bring a script to a producer, the first question he asks is not "what is your film like?" but "what *film* is your film like?" That's the way it is, we can only make *Zombie 2*, never *Zombie 1*.'

DAVID CRONENBERG

The Canadian writer/director is one of the very few SF/horror screenwriters to have developed a recognizable dialogue style:

'Sex is the invention of a clever veneral disease.'

(**Sign in** *Shivers*, 1975)

'I don't want to become the Colonel Sanders of plastic surgery.'

(**Dr Dan Keloid in** *Rabid*, 1976)

'Thirty seconds after you're born, you have a past; sixty seconds after, you start lying to yourself about it.'

(**Juliana Kelly in** *The Brood*, 1979)

Cameron Vale: 'I'm one of you.'
Ben Pierce: 'You're one of *me*?'

(*Scanners*, 1980)

'The battle for the mind of North America will be fought in the video arena, the Videodrome. The television screen is the retina of the mind's eye. Therefore the television screen is part of the physical structure of the brain. Therefore whatever appears on the television screen emerges as raw experience for those who watch it. Therefore television is reality, and reality is less than television.'

(**Dr Brian O'Blivion, in** *Videodrome*, 1982)

Although Cronenberg's favourite on-set declaration is apparently 'More blood! More blood!', he has proved as pointed and articulate as his characters.

'Seeing a horror film is like thinking of voting for Goldwater. It's something you want to see or do up on the screen where it's not irrevocable.'

'Sex and violence are very interesting, don't you think?'

'I'm not particularly insecure or paranoid, but I understand it very well. I always thought that I could much more likely be put in jail for my art than my Jewishness.'

On the cheeriness of *Scanners* when compared with the downbeat finish of *The Brood*: 'I'm feeling much more optimistic about things in general. Now that I'm feeling so good, I'm exploding heads, just like any other young, normal North American boy.'

On being called 'the King of Venereal Horror': 'It's a small field, Venereal Horror, but at least I'm king of it.'

CARRIE FISHER

Obviously interviewed to death during the hyping of *Star Wars* (1977), the actress was heard to declare, 'I want to be the next Peter Lorre!'

LUCIO FULCI

'Violence is Italian art. I find a lot of what I film repugnant to me, but it has to be done. The scene where the girl vomits out all her intestines and guts was very important – and was insisted upon by my co-writer – as it is the first time we see the evil priest and what he can do.'

BEVERLY GARLAND

The intrepid heroine who stopped *It* from *Conquering the Earth*, and also revealed her gutsiness in *Curcucu, Beast of the Amazon* (1956), *Not of this Earth* (1956), and *The Alligator People (1959)*,summed up her contribution to these Z-features. 'You don't have to act. All you have to do is possess a good pair of lungs. I can scream with more variations from shrill to vibrato than any other girl in pictures.'

HARRY HARRISON

'Charlton Heston for five years wanted to do *Make Room, Make Room* as a film. MGM said, "Aw, no. What's important about overpopulation? No one cares about overpopulation. That's not interesting. Can't do it." So they got a screenwriter, and he said: "The world doesn't care about overpopulation so, what we'll do, we'll bring in cannibalism. They'll eat that up, you know!" So MGM did *Soylent Green* (1973) because they thought they were doing a cannibalism picture!'

ROBERT A. HEINLEIN

Interviewer: 'In presenting speculative situations, does the film enjoy any advantage which you, as a writer, might envy?'

Heinlein: 'Yes, pictorial.'

Interviewer: 'Does the film have any disadvantages which you are glad to be without?'

Heinlein: 'Working in Hollywood.'

FRANK HENENLOTTER

Describing the stop-motion effects in his sleaze classic *Basket Case* (1982): 'Crude? Rather than putting in a credit for special effects, we were thinking of crediting *ordinary* effects.'

ALFRED HITCHCOCK

'Some films are slices of life, mine are slices of cake.'

'Always make the audience suffer as much as possible.'

BORIS KARLOFF

'When I was offered the part of the Monster in *Frankenstein* I knew that I'd found it at last. The part was what we call a *natural*. Any actor who played it was destined for success.'

'The Monster was the best friend I ever had.'

'Between horror characterizations I should like to be more of a human being. After all, you know, I am human and I would like the public to think of me in that light occasionally.'

Best known for his speechless role as the Frankenstein Monster, Karloff found a catch-phrase in the stage production of *Arsenic and Old Lace*, in which he admits to killing someone because 'he said I looked like Boris Karloff!'

JOHN LANDIS

On the plot of *Alien* (1979): 'There's an alien monster aboard the spaceship. No one's safe. Excuse me, I'm just going into this dark room by myself.'

Sticker on the cover of his original screen-play for *An American Werewolf in London*: 'You will personally be held responsible for the confidentiality of this screen-play. Violators will be killed.'

HERSCHELL GORDON LEWIS

'*Blood Feast* (1963) I've often referred to as a Walt Whitman poem – it's no good, but it's the first of its type and therefore deserves a certain position.'

'We still have the old-fashioned Victorian morality in our films. In *The Gore Gore Girls* (1972), the maniac pulls the eyeball out of a girl's head and *squeezes*. And you see the knuckles tighten, and you see this eyeball all the time. And finally it bursts, and this inky black glop squirts out all over the place. I have seen people faint, vomit, turn green, leave the auditorium, and go to the washroom because of that scene.'

On being told that *Cahiers du Cinema* classify him as 'a subject for further research': 'Well, they also say that about cancer.'

In conversation with John Waters, director of the infamous doggy-doo-eating scene in *Pink Flamingoes* (1973): 'The difference (between us) is that, in your films people eat defecation; in mine the audience is simply exposed to it.'

PETER LORRE

Fan letter: 'Dear Master: I would love to be tortured by you . . .'

Lorre's reply: 'You have been tortured enough by going to see my pictures.'

In answer to a personal communique from Adolf Hitler in which the Führer expressed admiration for Lorre's role as the child-killer in *M* (1939) and offered the actor a place in the German film industry: 'Thank you, but I think Germany has room for only one mass murderer of my ability and yours.'

JOHN MILIUS

'In *Star Wars*, the rebels are unequivocally good, the Force is better; The Empire is the bad guy. Why? Because the history books tell us that empires are bad, and that the rebels are the freedom fighters. But what are they rebelling against? We don't know anything. We assume everything. Whereas if I were *in Star Wars* I'd definitely want to be working for Darth Vader. I'd much rather be on *his* side.'

VINCENT PRICE

'There's a difference between horror and terror pictures. A horror picture depicts real problems as they exist today. They frighten you because you think the situation could involve you. Terror movies are make-believe. A hand comes out of nowhere. It's contrived to make you scared, just as comedy is contrived to make you laugh.'

'I'm always evil in a keen, clean way which makes me good in terms of an inverted aestheticism. Pure evil, as much as pure good, is poetic.'

'The cinemas have bred a new race of giant popcorn-eating rats.'

'They'd have to bury me before I retire, and even then my tombstone will read "I'll be back!" '

A favourite moment of Price villainy, from the *Batman* TV series. As Egghead, he has kidnapped the four most likely suspects, and strapped them into his combination electro-encephelograph/hairdryer in order once and for

all to reveal the caped crusader's secret identity. He explains how the machine works: 'If you're Batman, the little light will go on. If not, your head will explode!'

VINCENT PRICE/MICHAEL REEVES

On the set of *Witchfinder General* (1968), the star became irritated with his young director's insistence that the horror be played straight, and ventured to question Reeves' instructions.

Price, casting a withering glance at the twenty-four-year-old director, said, 'I've made seventy-four films, what have you done?'

Reeves replied, 'I've made three good ones.'

GEORGE A. ROMERO

On the popularity of explicitly violent 'splatter' movies: 'I find it interesting that my films, and Tobe Hooper's and Wes Craven's, have been championed by the generation that refused to go to war.'

BARBARA STEELE

On her decision to stop making Italian gothic horror movies: 'I never want to climb out of another fucking coffin again.'

HOWARD VERNON

A distinguished French character actor, also a familiar face from lurid sex-horror films like *Dracula contra el Dr Frankenstein* (1972), Vernon summed up the position of all name players in dire movies: 'I am not a modest or moral individual . . . I act without distaste or conviction.'

KURT VONNEGUT JR

'Every time a motion picture company buys a book they get cheated. There is no way an author cannot cheat them. There's always one character missing . . . the author. And the book is what it is because the author's there.'

JOHN WATERS

In *Pink Flamingoes*, Waters has his hero/heroine Divine exclaim 'Filth are my politics. Killing and blood make me *come*.' **In *Shock Value*, his autobiography, the auteur of *Multiple Maniacs*** (1979), ***Mondo Trasho*** (1969) **and *Female Trouble*** (1974), **writes** 'I pride myself on the fact that my work has no socially redeeming value.'

Justifying the sequence in *Pink Flamingoes* in which Divine eats dog excrement live on camera, Waters explains: 'I had ten thousand dollars to make a film. I had to compete with *Shampoo* (1975) and the big Hollywood films . . . I had to go out on a limb. I had to do something that people might not like, but they wouldn't ever be able to forget.'

'To me, bad taste is what entertainment is all about. If someone vomits watching one of my films; it's like getting a standing ovation. But one must remember that there is such a thing as good bad taste and bad bad taste.'

If you've been convinced that the people who make these films are completely loopy, consider now the people who pay time and again to watch them.

Stephen King: '*Prophecy* (1979) was a turkey, but I saw it three times. If you love horror movies, you've got to have a love for pure *shit*. You turn into the kind of person who would watch *Attack of the Crab Monsters* (1957) four times. You know how shitty it is, but there's something that appeals to you. It doesn't mean you don't want to do better.'

But for an insight into the diehard fan, ponder this red-inked letter that critic John Brosnan received after he confessed in the pages of *Starburst* that he was mildly dissatisfied with *The Empire Strikes Back* (1980): 'Brosnan (the thing), My friend and I are both friends of Yoda (not like you). We want you in a pill so we can flush you down the loo . . . We think Yoda's wise talk is very good even if you don't. And there are other things too, firstly Yoda is better looking than you (then again a Wookie is better looking than you) and secondly he doesn't turn up his nose at every film that comes his way . . . lots of spit on your jacket – Yoda's Best Fans.'

Just Testing

CATCH-PHRASES

Although catch-phrases might seem to be the prerogative of comedians, quite a number of zippy little expressions have become common usage in the SF and fantasy community. Can you identify the films, books, TV shows, songs, characters or institutions connected with the following:

1. 'The world has not heard the last of— ——!'
2. 'Exterminate!'
3. 'I do not grok.'
4. *See You Next Wednesday.*
5. 'I think we're property.'
6. 'Heeeeere's Johnny!'
7. 'You Need a Thneed!'
8. 'QX!'
9. 'Shoot 'em in the brain!'
10. '*Now* there is a God!'
11. 'It's clobberin' time!'
12. 'Tanstaafl!'
13. 'Klaatu barada nikto!'
14. 'I was the victim of a series of accidents, as are we all.'
15. 'More blood! More blood.'
16. 'Ground Control to Major Tom.'
17. '. . . for cats who like people!'
18. *Ph'nglui mglw'nafh Cthulhu R'lyeh fthagn.*

19. 'Mind the doors!'
20. Here is the race that shall rule the Sevagram.
21. 'You wouldn't like me when I'm angry.'
22. 'Look! Up in the skies! It's a bird, it's a plane, it's ——!'
23. 'Us needs you 'cause you're Younique.'
24. 'God told me to.'
25. Life, the Universe and Everything.
26. 'Don't dream it, be it!'
27. 'Feeed mee!'
28. 'You're all doomed! Doomed!'
29. 'The dilithium crystals canna take it, captain.'
30. 'Gobble gobble, one of us. We accept her, one of us.'
31. '— ——, we're needed.'
32. 'Was and will make me ill. I take a gramme and only am.'
33. 'May the Force be with you.'
34. 'By the hoary hosts of Hoggoth!'
35. 'Open Channel D.'
36. 'Who knows what evil lurks in the hearts of man?'
37. 'Do you want to see something *really* scary?'
38. 'We are the dead.'
39. 'I am not a number, I am a free man!'
40. '. . . calling International Rescue . . .'
41. E.T. Phone Home

CATCH-PHRASE ANSWERS

1. Fu Manchu, as played by Christopher Lee in a series of films, from fairly decent Don Sharp's *The Face of Fu Manchu* (1965) to Jesus Franco's atrocious *Castle of Fu Manchu* (1970). The finale would always find the insidious doctor's current hide-out exploding, while Lee's disembodied, superimposed head intoned the threat from beneath his absurd moustache. The original

version, spoken by Warner Oland in *The Mysterious Dr Fu Manchu* (1929) is more picturesque: 'When the moonbeam touches the dragon, I shall return!'

2. While *Dr Who,* in his various regenerations, has failed to come up with much that is quotable, his arch-enemies, the Daleks, did bequeath this mechanical-croak to successive generations of stiff-armed children with cardboard boxes over their heads. The tin cans from Skaro were also prone to say things like 'What-are-your-orders?' 'I-obey', and 'You-will-all-be-killed!' They may be the only alien race to receive, when their adventures were chronicled in the sorely-missed *TV 21* comic, their own type-face.

3. Uttered by Valentine Michael Smith in Robert A. Heinlein's *Stranger In A Strange Land.* To grok something is to understand it completely and all-embracingly, as in 'All the grokking world was enchanting and he wanted to drink so deep that his own grokking would be perfect.' *Stranger* also provided the pseudo-religious phrase 'Thou Art God,' and, with its philosophy of ritual cannibalism and 'water-sharing' ceremonies, a certain amount of the philosophy for Charles Manson's 'family'.

4. This may not sound like the snappiest line from *2001: A Space Odyssey* (1968), but it evidently caught the imagination of John Landis, who has worked references to a mythical film of this name into most of his own movies – memorably as the grotty British skinflick watched by an assortment of lycanthropes and zombies in the climax of *An American Werewolf in Paris* (1981).

5. Originated by Charles Fort, 'Prophet of the Unexplained', and quoted by Eric Frank Russell in his *Sinister Barrier.* A theory that human beings are actually the

property (like cows or sheep) of some super-powerful aliens, and used as the rationale of a number of subsequent SF stories by various authors.

6. Ed McMahon's introduction for Johnny Carson on *The Tonight Show*, of course, put to horrific use by Jack Nicholson and Stanley Kubrik in *The Shining* (1980).

7. The advertising slogan, coined by Dr Seuss, that nearly leads to the end of the world in the cartoon *How the Lorax Was Lifted.*

8. 'QX!' is E. E. 'Doc' Smith's future slang for 'OK' in his star-spanning *Lensman* series. As in 'QX Chris? *Really* QX?'

9. The policy of Sheriff McGowan and his posse, when faced with the flesh-eating ghouls of *Night of the Living Dead* (1968).

10. The punchline to a Fredric Brown short-short story, *Answer*, concerning the creation of a super computer. In context the quote reads:

> He turned to face the machine. 'Is there a God?'
> The mighty voice answered without hesitation, without the clicking of a single relay.
> 'Yes, *now* there is a God!'

Much quoted, but seldom attributed, unless occasionally to Isaac Asimov.

11. The battle cry of Benjamin Grimm, alias The Thing, in *The Fantastic Four* comics.

12. The rallying cry of Robert A. Heinlein's revolutionaries in *The Moon is a Harsh Mistress*. An acronym for 'There ain't no such thing as a free lunch.'

13. The instructions passed to the robot Gort by Klaatu the alien (Michael Rennie) via heroine Patricia Neal in *The Day the Earth Stood Still* (1952). Quoted by a lunatic schoolmaster in Mario Bellochio's *Nel Nome del Padre/In the Name of the Father* (1974).

14. Malachi Constant's first words upon returning to Earth in Kurt Vonnegut Jr's book *The Sirens of Titan.* Later used as a chorus to a song based on the book by English folk-rock singer Al Stewart. Other Vonnegut catch-phrases include 'So it goes' from *Slaughterhouse 5* and the irrtating 'Hi ho' in *Slapstick*.

15. Anyone who has seen one of David Cronenberg's movies – *Shivers* (1975), *Rabid* (1976), *The Brood* (1979), *Scanners* (1980) – will appreciate that the Canadian horror movie *auteur* says this a lot. During one particularly gruesome sequence in *Videodrome* (1982), he was heard to be experimenting with a new line, 'More cancer! More cancer!', but he was back on familiar territory with the scissors suicide scene in *The Dead Zone* (1983).

16. First line of David Bowie's first hit, 'Space Oddity', the story of an astronaut – Major Tom – who goes up and doesn't come down. Released in the aftermath of a Kubrick film with a similar title, it was re-released in 1977 and was a hit once more. A much-parodied song; the catch-phrase was also used by Fiona Richmond, in her sex-spoof SF *Galactic Girl.*

17. The unforgettable slogan of the unscrupulous catfood company who give household pets unsavoury tastes by recycling skid-row winos in the incredibly sleazy *The Corpse Grinders* (1971).

18. This would be a catch-phrase if anyone could say it. Introduced by H. P. Lovecraft in his short story *The*

Call of Cthulhu it translates as 'In his house at R'lyeh dead Cthulhu waits dreaming.' Subsequently used by innumerable 'Cthulhu mythos' writers as proof that they had read H. P. Lovecraft.

19. The only phrase that the subhuman cannibal (Hugh Armstrong) who roams the London underground in *Death Line* (1972, aka *Raw Meat*) is capable of uttering.

20. Last line of A. E. Van Vogt's *The Weapon Makers*. All the more mysterious for it being the first time that the Sevagram is mentioned, leaving readers either imbued with a sense of wonder, or, puzzled, to flip back through the book to see if two pages were stuck together somewhere.

21. Troubled scientist David Banner (Bill Bixby) trying to get pesky reporter Muckraking McGee (Jack Colvin) off his back before he turns into the jolly green giant (Lou Ferrigno) in the credit sequence of television's *The Incredible Hulk*.

22. Superman, of course. But this line, which served as the title of a Broadway musical *(It's a bird! It's a plane! It's Superman*!), originates not in the pages of *Action Comics* but in an American radio serial. Likewise, the Man of Steel's favourite exit line, 'Up, up, and away!'

23. Catch-phrase in Rudy Rucker's novel *Spacetime Donuts*. 'Us' is the new term for America, and the catch-phrase is a meaningless piece of government propaganda, in a book about the ultimate welfare state.

24. The excuse given to hard-bitten NY cop Tony LoBianco by various mass murderers in Larry Cohen's blasphemous *Demon* (1978, originally entitled *God Told Me To*). God turns out to be a luminous,

hermaphrodite hippie from outer space (Richard Lynch) who, in a slam-bang finish, offers to have the hero's baby and conquer the world.

25. In Douglas Adams' *Hitch Hiker's Guide to the Galaxy*, the question asked of Deep Thought, the almost-ultimate computer. After seven and a half million years of cogitation it proclaims that the answer to the great question of Life, the Universe and Everything is forty-two. Subsequently used by Adams for the title of his third book in the *Hitch Hiker* series. Other catch-phrases from the *Hitch Hiker* books include 'Don't Panic' (the message written on the front of the eponymous book), 'Life, Don't Talk to me about Life' – Marvin the android's catch-phrase, and many more.

26. The philosophy of Dr Frank N. Furter (Tim Curry) in *The Rocky Horror Picture Show* (1975), quoted by Amyl Nitrate (Jordan), the post-holocaust punk heroine of Derek Jarman's *Jubilee* (1977).

27. Audrey Junior, the ravenous killer plant in Roger Corman's cheerfully lurid *Little Shop of Horrors* (1960). She/he/it became Audrey II ('Tooey' for short) in the successful stage musical.

28. Crazy Ralph (Walt Goorney), echoing many other whiskery horror film Cassandras by trying to warn the kids away from Camp Crystal Lake in *Friday the 13th* (1980). Nobody takes any notice of him and, in *Friday the 13th Part Two* (1981), he gets garrotted with barbed wire by a pudgy, mongoloid psychopath with a flour sack over his head.

29. Engineer Montgomery Scott (James Doohan) in *Star Trek*, the show that also gave the world 'Illogical, Captain', 'He's dead, Jim', 'Phasers on stun', and 'Warp factor five'.

30. The ritual by which the circus folk accept Cleopatra (Olga Baclanova) into the brotherhood of the deformed in Tod Browning's *Freaks* (1932).

31. 'Mrs Peel, we're needed.' Steed (Patrick MacNee) tells Emma Peel (Diana Rigg) that another episode of *The Avengers* has started.

32. Along with 'All men are psycho-chemically equal' and 'When the individual feels, the community reels', catch-phrases for the hedonistic society in Aldous Huxley's *Brave New World.*

33. The science-fictional equivalent of 'Love means never having to say you're sorry', the pointless but much-quoted rallying cry of *Star Wars'* fanatics.

34. The favourite incantation of *Dr Strange*, who is also much given to swearing 'By the crimson bands of Cyttorak!'

35. Napoleon Solo (Robert Vaughn) talking into his pen in *The Man from UNCLE.*

36. *The Shadow* knows, in hundreds of pulp novels by Walter Gibson, several movie serials, and, immortally voiced by Orson Welles, on radio.

37, Dan Aykroyd about to turn into a monster in the prologue of the otherwise disappointing *Twilight Zone: The Movie* (1983).

38. Winston Smith and Julia's motto in George Orwell's *1984*. Less well-known than some of the others ('Big Brother is watching you', 'If you want a picture of the future, imagine a boot stamping on the human face – forever. And remember that it is forever', 'War is peace. Freedom is slavery. Ignorance is strength', 'Who

controls the past controls the future. Who controls the present controls the past'), it was adopted by David Bowie for his *Diamond Dogs* album song of the same title. (An album conceptually based around *1984* and Harlan Ellison's short story *A Boy and His Dog*.)

39. Patrick McGoohan, as Number 6, getting himself into the *Penguin Dictionary of Modern Quotations* during the extended credits of *The Prisoner*.

40. Any number of disaster victims, crouched over their radios, barely croaking out a plea for help as the flames/floods/earthquake/runaway spaceship/giant alligators/Barry Gray theme tune edges dangerously near in *Thunderbirds*.

41. We're not even going to dignify this with an answer.

On the following pages are details of Arrow books that will be of interest.

THE CLAW OF THE CONCILIATOR

Gene Wolfe

Winner of *The World Fantasy Award, The British Science Fiction Award* and *The Nebula Award*

Volume Two of THE BOOK OF THE NEW SUN

'Bravo! A moving, subtle, exciting work at the very top of the field' Gregory Benford

In the darkling depths of the fantastical future, the torturer Severian continues his journey of exile to the city Thrax. He carries with him the ancient executioner's sword, *Terminus Est,* and the Claw of the Conciliator, a gem of extraterrestrial power and beauty which no one man is meant to possess. In a world of magical beauty and awesome terrors, Severian travels the perilous road towards his destiny.

'Simply overwhelming' Algis Budrys,
Fantasy and Science Fiction

DIARY OF A SOMEBODY
Christopher Matthew

'Quite definitely the funniest book I've had the pleasure of reading.' *Tribune*

At weekend houseparties and the elegant gatherings of the London season, at trendy Workers' Workshops and in the expectant crowds at the new National, Simon Crisp is always noticed. He's the one with the coffee stains on his trousers, the air of punctured dignity and educated worry. Humiliated by hurled apple cores and exploding plastic pants, by practical jokes in the office and in his West London flat, he's a fall-guy for our times.

This is his diary. It curiously resembles that classic of ninety years ago, *The Diary of a Nobody*. Especially in one respect: Simon never sees the joke.

But we do. And deliciously so.

'A genuinely funny book.' *Benny Green, Spectator*

'Spellbinding. I read the diary in one sitting.' *The Times*

THE CRUCIBLE OF TIME

John Brunner

Life can be just too unpredictable . . .

So it became for the people of a doomed world crawling across the rubble-strewn arm of a spiral galaxy. For as their system moved into the galaxy's arm, their star swept up all manner of cosmic debris.

Ice ages and tropical heatwaves alternated rapidly. Peaks of radiation caused even higher rates of mutation.

And meteor's fell constantly . . . so that yesterday's fabled culture might be tomorrow's hole in the ground.

Till the only hope of long-term survival was to abandon the planet, and get out.

But how?

John Brunner has here produced a huge, engrossing science-fiction epic in the best tradition of *Stand on Zanzibar*.

'A splendid, heartwarming alien multi-generation saga . . . beautifully thought out . . . Brunner in top form' *Kirkus Reviews*

Fran Lebowitz
SOCIAL STUDIES

The American bestseller from the author of *Metropolitan Life*

With elegance and accuracy, Fran Lebowitz draws a knife through urban life, dissecting its pretensions, puncturing its sensitive joints and bursting more than one overblown bubble. Woody Allen may have his finger on the pulse of metropolitan society – but Fran Lebowitz has unblinkingly, unashamedly and unrepentantly cut out its heart.

'Should you make it through this book without laughing, have your vital signs checked – a deep coma is nothing to trifle with'
Cosmopolitan

'The funniest woman in America'
John Heilpern, *The Observer*

'You laugh out loud while wincing' *Washington Post*

'Right on target' *Punch*

THE SWORD OF THE LICTOR

Gene Wolfe

Winner of *The World Fantasy Award* and *The British Science Fiction Award*

Volume Three of THE BOOK OF THE NEW SUN

'A classic in the making' *Publishers Weekly*

Beneath the dying sun the disgraced torturer, Severian, at last comes to his place of exile — Thrax, the City of Windowless Rooms. But Severian's journeying is not ended, and high in Earth's ancient mountains he draws closer to his destiny.